Crimes, Harms, and Wrongs

On the Principles of Criminalisation

A P Simester and Andreas von Hirsch

·HART·
PUBLISHING

OXFORD AND PORTLAND, OREGON
2014

Published in the United Kingdom by Hart Publishing Ltd
16C Worcester Place, Oxford, OX1 2JW
Telephone: +44 (0)1865 517530
Fax: +44 (0)1865 510710
E-mail: mail@hartpub.co.uk
Website: http://www.hartpub.co.uk

Published in North America (US and Canada) by
Hart Publishing
c/o International Specialized Book Services
920 NE 58th Avenue, Suite 300
Portland, OR 97213–3786
USA
Tel: +1 503 287 3093 or toll-free: (1) 800 944 6190
Fax: +1 503 280 8832
E-mail: orders@isbs.com
Website: http://www.isbs.com

British Library Cataloguing in Publication Data

Data Available

ISBN: 978-1-84113-940-1(Hardback)
ISBN: 978-1-84946-699-8 (Paperback)

Typeset by Columns Design XML Ltd, Reading
Printed and bound in Great Britain by
CPI Group (UK) Ltd, Croydon CR0 4YY

CRIMES, HARMS, AND WRONGS

When should we make use of the criminal law? Suppose that a responsible legislature seeks to enact a morally justifiable range of criminal prohibitions. What criteria should it apply when deciding whether to proscribe conduct?

Crimes, Harms, and Wrongs is a philosophical analysis of the nature, significance, and ethical limits of criminalisation. The authors explore the scope and moral boundaries of harm-based prohibitions, proscriptions of offensive behaviour, and 'paternalistic' prohibitions aimed at preventing self-harm. Their aim is to develop guiding principles for these various grounds of state prohibition, including an analysis of the constraints and mediating factors that weigh for and against criminalisation. Both authors have written extensively in the field. In *Crimes, Harms, and Wrongs* they have reworked a number of well-known essays and added several important new chapters to produce an integrated, accessible, philosophically sophisticated account that will be of great interest to legal academics, philosophers, and advanced students alike.

Preface

A.T.H Smith, our colleague and friend, introduced us at Cambridge in 1993. APS had just arrived from Oxford to take up a Research Fellowship at Gonville and Caius College, while AvH had joined the academic staff of the Institute of Criminology after two decades' working at Rutgers University in the United States. At that time, AvH was developing an interest in criminalisation issues, following on from his earlier research on sentencing theory, while APS was working primarily in substantive criminal-law theory. Together, we instituted a new LL.M. course at Cambridge, on the Philosophy of Criminal Law, finding in the process that many of our ideas—and values—overlapped in a way that was both stimulating and instructive. Many of our early discussions centred around remote harms, since AvH was working on the paper that subsequently appeared in the 1996 collection, *Harm and Culpability*, edited by Simester and Smith.

Thereafter, we worked together from time to time, publishing a number of papers on criminalisation topics, including offence and paternalism as well as harm. Some of the papers were published individually, some jointly; and we worked also with other colleagues who shared our interest—yet invariably discussed the issues with each other in the course of our writings. The upshot of this approach was a rather unsystematic body of writings, but the process itself was invaluable in shaping our thinking on criminalisation. That changed at the beginning of 2009, when we resolved to try to synthesise our various ideas into a more coherent work.

The present book was conceived of as a monograph rather than an essay collection. We quickly discovered that its preparation called for considerably more thought and effort than was originally anticipated. Many of our earlier arguments required substantial revision and refinement. Juxtaposing them revealed additional issues needing to be addressed. And the entire project demanded a coherent theoretical structure. In short, we needed to write a new account, not just a synthesis of our earlier ideas. At the same time, we have not aimed in this book to be comprehensive, or to develop a complete theory of criminalisation. Our main concern is with the structure of criminalisation questions, with general principles rather than details. So the present effort is unavoidably selective. It leaves many questions to the future.

Along the way, we have incurred substantial debts of gratitude. Andrew Ashworth and Douglas Husak supplied extensive and detailed comments on an entire draft manuscript. Matt Matravers, Antje du Bois-Pedain, Victor Tadros, and Bob Sullivan all gave us valuable advice on individual chapters. Regular visits to Uppsala University supplied the opportunity to exchange ideas with an impressive group of criminal-law theorists working (or visiting) there and nearby, especially Petter Asp, Nils Jareborg, Claes Lernestedt, Nina Peršak, and Magnus Ulväng. AvH also worked with several German colleagues on related German-language criminalisation projects, including Ulfrid Neumann, Tatjana Hörnle, Kurt Seelman, Klaus Günther, and Vivian Schorscher. To all these friends and colleagues, we owe our sincerest thanks.

There was also valuable institutional support. We benefited by excellent secretarial assistance from Ann Phillips. Our meetings at Cambridge and Uppsala were facilitated by the Centre for Penal Theory and Penal Ethics at the Institute of Criminology in Cambridge, and by a Singapore Ministry of Education Tier One Research Grant (R241000045112). Perhaps most importantly of all, election to a fellowship at Wolfson College enabled APS to continue returning regularly to Cambridge, teaching the Philosophy of Criminal Law course and working together with AvH on the book. We hope that all those who have contributed, in so many ways, to this project will be pleased with the result.

A.P.S.
A.v.H.
Michaelmas 2010

Acknowledgements

In writing this book, we have drawn directly or indirectly from a number of our existing articles and book chapters, some of which were co-authored with other colleagues. These various sources include:

'Betrachtungen über Moral und Paternalismus' ['Reflections on Morality and Paternalism'] in A. von Hirsch and U. Neumann (eds), *Paternalismus im Strafrecht: Die Kriminalisierung von selbstschädigendem Verhalten* (Baden-Baden: Nomos Verlagsgesellschaft, 2010) (A.P. Simester)

Criminal Law: Theory and Doctrine (3rd ed., Oxford: Hart Publishing, 2007) (A.P. Simester and G.R. Sullivan)

'Direct Paternalism: Criminalizing Self-Injurious Conduct' (2008) 27 Criminal Justice Ethics 25 (A. von Hirsch)

'Enforcing Morality' in A. Marmor (ed.), *The Routledge Companion to Philosophy of Law* (New York: Routledge, 2011) (A.P. Simester)

'Extending the Harm Principle: "Remote" Harms and Fair Imputation' in A.P. Simester (ed.), *Harm and Culpability* (Oxford: Oxford UP, 1996) (A. von Hirsch)

'Harm and Offence: Schädigungsprinzip und Belästigungsprinzip als Kriterien für die Kriminalisierung von Verhalten' ['Harm-Principle and Offence-Principle as Criteria for the Criminalisation of Conduct'] in H. Putzke (ed.), *Strafrecht zwischen System und Telos: Festschrift für Rolf Dietrich Herzberg zum siebzigsten Geburtstag* (Tübingen: Mohr Siebeck, 2008) (A. von Hirsch)

'"Indirekter" Paternalismus im Strafrecht am Beispiel der Tötung auf Verlangen (§ 216 StGB)' ['"Indirect" Paternalism in Criminal Law: Punishing Killing on Request'] in A. von Hirsch and U. Neumann (eds), *Paternalismus im Strafrecht: Die Kriminalisierung von selbstschädigendem Verhalten* (Baden-Baden: Nomos, 2010) (A. von Hirsch and U. Neumann)

'Indirekter Paternalismus und § 216 StGB: Weitere Bemerkungen zur Bedeutung und Reichweite des Paternalismus-Begriffs' ['Indirect Paternalism and the Prohibition of Killing On Request: Further Comments on Scope and Meaning of the Concept of Indirect Paternalism'] in A. von Hirsch and U. Neumann (eds), *Paternalismus im Strafrecht: Die Kriminalisierung von selbstschädigendem Verhalten* (Baden-Baden: Nomos, 2010) (A. von Hirsch and U. Neumann)

'Nachwort: Indirekter Paternalismus und die normative Basis des Tötung-auf-Verlangen-Verbots' ['Postscript: Indirect Paternalism and the Moral Basis of the Prohibition of Killing on Request'] in A. von Hirsch and

U. Neumann (eds), *Paternalismus im Strafrecht: Die Kriminalisierung von selbstschädigendem Verhalten* (Baden-Baden: Nomos, 2010) (A. von Hirsch and V. Schorscher)

'Injury and Exasperation: An Examination of Harm to Others and Offence to Others' (1986) 84 Michigan LR 700 (A. von Hirsch)

'The Mental Element in Complicity' (2006) 122 LQR 578 (A.P. Simester)

'The Nature and Rationale of Property Offences' in R.A. Duff and S.P. Green (eds), *Defining Crimes: Essays on the Criminal Law's Special Part* (Oxford: Oxford UP, 2005) (A.P. Simester and G.R. Sullivan)

'The Offence Principle in Criminal Law: Affront to Sensibility or Wrongdoing?' (2000) 11 King's College LJ 78 (A. von Hirsch)

'Penalising Offensive Behaviour: Constitutive and Mediating Principles' in A. von Hirsch and A.P. Simester (eds), *Incivilities: Regulating Offensive Behaviour* (Oxford: Hart Publishing, 2006) (A. von Hirsch and A.P. Simester)

Proportionate Sentencing: Exploring the Principles (Oxford: Oxford UP, 2005) (A. von Hirsch and A. Ashworth)

'Regulating Offensive Conduct Through Two-Step Prohibitions' in A. von Hirsch and A.P. Simester (eds), *Incivilities: Regulating Offensive Behaviour* (Oxford: Hart Publishing, 2006) (A.P. Simester and A. von Hirsch)

'Remote Harms and Non-constitutive Crimes' (2009) 28 Criminal Justice Ethics 89 (A.P. Simester and A. von Hirsch)

'Rethinking the Offense Principle' (2002) 8 Legal Theory 269 (A.P. Simester and Andrew von Hirsch)

'Is Strict Liability Always Wrong?' in A.P. Simester (ed.), *Appraising Strict Liability* (Oxford: Oxford UP, 2005) (A.P. Simester)

'Toleranz als Mediating Principle' ['Tolerance as a Mediating Principle] in A. von Hirsch, K. Seelmann and W. Wohlers (eds), *Mediating Principles: Begrenzungsprinzipien bei der Strafbegründung* (Baden-Baden: Nomos, 2006) (A. von Hirsch)

Contents

Abbreviations

The following abbreviations for standard textbooks and statutory materials are used in the text and footnotes.

Harm to Others J. Feinberg, *The Moral Limits of the Criminal Law,* vol. 1: *Harm to Others* (New York: Oxford UP, 1984)

Harm to Self J. Feinberg, *The Moral Limits of the Criminal Law,* vol. 3: *Harm to Self* (New York: Oxford UP, 1986)

Husak, *Overcriminalization* D. Husak, *Overcriminalization: The Limits of Criminal Law* (New York: Oxford UP, 2007)

Incivilities A. von Hirsch and A.P. Simester (eds), *Incivilities: Regulating Offensive Behaviour* (Oxford: Hart Publishing, 2007)

Offense to Others J. Feinberg, *The Moral Limits of the Criminal Law,* vol. 2: *Offense to Others* (New York: Oxford UP, 1985)

On Liberty J.S. Mill, *On Liberty* (London: Parker, 1859)

Proportionate Sentencing A. von Hirsch and A. Ashworth, *Proportionate Sentencing: Exploring the Principles* (Oxford: Oxford UP, 2005)

Roxin, *Strafrecht AT* C. Roxin, *Strafrecht AT* (4th ed., München: Verlag C.H. Beck, 2006)

Simester and Sullivan A.P. Simester and G.R. Sullivan, *Criminal Law: Theory and Doctrine* (3rd ed., Oxford: Hart Publishing, 2007)

StGB *Strafgesetzbuch* (German Penal Code)

Table of Cases

Table of Legislation

Part I

Criminalisation and Wrongdoing

1

The Nature of Criminalisation

O UR CONCERN IN this book is with what to criminalise: with the moral question, when should the criminal law be deployed to regulate the behaviour of citizens? In what follows, especially Parts II through IV, much of our argument will build upon, refine, and in some places depart from the analysis by Joel Feinberg in his great work, *The Moral Limits of the Criminal Law*. In particular, we investigate the approaches that the criminal law ought to adopt regarding harm, offence, and paternalism. We shall argue that, on occasion, each can serve as a legitimate ground of criminal intervention, but only once certain normative distinctions are observed. Those distinctions underpin some powerful constraints upon the reach of the criminal law, constraints that go beyond those set out in the existing literature.

We begin, however, with a more general inquiry. The proper scope of the criminal law depends, in part, upon its nature and function. In order to know *when* to criminalise, we need first to think about what it means to do so.

Broadly speaking, we can divide the operation of the substantive criminal law into three stages. First, the state 'criminalises' certain activities by setting out, hopefully in advance and in clear terms, a catalogue of specified actions or omissions that are prohibited, together with ranges of sanctions for violations. Secondly, at trial, it convicts persons who are proved to have contravened those prohibitions. Finally, it imposes sentence upon those it convicts, a sentence that is drawn from a specified range of permissible sanctions.

In so far as this sketch goes, it seems uncontroversial. Indeed, much the same can be said of other branches of law. Torts are broadly articulated in advance, their commission followed by courtroom verdicts and sanctions. What, then, marks out the criminal law?

That question may be answered in different ways. One very common approach is to think of the criminal law by reference to its system of sanctions. On this view, the criminal law becomes a field *sui generis*—a special body of law that is distinctively motivated by its concern with the imposition of sanctions *as punishment*. Other bodies of law might occasionally punish, e.g. through exemplary damages, but they do so only incidentally, and then perhaps only for the kinds of conduct that might appropriately be criminalised. It is a short move from that line of thinking to retributivism: the criminal law exists *in order to* punish people for their culpable misconduct.

For a retributivist such as Michael Moore,[1] the question what to criminalise is secondary to the question, what to punish? Prima facie, one should criminalise, and punish, *whenever* there is a culpable wrong, *and not otherwise*.[2] An asymmetry between what is criminalised and what is punishable will no doubt open up in practice; but it does so on a different plane, for rule of law ('legality') reasons,[3] or for pragmatic reasons,[4] or perhaps owing to various rights-based exceptions.[5] On that view, the primary task when ascertaining the scope of criminalisation is to identify when conduct is morally wrongful.

At the other end of the spectrum, some writers see the criminal law as just another state regulatory tool, one that happens to involve fines and imprisonment rather than injunctions and damages. To them, there is no fundamental distinction between crimes and other branches of law that impose sanctions. The difference is one of degree: the criminal law exists to visit punishments such as imprisonment or fines in situations where other forms of disincentive make for an insufficient deterrent.[6] The point of punishment then becomes, like other forms of sanction, to foster compliance by creating strong prudential reasons for abiding by the law; and we should criminalise especially when other forms of regulation are ineffective to achieve that end. Beyond that immediate purpose, the ultimate aims of criminal law are no different from those of the civil law; which, although themselves disputed, generally involve the co-ordination and regulation of behaviour so as to facilitate the well-being of community members.

The truth is, we think, somewhere in between. The criminal law *is* a regulatory tool for influencing behaviour, and in some respects no more than that; but it is a special kind of tool. The essential distinction between criminal and civil law lies in the social significance of the former—in the way criminal laws, convictions, and sanctions are understood. The criminal law has a communicative function which the civil law does not. It speaks with a distinctively moral voice, one that the civil law lacks.

---

[1] M. Moore, *Placing Blame: A Theory of Criminal Law* (Oxford: Clarendon Press, 1997).

[2] We take it here that eligibility for punishment depends on considerations of blameworthiness ('desert'), which in turn is predicated on the commission of a culpable wrong. More on this below, and in Chapter 2.

[3] Below, §§ 11.3–11.4.

[4] See, e.g., § 11.5 below.

[5] cf. Moore, above n. 1, § 18(v).

[6] e.g. R. Posner, 'An Economic Theory of the Criminal Law' (1985) 85 Columbia LR 1193.

We may observe this in all three stages of operation. The act of criminalisation itself constitutes a declaration that designated conduct is, so far as the state is concerned, wrongful and should not be done. *Ex post*, the conviction and the punishment also express disapprobation. D is labelled as a particular sort of criminal (a 'murderer', 'fraudster', etc.), a labelling that conveys a public declaration of culpable wrongdoing. Recognition of the significance of convictions can be seen in disclosure requirements of applications for a visa, or for admission to practise as a lawyer, which call for information about prior convictions but not about lost civil lawsuits. The very labelling of a defendant as 'criminal' imports all the resonance and social meaning of that term—quite different from publicly calling her a 'tortfeasor'(!) This is one reason why it is intelligible to have a conviction accompanied by discharge without punishment.[7] Punishment, in turn, is imposed with censure as an integral aspect. It responds to the fact that the defendant has done something wrong. Indeed, quite apart from deterrence considerations, the level of sentence is one way in which a court proclaims the wrongfulness of the defendant's actions and the gravity of the wrong.

Yet the crime-preventive aspect of the criminal law, and of its sanctions, is also significant. There is certainly evidence that the criminal law has some deterrent effect.[8] The criminal law does not ask: 'Do not assault others, *please.*' It tells: 'Do not assault others, *or else....*' The threat is straightforwardly coercive. And this generates a puzzle. Is the preventive effect incidental, as a retributivist might argue, or is it part of the point of the criminal law? Are the sanctions imposed purely because deserved, or are they intended to help influence the behaviour of citizens, notably of those who would not otherwise be inclined to conform to the law's requirements?

We think the latter; that deterrence is part of the point. At the same time, it is easy to see why writers have questioned whether a deterrent motivation is compatible with the morally-loaded, desert-based sanctioning system that, in our view, is rightly *also* characteristic of the criminal law. How can a system of culpability-driven sanctions be reconciled with deterrence?

---

[7] e.g. Sentencing Act 2002, s. 108 (NZ).

[8] See, e.g., A. von Hirsch, A. Bottoms, E. Burney, and P.-O. Wikstrom, *Criminal Deterrence and Sentence Severity: An Analysis of Recent Research* (Oxford: Hart Publishing, 1999) ch. 2, referring to the crime-preventive effects of drink-driving prohibitions. By contrast, altering sentence severity of already-prohibited conduct seemingly has little if any deterrent impact: *ibid.*, ch. 10.

1.1   THE ACT OF CRIMINALISATION

Hybrid accounts exist already in the literature,[9] though they seem to us unsuccessful. A difficulty is that they focus on justifying the criminal law as an *ex post*, punishing institution.[10] Seen purely in isolation, as a response to instances of wrongdoing, the imposition of a punitive sanction cannot (save contingently) discharge both deterrence and desert motivations at the same time. Unless both goals happen to converge on the same quantum of penalty, one must corrupt the other. Systematically, conflict is inevitable. So, unless we are prepared to give up on one of those two goals, we should abandon the attempt to justify punishment on a purely *ex post* basis.

Instead, let us start earlier: with the act of criminalisation. This is a complex, public, and coercive act, one that articulates both deterrence and desert *ex ante*. To criminalise an action is both to declare that the action should not be done and to deploy desert-based sanctions as supplementary reasons not to do it. More fully, by criminalising the activity of ϕing,* the state declares that ϕing is morally wrongful; it instructs citizens not to ϕ; it warns them that, if they ϕ, they are liable to be convicted and punished within specified ranges (the levels of which signal the seriousness with which ϕing is regarded); and, further, the state *undertakes* that, on proof of D's ϕing, it will impose an appropriate measure of punishment, within the specified range, that reflects the blameworthiness of D's conduct.

Clearly, this act is coercive. The warning is no mere advice but a threat, in as much as it communicates an intention to inflict unwelcome consequences upon D, conditional upon D's ϕing; moreover the consequences will be inflicted not just if but *because* D ϕs, and *because* they are unwelcome.[11] Typically, moreover, the threat is made *in order* to give D reason not to ϕ; that deterrent element does not arise just incidentally. (Indeed, even if a particular state's motivation were purely retributivist, the coercive *effect* of criminalisation would still call for justification—whether aimed at or not.)

However, actions can be coercive in different ways. Various forms of ('non-rational') coercion operate through bypassing the subject's rational capacities: for example, by simple physical restraint; or through a technique of psychological compulsion, such as the state's use of the rat against Winston Smith in Orwell's *1984*. Imprisonment, itself, is non-rationally coercive. But the type of coercion involved in criminalisation is what we might term *rational coercion*. Rational coercion operates via, and appeals

---

* For explanation of this usage, see the note to page 22 below.
   [9] We are thinking in particular of H.L.A. Hart's model and of the German theory of *Integrationsprävention*, critiqued in *Proportionate Sentencing* § 2.3.
   [10] A similar problem afflicts John Kleinig's attempt to justify the hard treatment element of punishment from its other element, censure. For discussion, see *ibid.*, § 2.5(1).
   [11] The latter criterion helps to distinguish unwelcome consequences that follow D's action but which are not punitive—such as damages in tort.

to, the subject's responsible agency; it offers her reasons for action, reasons that she may choose to ignore. It does not make the decision for her.[12]

a. An Archetype

Clearly, it is *possible* for the state to take coercive measures of the form we have outlined above. The very possibility of such a regulatory tool is sufficient to raise normative questions about its use and limitations, many of which are addressed in this book. But we think the account of criminalisation we have stated is more than a possible form of legal coercion. It is an archetype: as well as being a paradigm or standard account of what is done when the state enacts a criminal law, it is also a point of reference. It is an ideal type, at the normative heart of criminal law.

Conceived of as a paradigm, we think our account describes the structure of core, traditional acts of criminalisation, the declarations made (and subsequent punishments inflicted) in the context of offences such as murder, rape, theft, and the like; and it is the association of criminal law with such offences that tends to underpin the moral resonance of the criminal law in the public mind. But as a paradigm, our model is not always followed. Much punishment in England is explicitly preventative, involving terms of imprisonment that are disproportionate to the circumstances of the offence.[13] And, notoriously, many English and American criminal prohibitions impose strict liability, where convictions and sentences are imposed without proof of fault.[14] The distance of such offences from our paradigm can be observed in the common thought that such ('public welfare regulatory') offences are, in some sense, not 'truly' criminal. But we cannot deny altogether that they are criminal laws. Unfortunately, the common law knows no systematic and clear distinction between 'true' crimes and regulatory or administrative violations. We lack formal categories such as the German *Ordnungswidrigkeiten* or the French *contraventions*. So, at least in England, they fall within the domain of the criminal law. Indeed, nowadays they may even represent a second paradigm.

We say unfortunately because, normatively speaking, they *are* defective. *Our* paradigm account is an archetype because it contains, we think, the features that can make criminalisation morally legitimate. To the extent

---

[12] Akin to the kind of compulsion found in duress, which similarly does not deny the actor's moral responsibility: cf. J. Gardner, 'The Gist of Excuses' (1998) 1 Buffalo Criminal LR 575.

[13] cf. the power to impose 'public protection' sentences, critiqued by A. Ashworth, *Sentencing and Criminal Justice* (5th ed., Cambridge: Cambridge UP, 2010).

[14] See A.P. Simester (ed.), *Appraising Strict Liability* (Oxford: Oxford UP, 2005).

that the constraints our account generates are breached in practice, we argue, the state acts unjustifiably. There is much to be said for moving toward the continental approach,[15] and entrenching into English law a distinction between criminal laws and non-censorious administrative violations—the latter covering minor wrongs, punishable only by modest fines, where it may conceivably be legitimate to deploy strict liability.

b.   Normative Implications of an *ex ante* Perspective

We have described criminalisation as a type of conditional threat. That it involves rational coercion is necessary, albeit not sufficient, to ensure that criminalisation treats D with the respect due to human beings as deliberative agents—rather than as a creature merely to be intimidated, a dog addressed by a stick (or a cow by an electric fence). The rational agency component permits its addressees *ex ante* to evaluate the conditionally threatened consequence, to decide for themselves upon compliance. Rational coercion thus acknowledges D's independent identity as a responsible agent; in the context of state prohibitions, it acknowledges D's individual standing as a subject-citizen. Notice that this is why rational coercion necessarily operates *ex ante*, and why it is mistaken to focus (as retributivists tend to do) upon the imposition of punishment when seeking to justify the coercive nature of the criminal law. It is the prohibition, not the punishment that results from its violation, that is the relevant act of rational coercion,[16] at least when prohibition is accompanied by a conditional threat of unwelcome consequences—such as, though it need not be, of punishment.

   Rational coercion may or may not be justified. That the threatened consequence is *deserved* punishment becomes crucial, however, to the justification of criminal prohibitions. It matters to the moral legitimacy of the act of coercion, as well as to the *ex post* act of punishment. It is still a threat, but it is a moral threat. This is the key move: punishment is (and will be, the threat goes) imposed only to the extent it is deserved—that is, justified on retributive grounds, and not determined by considerations of deterrence.

   Our analysis thus addresses the worry expressed by Antony Duff's suggestion that a justification of punishment based partly on prevention is

---

[15]   Although see *Öztürk v. Germany* (1984) 6 EHRR 409, holding that *Ordnungswidrigkeiten* can be criminal in substance.

[16]   Admittedly, the imposition of punishment may itself involve further acts of rational coercion, in jurisdictions where it is backed up by supplementary threats for those who fail to observe the punishment. But that is a secondary matter.

morally embarrassing, and doesn't treat V as a moral agent.[17] Within the archetype we have set out, there is no corruption of goals, or failure to respect D as a moral agent. There are no mixed messages. At the stage of imposing punishment, the state's punitive response is legitimate just in so far as it responds to D's own, wrongful conduct. There is no corruption of goals because deterrence elements, by their nature, operate *ex ante*. Indeed, it is only with *ex ante* analysis that we can explain the role of deterrence; which is embedded in the act of criminalisation, not the act of punishment.[18]

c. Linking the *ex ante* Threat to the *ex post* Punishment

Even so, one might ask what reason the state has *ex post* to punish. Surely the actual imposition of sanctions presents a distinct, further problem of legitimacy beyond the act of regulation? *Ex hypothesi*, where punishment is deserved, the initial deterrence has failed, and it might be thought vindictive to pursue acts of punishment unless there were, at the point of sentencing, some further aim of general deterrence—*pour encourager les autres*—that threatens, once again, to corrupt the desert-based rationale. Perhaps D may *deserve* punishment for some instance of wrongdoing. But it does not follow that anyone (D's neighbour?) has a right to inflict it. Why should the state be the one to do so?

This is a particular challenge for pure retributivist theories. Unless *anyone* is entitled to punish wrongful conduct, it follows that the state's entitlement to punish D cannot be grounded in D's deservingness, *simpliciter*. On our account, however, this is not a distinct problem, because the relationship between prohibition and punishment goes both ways. By embedding the threat of punishment in the proscription, the state *commits* itself to responding to a subsequent act of ɸing in that manner. This commitment takes the form of an undertaking to respond to proved ɸing with justified punishment, an undertaking publicly made: to the potential defendant, to any potential victim, and more generally to members of the community as a whole.[19] Commitments of this sort are a conceptual element of threats. As Grant Lamond helpfully explains,[20]

[17] R.A. Duff, *Punishment, Communication, and Community* (Oxford: Oxford UP, 2001) §§ 3.1–3.2.
[18] Of course, the act of imposing deserved punishment may be relevant in terms of general deterrence, by confirming the credibility of the *ex ante* criminalisation-threat, going forward.
[19] Hence the need for even-handed generality in prohibitions: below, § 12.3(c).
[20] G. Lamond, 'Coercion, Threats, and the Puzzle of Blackmail' in A.P. Simester and A.T.H. Smith (eds), *Harm and Culpability* (Oxford: Oxford UP, 1996) 215, 228–29 (emphases omitted).

A coercive threat does not simply involve the communication of an intention to do something unwelcome. The non-performance of a threatened consequence is made dependent upon the recipient doing as demanded. The making of a threat thus creates a commitment to the carrying out of the intention. This is reflected in the fact that threats can be made by 'promising' to do something to the recipient. Coercive threats belong to a class of undertakings, including promises and vows, which commit the maker to a certain course of action. To be 'committed' to a course of action is to have a reason for carrying it out with the same sort of peremptory status as the reasons created by promises and vows. Such a reason pre-empts most ordinary reasons for or against an action. This feature of coercive threats is central to understanding their social function and point.

Thus the commitment itself constitutes a reason to punish; indeed, a duty to do so. There are a number of grounds for that conclusion. First, and most obvious, is the constraint of truthfulness—the threat is not a bluff. That constraint has intrinsic value, but it is backed up by instrumental reasons of credibility: that in the context of an ongoing legal system, a willingness to carry out threats is essential to their deterrent force. Moreover, it will not do to prosecute on a random basis, since that would violate rule-of-law norms which require treating citizens even-handedly.[21] Perhaps most importantly of all, since the undertaking is made publicly, citizens are entitled to rely on it, and to expect the state to see its commitment through. Obviously, this does not resolve the prior question of the state's entitlement to issue an *ex ante* proscription: *that* issue will dominate much of this book.[22] But it does show how the state's entitlement to punish is partly dependent on its prior entitlement to criminalise. Justifying that earlier act is where we should start.

1.2   THE MORAL VOICE

On this view, the criminal law is indeed a regulatory tool, one of many options available within the state's toolbox. Its deployment *ex ante* as a coercive, autonomy-restricting device must meet the stringent demands of social regulation that any form of authoritative legal regulation must satisfy; and in the following chapters, we will have something to say about those more general constraints upon coercive state intervention. But it is also a special kind of tool, a morally loaded sledgehammer; and there are some unique constraints that govern its use. In this book, our focus will be

---

[21] This is not to assert that every crime must be prosecuted: there may be insufficient evidence, for example, or the obligation to proceed may be otherwise defeasible. Cf. StGB § 60; also the public interest constraint on prosecutions in the common law, below, § 11.4(c).
[22] See further below, § 1.4.

primarily upon the special features of *criminal* regulation, and upon the particular constraints upon criminalisation that it imports.

a. Prohibitions and Censure

Let us begin, therefore, by saying a little more about the distinctiveness of the criminal law as a morally-loaded regulatory tool.[23] We take it to be conceptually true that punishment connotes blame. By extension, the action being punished must be censur*able*. Unlike blame in everyday contexts, the criminal law announces in advance that specified categories of conduct are punishable. Just as the prescribed sanctions are of a kind that express reproof, the announcement conveys the message that the conduct is deemed reprehensible. This is one of the labelling effects of criminalisation—to declare publicly that the proscribed conduct is wrongful.

As such, the censure embodied in the prescribed sanction has a central role to discharge as a public moral appeal, that people should refrain from the conduct in virtue of its wrongfulness.[24] The conduct is disapproved and, should D nevertheless perpetrate it, the subsequent act of punishment conveys to D, and others, a critical normative message concerning his conduct; that he has thus behaved reprehensibly.

It is, of course, possible for the state to enact a regulatory norm accompanied by other, non-desert-based forms of sanction, and that frequently occurs. The same assault may constitute a tort and a crime. Why, then, differentiate between the two? Why should there be a blaming response to the core conduct with which the criminal law deals? Why not replace criminal sanctions by some other, perhaps more cost-efficient institution that has no censuring implications, such as a deterrent tax?

There is no reason of principle why assaults cannot be regulated by tax, torts, and the like. The criminal law is just one response amongst many. But each form of regulation, the use of each tool, must be justified in its own terms. A disincentivising tax—say, a levy on cigarette sales—lacks the condemnatory bite of the criminal law, and offers only prudential reasons for refraining from given courses of conduct, although it may be warranted

---

[23] See also *Principled Sentencing*, especially § 2.4.1, on which parts of the following sections are based. We acknowledge our debt to Andrew Ashworth, co-author of that analysis.

[24] This is not necessarily, though on occasion it may be (cf. drink-driving legislation), a matter of teaching people that the conduct is wrongful, for those addressed (or many of them) may well understand that already. In other cases, the wrongfulness may arise only post-legally: more on this below, §§ 2.3(b), 3.1(a). In either case, the censure is, in principle, to be directed at the substance of the wrongdoing involved in the conduct. Thus the censure due for a criminal assault, for example, should relate to the wrongfulness of injuring someone, and not just to the fact that assaults are prohibited (which would be circular).

as a means to correct externalities in the pricing of goods.[25] To the extent that tort is justified in terms of disincentives, much the same is true; although tortious sanctions may frequently also be justified, e.g., by reference to the victim's deservingness of compensation relative to D.

Yet if we want to communicate the wrongfulness of assaults, we need criminal laws. A central reason for the blaming responses embedded in criminal law concerns censure's role as critical moral *communication* to perpetrators, potential and actual. Criminalisation speaks directly to subject-citizens, and in turn to wrongdoers, in clear moral terms, treating them as agents capable of moral reflection. It makes an official valuation concerning the moral status of ϕing. This appeal to the addressee of a criminal prohibition as a moral agent gives her the opportunity to reflect on the appropriateness of the conduct. The message conveyed by the censure is that the behaviour is wrongful, and that the person should consider its wrongfulness (and not just the threat of adverse consequences) as reason to desist. This is not just a matter of informing or teaching addressees that the conduct is inappropriate: they may know that already. Rather, the censure embodied in the prohibition serves as an appeal to desist, on the basis of the conduct's wrongfulness.

Subsequently, when an offence occurs, wrongdoers are confronted, through conviction and punishment, with disapproval in virtue of the wrongfulness of their ϕing; because, for example, they have culpably harmed someone. They are addressed as moral agents in themselves, and not just for the sake of preventive or other societal benefits that such censure might achieve. When an actual offender is punished—and thus censured—for his conduct, no doubt a moral response on his part would be hoped for: an effort at greater self-restraint or even, perhaps, an expression of concern or acknowledgement of wrongdoing. However, on our account, punitive censure is retrospective and desert-based, and is not imposed *in order* to give D the opportunity to make such a response. Our view thus differs from penance theories, according to which the sanction should aim at eliciting certain sentiments in the actor, e.g. shame, repentance, or the like.[26]

It follows that, within the criminal law, transgressions should not be dealt with through a neutral system of disincentives that convey no disapproval. Such disincentives—even if they were no less effective in discouraging the behaviour—would fail to respect persons as agents capable of moral understanding. Of course, any threat of a sufficiently

---

[25] e.g., in the case of tobacco, where the pre-tax market price does not reflect the true social cost of the product.

[26] See Duff, above n. 17, chs 2–3; critiqued in *Proportionate Sentencing* ch. 7. On our view, there is no need to tailor the censuring response to the actor's supposed degree of receptivity.

large sanction might happen to function as a deterrent: but if the response does not track the wrongfulness of the conduct, then it loses its moral voice.[27]

b. The Authoritative Character of Penal Censure

Ordinary language tends to distinguish *blame*, which expresses disapproval in everyday discourse, from *censure,* which generally involves authoritative expressions of disapproval. When someone carelessly steps on my toe, my disapproving response expresses blame. When she plagiarises my latest article and is subjected to a university disciplinary proceeding, the disciplinary board may issue a formal judgment of disapproval, a visitation of censure. It is the authoritative character of such disapprobatory judgements that makes them expressions of censure.

An act of censure is especially significant when it is done by the state. The criminal law's authoritative judgements of wrongfulness, both *ex ante* and *ex post*, are made on behalf of the wider community, and not just of victims or even specialist bodies such as universities. They provide a public valuation of the conduct, one that stems from the state's community-wide authority. What constitutes unacceptable conduct, the criteria for criminal liability, and what punishment D should receive are all determined via the formal criminal law, not by negotiation between the censuring agency and individual actors. Through criminalisation, the state delineates boundaries between acceptable and unacceptable forms of behaviour; these are not matters to be settled through discussion in individual cases.

The same holds for convictions and punishment. In everyday contexts, the reproof is characteristically private; it may affect D, and even harm D's relationship with other persons who are immediately involved; but it lacks the authoritative voice of the state and normally does not affect D's status in the community. An ascription of blame may bring D into conflict with P—or, in the case of a university, with the body of which D is a member—but it normally does not affect D's membership of the larger society.[28] By contrast, convictions are official. They condemn D on behalf of the community. To say that D has a criminal record is to say that he has been designated, officially, as a wrongdoer; that the state has made a formal adverse statement about *him*. Moreover, the statement marks D out in a way that may affect, within the community, the regard in which he is held. Certain exclusions, both social and professional, may legitimately

---

[27] This is not to conclude that neutral systems (cf. taxes) should never be used. Rather, their justification must be located, if at all, elsewhere in the legal system, resting on compensation or other rationales.

[28] Save in special cases, e.g. where the sentiments are pervasively held, or where P (the one casting blame) has representative standing in the community.

follow. Depending on the crime for which D is convicted, he may be ostracised by his peers, excluded from certain professions,[29] disqualified as a company director or from owning a pet,[30] prevented from working with children, refused insurance coverage, and so on. As such, the criminal record becomes part of the material that frames D's engagement with his community, with adverse implications for D's ability to live his life—a life that is, in part, defined in terms of D's interactions within, and membership of, his society. The conviction and the punishment (in its censorious aspect) tend not only to censure D for the particular act that is proscribed, but also to affect D's participation in the society itself.

1.3 HARD TREATMENT AND DETERRENCE

At the same time, the censure in punishment is expressed through the imposition of a deprivation—hard treatment—upon the offender. It is this other constitutive element, the hard treatment, that invokes preventive considerations in the criminal law, and which raises the apparent contradiction that we noted in § 1.1(b).

In our analysis, the hard-treatment element in sanctions supplies, *ex ante*, a prudential reason for desistance from offending, but one that is tied to the normative communication in penal censure. Through its act of criminalisation and the censure embodied in its prescribed sanctions, the state conveys that the conduct is wrong, and a moral agent is thus furnished with a moral appeal to abstain. Given human fallibility, however, D may be tempted nevertheless. Hard treatment, instead of *purely* symbolic means, is therefore incorporated in the censuring vehicle in order to provide him with a further reason, a prudential one, for resisting the temptation.

A certain conception of human nature, and of reasons for action, underlies this account. Persons, it is assumed, are typically neither like angels, for whom purely normative appeals suffice, nor like brutes, to be influenced only by threats. Human beings, instead, are moral but fallible creatures—capable of being motivated by normative appeals, but sometimes inclined to offend nevertheless. As Anthony Bottoms has suggested,[31] human choice should be seen as a complex interactive process, involving both a distinctively human capacity for moral reasoning and strong instincts and inclinations—e.g., of greed, aggression, and the like. On this

---

[29] See A. von Hirsch and M. Wasik, 'Civil Disqualifications Attending Conviction: A Suggested Conceptual Framework' (1997) 56 CLJ 599.

[30] cf. Dog Control Amendment Act 2003 (NZ).

[31] A. Bottoms, 'Five Puzzles in von Hirsch's Theory' in A. Ashworth and M. Wasik (eds), *Fundamentals of Sentencing Theory: Essays in Honour of Andrew von Hirsch* (Oxford: Clarendon Press, 1998) 53, 81–82.

view of human nature, we require a response that both takes humans' capacity for moral judgement seriously yet provides them with disincentives that can help them to control certain inclinations. Persons' character as moral agents makes them capable of taking into account the censuring message conveyed through the sanction, that the conduct is reprehensible. Given human fallibility, however, the temptation to offend becomes easier to resist if the censure of some activity is expressed through its prohibition in a manner that operates also as a prudential disincentive against the conduct. But providing such a disincentive does not render the sanction purely coercive: it does not make fear of unpleasant consequences the *only* basis for compliance.

Deterrence, on this account, does not stand alone. The prohibition conveys moral disapproval—embedded in the sanction's censuring character and in the commitment to impose *justified* punishment—while its mode of expression contains a prudential disincentive. By contrast, a proscription that offers hard treatment only to beget compliance is purely coercive, a naked threat. Granted, a morally committed person might find that even a neutral, non-condemnatory sanction makes it easier to resist temptation, and thus to comply with moral obligations he himself recognises. But the prohibition itself would lose its moral voice. Whatever the actor's reasons for compliance, the effect of the prohibition would be to treat subject-citizens as creatures to be manipulated rather than engaged with; not as persons for whom normative reasons for action matter.

The censure and the hard treatment are thus intertwined. A penal measure provides that a specified type of conduct is punishable by certain onerous consequences. Those consequences both constitute the hard treatment and express the censure and its degree. The preventive function operates, therefore, *within* the framework of a censuring institution.[31a] Indeed, this account would permit the abolition of the institution of punishment, were it not needed for preventive purposes. Imagine a hypothetical society in which social and economic conditions had improved so much that predatory conduct became much more infrequent than it is today. The criminal law—with its expensive armada of police, courts, correctional agencies, and the like—might conceivably no longer be required in order to keep such conduct within tolerable levels. Would such a society, in that event, be obliged to preserve the institution to deal with the occasional predatory act? Not necessarily. While it still might be appropriate to retain some form of official censure to convey the requisite disapproval of such acts, there would be a considerably weaker case for so ambitious, intrusive, and burdensome an institution as the criminal sanction.

[31a] Hence the penalty should be proportionate: see *Proportionate Sentencing* 26–27, 134–37.

a.   Moral Agency and Threats

We have argued that supplying deterrent incentives is compatible with desert-based punishment. But one might still wonder whether the element of prevention, even within a censuring framework, fails to respect subject-citizens as autonomous moral agents. On a narrow view of moral agency, sometimes (inaccurately) attributed to Kant,[32] an agent makes a moral choice only if the reasons for action she is offered and takes into account are 'purely' moral reasons in which the agent is not treated instrumentally. On that view, the introduction of prudential considerations, whether incentives or disincentives, would divest the appeal to the agent of its essentially moral character.

This view is too restrictive. One can be respectful of another's moral agency even when supplying her with prudential disincentives, provided one does not treat the person *purely* in this fashion. A demand by the state can address persons respectfully as autonomous moral agents even if it doesn't do so exclusively. A purely deterrence-based scheme would not meet this standard; the actor is informed that he had better comply or suffer the consequences, but is not offered any moral claim that he *ought* to comply. On our suggested account, however, the actor is given such grounds: through the censure embodied in the prohibition and sanction, the actor is conveyed the message, issued by an authoritative source, that the conduct is reprehensible and should therefore be eschewed. Concededly, this is not the only type of reason being put forward: the proscription also threatens hard treatment, which serves also as a disincentive. But if one accepts the conception of humans that has been propounded here, as fallible agents capable of acting on moral reasons but sometimes requiring practical disincentives to reinforce those reasons, this still takes seriously their capacity for moral agency.

1.4   THE ROLE OF THE STATE

Let us assume that prohibitions and punishment may, vis-à-vis the addressees, sometimes be justified. Wherefore by the state? Even when it can be shown that punishment is deserved, it does not necessarily follow that its imposition is an appropriate task for the state. In § 1.1(c), we answered this question in part, by grounding the reason the state has to punish in the undertaking it makes to do so when it enacts the original proscription.

---

[32]   While Kant famously divided prudential from moral reasons, his views in this context are more differentiated, in as much as he distinguishes between reasons for acting that have personal moral worth for the actor, and reasons which the law may legitimately invoke in its public standards.

This, however, brings us to the more important question: why is the *ex ante* issuance of morally-loaded, prohibitory norms itself one of the state's proper functions?

One familiar argument is based on the state's monopoly of coercion; that only the state should have coercive powers over its citizens. To grant such powers to private parties would invite retaliation on the part of those coerced and would open the way to injustice, given the partiality of those involved. There are, however, two difficulties with this line of argument. For one thing, it tends to be over-inclusive. It needs refinement to explain why limited powers of coercion may be vested in non-state agents, such as parents and indeed bodies like universities.[33] More importantly, the argument is purely negative. It suggests why it might be wrong to entrust penalising responses primarily to private citizens. But it does not develop affirmative reasons for the state, in particular, to be involved in a system of criminal proscriptions.

This is a large topic and, in keeping with the spirit of this chapter, we seek here only to sketch our account. There do exist positive reasons, we think, that underpin the state's involvement in legal regulation more generally, through both criminal and civil law. They concern the principal reasons for the state's existence, as an institution for helping to secure and improve the lives of its citizens.[34] There are various means of going about those aims. One is by generating public goods such as education, roads, hospitals, and the like. Another is by setting certain basic rules of engagement, or terms of interaction, among citizens. Indeed, one may even describe it as a defining role of the state to facilitate peaceable co-existence among citizens, and to safeguard the basic means by which citizens can live good lives. A paradigm mechanism for doing so is through the issuance of prohibitory rules, with sanctions attached as a disincentive to the behaviour.

Yet why should these state-imposed regulations involve censure? Suppose, though we think it unlikely, that a system of tort laws could provide sufficient protection for citizens.[35] None the less, criminal law may be the

---

[33] Above, § 1.2(b).

[34] Arguably, too, for the sake of ensuring that human beings meet their obligations to the rest of the planet (something that would allow for harm to non-human victims; below, Chapter 3 n. 10).

[35] Unlikely because, *inter alia*, initiation of tort proceedings depends on the person ostensibly injured: if no injured party brings an action, the tortfeasor will not be held to account. The criminal law, by contrast, is supported by state agencies such as police and prosecutors whose function is to identify and prosecute wrongdoers even where there is no identifiable victim. This is particularly important where the conduct merely risks harm but none results, so that there are no grounds for compensation in tort; whereas the criminal law can regulate activities that create such risks of harm (below, § 3.2(a)).

better tool.[36] Sometimes, it is important to recognise wrongdoing, to articulate a public evaluation of conduct. A 'neutral' regulatory response would not only fail adequately to engage in moral dialogue with actual and potential wrongdoers; it would also fail those injured or placed at risk—because it would not provide them with official acknowledgement of the wrongdoing involved. The state would be seeking to discourage the conduct, but in a manner that did not testify to its wrongful character.

1.5   CONCLUSION

The institution of the criminal sanction contains both preventive and deontological features. Its prohibitions and its punishments involve a moral appeal that cannot properly be reduced to mere disincentives. At the same time, the criminal sanction has features that seem clearly oriented toward inducing people to comply. The most plausible direction of analysis, therefore, is toward a principled account that accommodates both deontological and consequential values. As a censuring appeal, addressed to actors capable of moral deliberation, it speaks with a potent moral voice, authoritatively condemning wrongdoing and wrongdoers on behalf of the community as a whole. At the same time, it threatens and imposes hard treatment as an integral aspect: both as the means through which the censure is expressed, and as a prudential disincentive against offending that operates within the censuring framework.

In discussing the appropriateness of criminal proscriptions, therefore, we need to be mindful of the interaction of these concerns. Institutions such as the criminal law call for moral justifications; but those arguments need to address the law as a social institution, involving the exercise of state power, that must have pragmatic goals concerning the welfare of citizens. The state is an instrumental actor and not a moralising institution *per se*.

Moreover, while this book argues that criminal prohibitions are quite often justified, we should remain mindful that this is a regulatory tool with enormous drawbacks. It takes away important rights to which people are ordinarily entitled. Its coercive prohibitions deprive people of freedoms. Its more onerous sanctions, particularly imprisonment, take away critical social and economic opportunities as well as basic freedoms. The power to proscribe generates strong temptations to misuse it as a weapon of social control. In the rest of this book, we investigate the moral limits upon its use.

---

[36] By implication, we reject the principle that criminal law should always be the mechanism of last resort. See further below, § 11.2(e).

2

Wrongfulness and Reasons

W*HEN* SHOULD THE criminal law be invoked? We have observed that the criminal law is an emphatic condemnatory response by the state. It is also a coercive system, directed at controlling the behaviour of citizens. No one, including the state, should coerce others without good reason, all the more so when the measure involves censorious hard treatment of those who do not comply. The criminal sanction is the most drastic of the state's institutional tools for regulating the conduct of individuals. As such, it should be deployed only where supported by convincing justifications.

2.1   A GENERAL LIMITING PRINCIPLE

On the account we set out in Chapter 1, the criminal law is distinctive because of its moral voice. It removes specified activities from the permissible and punishes individuals who venture or stray into its realm. It is a complex, authoritative, censuring device. Conduct is deemed through its criminalisation to be, and is subsequently punished as, *wrongful* behaviour that warrants blame.

This official moral condemnation of activity and actor generates a truth-constraint. When labelling conduct as wrongful, and when labelling those it convicts as culpable wrongdoers, the state should get it right. There are reasons to do this even apart from the intrinsic wrongness of telling untruths. For one thing, people have a moral entitlement not to be designated, officially, as miscreants when they do no wrong. Morally speaking, those whose conduct is not reprehensible ought not to be convicted and made punishable. If a person does not deserve such treatment, then she has a right that it not occur; and neither her conviction nor her punishment can be justified by such consequential considerations as deterrence. A conviction for ϕing has the effect of designating D as a criminal (in respect of that particular offence), a designation communicated to the public as well as to D. Where ϕing is not wrongful, this amounts to moral defamation by the state.[1] The state is no longer telling the public the truth about D. People have, we think, a moral right not to be censured falsely as criminals, a right that is violated when one is convicted and punished as a criminal without having perpetrated culpable wrongdoing.

Moreover, and thinking instrumentally, extending criminal liability to conduct that is not wrongful is likely to be bad for the criminal law. In the long term, it risks undermining the moral authority of the criminal law generally, by weakening the association of criminal laws with culpable wrongdoing. Blurring the moral voice leaves criminal law less distinct from civil law. It diminishes the criminal law as a distinct, valuable, tool for social control and doing justice. It gunks up the censure machine.

Consequently, when we ask, what sort of conduct should be criminalised, one starting point is: conduct that is (for some reason) wrongful. Much of the most familiar types of conduct which the criminal law addresses can straightforwardly be characterised as wrongful—because, for example, they involve culpably harming someone (theft, say), creating unwarranted risks of injury (driving while intoxicated), or flouting important communal obligations (tax evasion). Sometimes, the very act of criminalisation plays a constitutive role in marking conduct out as wrongful, and this is a matter to which we return below. But either way, morally legitimate criminalisation requires that the prohibited conduct be in some manner reprehensible, wherefore one who culpably perpetrates the behaviour may be considered as a candidate for censure. Recognising that the criminal law essentially involves censure provides a foundational critical principle; it furnishes a reason to decriminalise conduct that cannot reasonably be accounted for as involving wrongdoing of some kind.

2.2   WRONGFULNESS AS THE DETERMINANT OF CRIMINALISATION?

But is wrongfulness really the starting—perhaps even the finishing—point? From the perspective of legitimate criminalisation, no doubt it is a vital concern; but as we shall see, activities can be wrong for different kinds of reasons. Sometimes, for instance, when considering whether a particular action is wrongful, it seems that we should begin with its *harmfulness*. Certain actions, such as murder and vandalism, are wrongs because of the harm they produce: the wrong derives from the harm.[2] On the other hand,

---

[1] 'Morally defamed', as opposed to defamed in law, since the state is a privileged wrongdoer in such cases (and thus exempted from tort liability). The phrase is used here to convey the sense of an untrue and adverse labelling by the state, in that the defendant is labelled with a stigmatic criminal conviction where the implicit social meaning of that label is unjustified.

[2] We return to these distinctions in § 3.2.

actions such as perjury and blackmail are wrongs independently of the harms they directly cause—they are, if you like, non-derivative wrongs.[3] If asked, 'which comes first, the wrong or the harm?' we can only say: it depends.

When deciding whether to *criminalise* that action, however, a parallel question may not receive the same reply. Famously, for Mill, 'the only purpose for which power can rightfully be exercised over any member of a civilised community against his will is to prevent harm to others.'[4] Perhaps, like Feinberg, we might require that the harm *also* be wrongful,[5] but part of the point of Mill's Harm Principle is to focus attention on the harm—and to reject wrongfulness *per se* as a ground of prohibition. On the other hand, Patrick Devlin notably asserted that 'it is not possible to set theoretical limits to the power of the State to legislate against immorality ... or to define inflexibly areas of morality into which the law is in no circumstances allowed to enter.'[6] Indeed, from Michael Moore's retributive perspective, an action may warrant proscription only on the ground of its moral wrongfulness.[7]

Ultimately, these two approaches are incompatible. But they share common ground, and Devlin's challenge helpfully focuses our attention on the necessary requirements of justified criminalisation. It follows from what we said in § 2.1 that there is nothing special, or objectionable, about confining prohibitions to morally wrongful actions, i.e. actions that one ought not to do. In our view, these are exactly the sorts of action that prohibitions should address. Establishing that an action is wrong, in other words, is indispensible to justifying its prohibition. As we shall see, wrongfulness is not sufficient; but if there are harm-based constraints on state intervention to regulate wrongs, they complement and do not displace the wrongfulness requirement.

Indeed, an exclusive reliance on harm is apt to mislead. It diverts attention from the more general inquiry when we should prohibit *wrongful* conduct. As we shall see, that latter inquiry yields more variegated answers than focusing solely on harm would suggest.

---

[3] Discussed below, § 3.3.

[4] *On Liberty* (1859) ch. 1, para. 9.

[5] *Harm to Others* 34–36; cf. J. Raz, 'Autonomy, Toleration, and the Harm Principle' in R. Gavison (ed.), *Issues in Contemporary Legal Philosophy* (Oxford: Oxford UP, 1987) 313, 328.

[6] P. Devlin, *The Enforcement of Morals* (Oxford: Oxford UP, 1965) 12–13.

[7] M. Moore, *Placing Blame: A Theory of Criminal Law* (Oxford: Clarendon Press, 1997).

2.3   THREE THESES CONCERNING WRONGFULNESS

Even so, taking morality and wrongfulness as a starting point may seem counterintuitive. It is often said that the law should not be in the business of prohibiting 'immoral' behaviour, and at least one version of that claim is surely right. But we need to be careful about what is meant by the claim, and about how convincing it really is. Clarification is required. Here are three possible interpretations:

1. That φing* is wrongful is insufficient to justify its criminalisation (Insufficiency Thesis).
2. That φing is wrongful is necessary to justify its criminalisation (Necessity Thesis).
3. That φing is wrongful is insufficient to establish even a pro tanto ground for its criminalisation (Non-qualifying Thesis).

The first thesis, that moral wrongfulness is insufficient to justify criminalisation, seems uncontroversial. Even Devlin and Moore could embrace it. Suppose that φing ought not to be done. Accept too, for the moment, that this generates a reason to prohibit it. It does not follow that, *all things considered*, we should prohibit φing, because the reason favouring prohibition may be defeated by other considerations.

One set of counter-considerations is operational. Even if a prima facie case can be made for prohibition, and φing lies within the range of conduct for which there is reason to criminalise, that case must still overcome various negative constraints, to be discussed in Chapter 11, which militate against criminalisation generally. At the very least, to make an all-things-considered case for criminalisation, we need to show that the criminal law offers an appropriate method of controlling φing, and is preferable to other methods of legal regulation available to the state. Recall the disastrous attempt by many western governments in the twentieth century to outlaw alcohol sales through criminal prohibitions, which created a black market ripe for extortion and racketeering. Rightly, regulation of sales through licensing and taxation laws is now preferred. Other constraints include the practical challenges of crafting an offence definition in terms that are effective, enforceable, and which meet rule of law and other concerns. It may be, if these demands cannot be met, that the state ought not to prohibit φing despite the prima facie case for doing so.

The in-principle case must also be weighed up against the burdens of prohibition itself, most notably in terms of freedom and lost opportunities.[8]

---

* The Greek symbol, phi, is used here to designate an (unspecified) action. It is used as conventional shorthand in the philosophical literature, in preference to alternatives such as 'Xing'.

[8]   See, e.g., *Harm to Others*, 216.

Ordinary mendacity, for example, should not be made criminal merely in virtue of its wrongfulness, because of the extensive intrusions that its prohibition would involve.[9] For all of these reasons, we should concede the Insufficiency Thesis. But we can do so without concern. For it is a long step from that thesis to concluding (i) that wrongfulness is *unnecessary* to justify criminalisation, or (ii) that even an in-principle case for criminalising ɸing requires *more* than that ɸing is morally wrong.

a. The Need for Wrongfulness

A very long step. Indeed, conclusion (i) would be a mis-step, because the truth is the other way around. This is the claim we made in § 2.1, that the wrongfulness of the conduct is an *indispensable* requirement of criminalisation. It is the Necessity Thesis, not an 'un-necessity' thesis, to which we should subscribe: any prohibition of ɸing can be justified only when ɸing is a morally wrongful action.

The Necessity Thesis is most easily defended, as we saw, by reference to the distinctive nature of the criminal law, which punishes, and censures, the offender for his conduct. One cannot blame a person unless that person does something morally wrong; that is, unless she does something that, all things considered, she ought not to do. One can, of course, also judge people morally for their good deeds: yet such judgements are not blaming judgements. Blame lies only for actions that, all things considered, it is wrong to do.[10]

This requirement for wrongfulness is sometimes confused with the requirement for culpability elements. There is a general objection to punishing the blameless in criminal law, one that is central to academic critiques of strict liability in Anglo-American criminal law.[11] But blameless-ness can derive from two sources, and strict liability is concerned with only one of them. One may be blameless because, although one's conduct was wrong, one was not culpable in respect of that conduct. Perhaps I inadvertently did that which I had all-things-considered reason not to do; however, my inadvertence was not negligent. The absence of that second element is what is objectionable about strict liability. But one may also be

---

[9] It may be quite a different matter when lies are told in certain contexts, e.g. for financial gain.

[10] 'Actions' here include omissions. For the sake of simplicity, we have disregarded special cases involving unknown justifications, such as in *Dadson* (1850) 169 ER 407 (noted below, § 2.5).

[11] See, e.g., A.P. Simester (ed.), *Appraising Strict Liability* (Oxford: Oxford UP, 2005).

blameless because one's conduct was not wrong in the first place. Thus the primary step is to establish whether the conduct is eligible for blame at all.[12]

As it happens, while the argument in § 2.1 is specific to the criminal law, a version of the Necessity Thesis holds also for the civil law; and, indeed, for all of us. No moral agent should act wrongfully. And the state is, like the rest of us, subject to requirements of morality. This matters because unless, all things considered, it is wrongful for D to φ, it generally follows that third parties—including the state—should not object to D's φing;[13] let alone prevent it. Notwithstanding that D's reason (or duty) to φ may be personal to D, the existence of those reasons is itself a general matter.[14] That D has reason to φ, therefore, is something that commands our allegiance too. This is not so much because D herself is entitled to respect—since respect for another human being does not imply that we must always respect the reasons for which that person acts. Rather, it is because the reasons themselves are entitled to respect—that is, because they are (good) reasons.

b.   Offences *Mala Prohibita*

But what about regulatory offences? It is a commonplace that the state frequently prohibits conduct that is not pre-legally wrong. Indeed such offences, which lawyers call *mala prohibita*, form the major part of the criminal canon. They vastly outnumber *mala in se* proscriptions of conduct that is pre-legally wrong. Frequently, conduct that is *malum prohibitum* seems not to be wrongful at all. Yet, if φing is not morally wrongful, how can we justify its prohibition and punishment? Is the Necessity Thesis incompatible with *mala prohibita* offences? This worry has concerned many writers.[15] As Douglas Husak complains, 'I fail to understand why persons behave wrongfully when their conduct is *malum prohibitum* but not *malum in se*.'[16] While accepting that some *mala prohibita* prohibitions

---

[12]   These steps cannot be merged, because they are asymmetrical. The asymmetry is most easily demonstrated in respect of praise, although it exists also in blame. One may do something praiseworthy without being deserving of praise, e.g. when one does the right thing inadvertently or for the wrong (e.g. unrelated and selfish) reasons.

[13]   Admittedly, on occasion the existence of reasons may depend on the status of the agent; thus it is possible that some reasons for individuals to φ may be excluded in the hands of certain other agents, such as the state, and vice versa. I cannot build on your land without your consent, even if I pay you a fair price and the building would benefit the community. But the state can and does do just that. We cannot pursue those cases in detail here.

[14]   For discussion of this point, see J. Gardner, 'Complicity and Causality' (2007) 1 Criminal Law and Philosophy 127, 131.

[15]   See, e.g., Husak, *Overcriminalization* 76, 103f.

[16]   *ibid.*, 112.

may give substantive content to underlying, pre-existing wrongs, Husak doubts that many modern offences do that.

This line of criticism is partly right and partly misleading. It is right in so far as it reflects the truth—and it *is* a truth—that φing does not become (morally) wrong just because the state declares it so.[17] But it is misleading in that it doesn't sufficiently distinguish criminalisation, which is forward-looking, from punishment, which is retrospective and *ex post*. This was one of the lessons from Chapter 1. Because they are different acts, the justification of an act of criminalisation is not the same as the justification of an act of punishment. The former can play a role in justifying the latter.

How so? Because the state can contribute to the *creation* of moral reasons. Moreover, it can do so in a variety of ways.[18] Indeed, that power is not restricted to the state. When the soccer referee shows a player a red card, the player thereupon has a reason (indeed, a duty) to leave the pitch. Any moral agent in a position of authority can help to create reasons: the power to do so is part of the very idea of authority.[19] Prior to law, there is no reason to drive on any particular side of the road, but one arises as soon as the state stipulates on which side the citizens should drive.[20] If the state rules that we must drive on the left, it thereby makes it a post-legal wrong to drive on the right.

In these kinds of cases, the state has good *ex ante* reason for passing the relevant law. In effect, the state acts as a conduit, crystallising those *ex ante* reasons into a more particular, practicable form—the moral force of which derives not from the enactment itself, but from the purposes it serves and which lie behind its enactment. Conversely, as will be seen below, we do not argue that it is wrongful to break laws that lack good *ex ante* reasons for their creation.

Many standard examples of successful norm creation involve conventions, typically as co-ordinating rules or as content-determinations of some more abstract, pre-conventional norm. How many players to field on a soccer team? How should we return the ball into play? Which side to drive

---

[17] John Gardner has asserted that 'it is the law's recognition of the [*malum prohibitum*] wrong that makes it a wrong': J. Gardner, *Offences and Defences* (Oxford: Oxford UP, 2007) 239. We can be confident that he did not mean 'recognition, *simpliciter*' but rather (as we suggest here), 'recognition for good reasons'.

[18] Two classic discussions are by A.M. Honoré, 'The Dependence of Morality on Law' (1993) 13 OJLS 1 and J. Finnis, *Natural Law and Natural Rights* (Oxford: Oxford UP, 1980) 284ff.

[19] cf. J. Raz, *The Authority of Law* (Oxford: Oxford UP, 1979) ch. 1.

[20] We assume here that the authority is not merely legitimate but effective, so that there is a reasonable expectation of conformity with the rules it creates; both because it is authoritative, and because others are likely to rely on those rules in their own conduct. But this does not seem too much to require, since effectiveness is a condition of the instrumental reasons underpinning a state's authority. (The need for such an assumption militates, incidentally, in favour of a doctrine of *desuetude*, as is found in many civilian legal systems.)

on? The answers to these questions may be to some extent arbitrary, even suboptimal; yet the very existence of an authoritative answer is itself valuable. Now we can have an organised game. Now we can drive, faster than a crawl, with more safety. And so on. The precise content of these co-ordinating rules may be less important than the purpose they serve. Even a rule about the age of consent in underage sexual intercourse, which most people would regard as a *mala in se* offence, is partially conventional. It varies widely across jurisdictions and history. But the rule is valuable—morally valuable—in virtue of helping to articulate one boundary of permissible sexual activity, benefiting potential offenders as well as potential victims by its clarity.

Yet is this enough to make violation of *malum prohibitum* rules wrongful? Some writers have argued that an extra ingredient is involved—that the rule-violation is wrongful only in virtue of exhibiting some further characteristic, some vice, such as being defiant or exploitative of the rule. Thus Antony Duff suggests that punishment is appropriate only when and because the *malum prohibitum* offender exhibits 'civic arrogance', arrogating to herself an exception to the rule and thereby ('arrogantly') setting herself above her fellow subject-citizens.[21] Similarly, Stuart Green argues that violations are wrongful in virtue of being a kind of 'cheating', or unfair play—taking unfair advantage of more compliant fellow citizens.[22]

We disagree with this approach. It seeks to introduce an additional element that can do no work, since its existence is constituted by nothing other than violation of the rule.

Why? After all, arrogance is a real phenomenon. Indeed, it is a vice. But to the extent that Duff's extra-ingredient approach appeals to the real phenomenon, the existence of arrogance must rest on something more than a mere norm-violation: it requires that the violation be done for certain kinds of reasons, be motivated by a certain kind of objectionable self-preference. By reverse implication, in the absence of such motivation, the rule-violation would not be wrongful. Ignorance of the rule, for example, would go not just to culpability but to the very wrongfulness of the conduct. Moreover, the wrongdoer's deserved punishment should then depend upon the degree of arrogance displayed, rather than upon the wrongful nature of the underlying, norm-violating conduct. The extra-ingredient approach, in other words, puts the wrongdoing in the wrong place.

The same is true of Green's analysis. Suppose that D fishes without obtaining a legally-required licence. On Green's account, the wrongdoing is a kind of free-riding: namely, that D takes unjustified advantage of other

---

[21]   R.A. Duff, *Answering for Crime: Responsibility and Liability in the Criminal Law* (Oxford: Hart Publishing, 2007) 104.

[22]   S. Green, 'Cheating' (2004) 23 Law and Philosophy 137.

rule-abiding persons. He may benefit by his fellow-citizens' obtaining the licence and observing its conditions, thereby (say) protecting the local fishing stocks for D to exploit; but spares himself the inconvenience and expense of doing the same himself. The wrong, on this perspective, is not concerned with the local fish stocks. It is, rather, one of not playing fair, perpetrated against those who were prepared to observe the rules. While that may be a secondary wrong, it does not characterise the primary wrongfulness of fishing without a licence—which concerns the reasons for having that rule in the first place.

The wrongfulness of a rule-violation depends on the moral force of the rule. In the case of a *malum prohibitum* rule, the moral force comes from its instrumental value; which depends, in turn, on the purposes the rule serves and how well it serves them. It depends, that is, on whether the creation of the rule itself is justified. Well-designed fishing licence regulations, for instance, are valuable because their observance helps to prevent exhaustion of fish stocks.[23] The strategy of which they form part thus safeguards against a form of conjunctive harm,[24] and it is their contribution to that strategy which gives citizens reason to comply.

Of course, not all prohibitions are justified. They are certainly not self-justifying. Neither does the mere act of rule-creation, in itself, justify the punishment of violations. Under our analysis, however, that does not present the problem Husak thinks it does, because there is a normative gap between criminalisation and punishment. Husak insists that punishment is appropriate only if ϕing is wrongful. We agree. But it need not be wrongful *independently*. Whether ϕing is wrongful depends on whether it is, all things considered, wrong to ϕ; and at the stage of punishment, the reasons not to ϕ are to be assessed *post-legally*, not pre-legally.

What's the difference? When does the state succeed in creating reasons not to do something that, pre-legally, was morally permissible? What counts is whether the authoritative agent creates those reasons *for good reasons*. More precisely, we have suggested, what counts is whether the agent's legislative act is justified. (The refinement allows for the possibility that the state might properly set out to regulate some activity, but where the scheme or rule it adopts is inappropriate, e.g. because overly intrusive or ineffective.) In the driving case, the reason we now have to drive on the left is created as a particular determination of the more general reasons we have to drive safely. Even though the content of the rule may be largely conventional, it acquires moral force in virtue of the function it performs. Here, the particular crystallises the abstract; but notice that it is the

---

[23] As we note in Chapter 3 n. 10, we are open to the argument that this goal is valuable in itself; but a sustainable fish population is likely also to be valuable to human beings, both as food source and through facilitating recreational activity.

[24] A form of remote harm: below, Chapters 4–5.

abstract which gives the particular its moral force. Even here, the state should do what morality gives it *ex ante* reason to do. Even authorities need a basis for their actions.

Authorities do not have to be right. They just have to generate reasons. The referee who makes an error still creates a duty for the player to leave the pitch. On the other hand, those reasons have to be sufficient,[25] and that depends on why they were created. The hard cases are the marginal ones, where the state has pressing need to regulate μing but cannot practicably do so without also regulating φing. Speed limits, drink-driving limits, and age-of-sexual-consent rules are examples where a prohibition is unavoidably *over-inclusive*, capturing both pre-legally immoral and pre-legally permissible instances of their perpetration.[26] A prohibition is over-inclusive when it proscribes a wider range of conduct than is required by the reasons motivating the prohibition. For example, a prohibition on driving above a certain speed limit may criminalise both safe and unsafe instances of such conduct, even though it is only the unsafe instances that motivate the prohibition. Since driving above the speed limit is not always dangerous, and the actor may know this is the case, Husak questions,[27]

> In these circumstances—when a defendant commits a hybrid offense by engaging in conduct that is *malum prohibitum* although not simultaneously *malum in se*—how can punishment be justified within a theory of criminalization that includes the wrongfulness constraint? ... In the circumstances I have just described, how can punishment be justified at all?

We should flip Husak's question around. The primary issue is not whether punishment of φing is itself justified, but whether the state is justified in criminalising φing.[28] If the proscription is justified, we don't need supplementary grounds to show why φing is then wrongful. We don't need complicated and unconvincing arguments about the 'civic arrogance' or 'cheating' exhibited by those whose *malum prohibitum* act of φing is not, apart from being prohibited, wrongful.[29] We don't need, in other words, to look for a supervening vice to explain why it is wrong for D then to φ. If

---

[25] It is also possible that the state-created reasons not to φ, while valid, are insufficient to make φing wrongful. Where this happens only occasionally, the prohibition of φing may best be ameliorated by means of defences; where it is true generally, the proscription itself should be abandoned.

[26] See Husak, *Overcriminalization* 106–107. We assume for the sake of argument that these over-inclusions are, for practical reasons, unavoidable: to the extent they aren't, the over-inclusions are likely to be illegitimate. See below, § 11.4(c).

[27] *ibid.*, 107.

[28] Note that the restriction need not be through criminalisation. The civil law can create wrongs too, e.g. through the allocation of property rights: below, § 3.1(a).

[29] Husak refutes such explanations in *Overcriminalization* 108ff.

the state's exercise of authority was justified,[30] then φing is already wrongful and, post-legally, D ought not to do it.

c. Mere Immorality?

So, we think, the Necessity Thesis is right too. But what about the third claim, that the in-principle case for criminalising φing requires more than that φing is morally wrongful? This is a much stronger version of the Insufficiency Thesis. According to this third claim (the Non-qualifying Thesis), immorality *per se* does not generate even a prima facie reason to prohibit. Only certain kinds of wrongfulness qualify. Something extra is needed.[31]

Our own view is that the Non-qualifying Thesis is correct. In particular, we will argue in Parts II–IV that legitimate grounds for coercive state intervention arise only when conduct directly or indirectly affects people's lives, such that its regulation would tend to prevent harm. A harm-based constraint applies, we think, even to conduct that is offensive to others. *A fortiori*, the constraint rules out criminalising purely self-regarding immoral behaviour.

We have no knock-down argument to demonstrate the logical truth of our position. In the course of the following chapters we will discuss various reasons why, morally speaking, a harm-based constraint is desirable. In particular, while an act of wrongdoing may by itself warrant censure *ex post*, something more is required to justify the *ex ante* step of criminal prohibition. That your φing would be wrongful doesn't entitle me to *coerce* you not to do it. Partly, this is because coercive prohibitions can significantly affect people's lives. They foreclose options that some individuals may value, and which (even if themselves wrongful) may form part of a valuable way of life. Indeed, because of their general nature, they tend in practice to be over-inclusive, even ruling out instances of the proscribed

---

[30] If the restriction of φing is itself (as so often) unjustified, punishment then compounds the wrong done by the state. But the objection to punishment is dependent.

[31] Interestingly, discussion of this claim is more developed in Anglo-American theory than in Germany, notwithstanding the sophistication of that country's criminal law and theory. German discussion has depended, in large part, on the proposition that conduct should be criminalised only if it intrudes upon a *Rechtsgut*—a legally-protected interest. However, comparatively little progress has been made in developing normative criteria for the recognition of a legitimate *Rechtsgut*. Only in the last decade, when the notion of the Harm Principle began to attract the interest of German scholars, have discussions of criminalisation theory begun to flourish. For a valuable English-language discussion of these developments, see N. Peršak, *Criminalising Harmful Conduct: The Harm Principle, its Limits and Continental Counterparts* (New York: Springer, 2007). In the context of paternalism, see now A. von Hirsch, U. Neumann and K. Seelmann (eds), *Paternalismus im Strafrecht: Die Kriminalisierung von selbstschädigendem Verhalten* (Baden-Baden: Nomos, 2010).

conduct that are not wrongful at all. It is hard to see how these effects of coercion can be justified when that conduct has no adverse effects on anyone's well-being.

But it is also a matter of one's conception of the state. As we said in § 1.4, we take the state to be an instrumental actor, an artificial creation that exists in order to advance the welfare of its subjects. On that view, the state has no interest in regulating conduct that does not affect people's lives. Pure moral wrongs fall outside its remit.[32] This means that we should consider disavowing the thought that moral wrongfulness is the starting point for justifying criminalisation.[33] It is indispensible, yes—a *sine qua non* of deploying criminal law as the preferred regulatory tool. The starting point, however, is the lives of people.[34] The state has an interest in regulating conduct that affects those lives. And where such conduct is wrongful, it may be appropriate to regulate it by the criminal law.

2.4   OTHER CONSTRAINTS

No other constraint upon justified criminalisation is so fundamental as the requirement that the prohibited conduct be wrongful. In Parts II–IV, we shall focus on some more detailed grounds for state intervention (harm, offence, paternalism), and consider the extent to which they support the choice to criminalise particular forms of conduct. Later, in Chapter 11, we will briefly discuss some practical and other limiting barriers that must be surmounted before criminalisation is justified. Before that, however, it is worth mentioning some further universal constraints. Closely related to the wrongdoing requirement and its justification is a general requirement for culpability elements to be specified, or at least implied, in any criminal prohibition. The censuring response of the criminal law is appropriate only to culpable wrongdoing, and not on a strict liability basis wherever some unwanted action occurs.

Why is punishment inappropriate when the actor acts without fault, so that it is illegitimately imposed by strict liability offences? The reason, outlined in Chapter 1, is that punishing someone conveys disapprobation of the person for her act, and that is appropriate only when the act speaks badly of the person doing it. Where the wrong is done purely accidentally—without awareness or negligence—this does not reflect adversely upon the character or choices of the wrongdoer. Certainly, the action forms part of her history, and may provide her with grounds for

---

[32] *A fortiori* if the conduct is not wrongful at all: cf. Moore, above n. 7, at 662, for one legal moralist's restrictive view of what counts as wrongful in contexts such as sexual practices.

[33] Note that the special case of moral paternalism will be discussed below, § 9.1(b).

[34] And also, perhaps, the needs of other creatures to whom humanity owes duties.

regret. Thus it can be meaningful to speak of faultless wrongdoing.[35] But where there are no unreasonable risks of which, from an *ex ante* perspective, she should have been aware when embarking on the conduct, she does not behave reprehensibly. The wrongdoing is accidental, and not fit for penal censure

In *Overcriminalization*, Douglas Husak proposes certain additional constraints, some of which we discuss in later chapters.[36] At least one of them seems uncontroversial: a burden-of-persuasion principle, according to which the burden of establishing the moral case for prohibition falls upon the would-be legislator.[37] Given the onerous nature of criminalisation, it is surely right that the default presumption should be against its use—unless the case for doing so, and for doing so in preference to other regulatory tools, is clearly established. Of course, a principle of this sort lies outside the structure of criminalisation arguments. It cannot tell us what are the requirements of a good argument, which reasons for prohibitions are legitimate and which are not; what shape the case must take. For that, we must turn to the more detailed discussion in the rest of this book.

2.5 TWO PROVISOS

Out of caution, however, two provisos. Our concern here will be with the *moral justifiability* of criminal proscriptions, and not with whether they are actually justified or indeed lawful when imposed on particular occasions. Many writers think that, for any action (including an act of criminalisation) to be justified, not only (i) must an in-principle justification exist, but (ii) that must also supply the motivation why the action is actually done.[38] As criminal theorists well know, an analogous principle holds in the substantive criminal law of many countries.[39] Similarly, under US constitutional law, government legislation and other actions limiting fundamental rights are subjected to 'strict scrutiny', whereby the legislation must be necessary and proportionate to achieving an essential government

---

[35] For an excellent discussion, see J. Gardner, 'Wrongs and Faults' in A.P. Simester (ed.), *Appraising Strict Liability* (Oxford: Oxford UP, 2005) 51.

[36] See especially §§ 5.1–5.2 and § 11.4(c). For more direct attention, see A.P. Simester and A. von Hirsch, 'Remote Harms and Non-constitutive Crimes' (2009) 28 Criminal Justice Ethics 89, 91–93.

[37] *Overcriminalization* 100.

[38] cf. Moore, above n. 7, § 18(iv), discussing a 'derived right to liberty' of citizens not to be coerced by the government 'for the wrong reasons'.

[39] See, e.g., *Dadson* (1850) 169 ER 407; *Thain* [1985] NILR 457; G.R. Sullivan, 'Bad Thoughts and Bad Acts' [1990] Crim LR 559 (defences such as self-defence unavailable when D acts without knowing about the existence of the threat). *Pace* P. Robinson, 'Competing Theories of Justification: Deeds v. Reasons' in A.P. Simester and A.T.H. Smith (eds), *Harm and Culpability* (Oxford: Oxford UP, 1996) 45.

purpose; *and* that purpose must be the very reason for which the government acted.[40] Rightly so—but this is, for our purposes, an extraneous matter. We are concerned here only with (i)—with what reasons for criminalisation can support an in-principle justification.

Moreover, our investigation is moral rather than constitutional: with the question, what conduct *should* a responsible legislator criminalise? and not the question, what does she have the legal authority to criminalise? Most legislatures are empowered to proscribe a wide variety of conduct for a wide range of reasons, subject to whatever constitutional constraints the particular legal system affords. A conscientious legislator, however, should support proscription only when good moral reasons exist for so doing. In what follows, we consider the nature of those reasons and the ways in which they apply to different kinds of eligible conduct. While we hope that the arguments have an overall coherence, we do not seek to be comprehensive or fully systematised; to some extent, the discussion reflects our own scholarly interests. And the principles we identify are not *handfeste Kriterien*, handily-useable criteria, for resolving which forms of wrongdoing should be criminalised. They lack the necessary specificity. Rather, they are offered as guides for the direction of argument, *Argumentationsmuster*, pointing to the distinctive shapes of the different grounds for criminalisation.

---

[40] Moreover, the burden of proving its purpose rests with the state, since it has control over the public record. See E. Chemerinsky, *Constitutional Law: Principles and Policies* (New York: Aspen, 1997). Contrast the 'rational basis' test that applies to most other government legislation, which requires only that the legislation be rationally related to a conceivable legitimate governmental purpose, regardless of whether this was the actual purpose of the legislation: *Fed. Communications Commission* v. *Beach Communication* 113 SC 2096 (1993).

Part II

Harm

3

Crossing the Harm Threshold

A FAMILIAR TENET of liberalism is the proposition that the state is justified in intervening coercively to regulate conduct only when that conduct causes or risks *harm to others*. Conduct that merely harms oneself, or which is thought to be immoral but otherwise harmless, is on this account ineligible for prohibition. First articulated by John Stuart Mill,[1]

> The principle is, that the sole end for which mankind are warranted, individually or collectively, in interfering with the liberty of action of any of their number is self-protection. That the only purpose for which power can rightfully be exercised over any member of a civilised community against his will is to prevent harm to others. His own good, either physical or moral, is not a sufficient warrant.

Expressed in this way, the Harm Principle is a negative constraint: in the absence of harm, or risk of harm, the state is not morally entitled to intervene. Feinberg, however, rightly presents it as supplying a positive (though not conclusive) ground to prohibit:[2]

> It is always a good reason in support of penal legislation that it would be effective in preventing (eliminating, reducing) harm to persons other than the actor (the one prohibited from acting) and there is no other means that is equally effective at no greater cost to other values.

Harm is not merely a licensing condition. It is integral to the justification for intervening. Indeed, on Feinberg's approach it need not even be a necessary condition. Feinberg's analysis leaves room to accept the legitimacy of supplementary grounds for criminalisation, such as offence and paternalism, which we consider later in this book. As we shall see, however, those supplementary grounds also involve certain forms of harm.

Part of the point of the Harm Principle is that it forces an enquiry into the consequences of conduct—does it hurt anyone? According to the Harm Principle, proponents of a given criminal prohibition cannot simply allege that the relevant conduct is immoral. Rather, they must identify the

---

[1] *On Liberty* ch. 1, para. 9.
[2] *Harm to Others* 26.

particular effects of that conduct:[3] the way in which it damages the lives of other persons. That claim can then be subjected to public debate. Empirical evidence of a link to the alleged harm can be demanded and scrutinised.

Consider, for example, the decision by the House of Lords in *Brown*[4] that, in the context of sadomasochistic sexual activity, it is an offence to inflict minor bodily harm on another person notwithstanding that the 'victim' consents. One justification offered for this conclusion was that the legalisation of such activities might encourage the seduction and 'corruption of young men'.[5] But would it? It is an easy claim to make when no supporting data is offered. Given the presumption against criminalisation, the onus is on its proponents to supply evidence that creating a new offence *will* help to prevent harm from occurring.

What counts as harm? Mill offers no clear response to that question, without which the application of the Harm Principle is indeterminate. Broadly speaking, the answer is consequential. A harm, on Feinberg's account, is a 'thwarting, setting back, or defeating of an interest.'[6] We are harmed when one or more of our interests is left in a worse state than it was beforehand. In Feinberg's words,[7]

> One's interests ... consist of all those things in which one has a stake ... These interests, or perhaps more accurately, the things these interests are *in*, are distinguishable components of a person's well-being: he flourishes or languishes as they flourish or languish. What promotes them is to his advantage or *in his interest*; what thwarts them is to his detriment or *against his interest*.

Satisfaction of the Harm Principle, thus, requires an adverse *effect*, upon something substantial; a diminution of the kinds of things that make one's life go well.

When we are harmed, our prospects are changed for the worse. The implications for our well-being are forward-looking and contingent. It does not follow that our lives will actually go less well. Things may still work out. Our interests merely serve our well-being. They augment our opportunities for success. They do not determine it. But when our interests are set back, there is a diminution of our wherewithal, our means and capacities, for pursuing a good life and facing its challenges. What matters, therefore, is not a wrong *per se* but the implications of that wrong for a person's well-being. Broken limbs are harms because of the loss of capacity to serve the victim's

---

   [3] H.L. Packer, *The Limits of the Criminal Sanction* (Stanford: Stanford UP, 1968) 262.
   [4] *Brown* [1994] 1 AC 212.
   [5] *ibid.*, 246 (Lord Jauncey).
   [6] *Harm to Others* 33.
   [7] *Harm to Others* 34 (emphases in original). See, too, his 'Harm to Others: a Rejoinder' (1986) 16 Criminal Justice Ethics 26, where Feinberg recapitulates: 'I argued that to harm a person was to set back his interest and violate his right. To have an interest, in turn, is to have a stake in some outcome, just as if one had "invested" some of one's own good in it, thus assuming the risk of personal harm or setback.'

needs;[8] vandalism is analogously harmful because, as Raz notes, it diminishes the victim's opportunities.[9] The value immediately protected is instrumental: what counts, ultimately, is people's lives.[10] We protect proprietary rights because of the contribution they can make to that end.[11]

Characteristically, the kind of adverse effect that counts as harm occurs through the impairment of some resource (physical, proprietary, or otherwise) over which the harmed person has a legitimate claim. By 'resource', we do not intend a proprietary analogy, though a person's property is certainly a part of her resources. The idea here is that one's interests comprise of the longer-term means or capabilities that one has. These are the assets one has in life, those things one can rely upon to sustain or enhance well-being. Their contribution to well-being may be either instrumental or constitutive. Indeed, some resources may be both: good health, for example, is valued both because it facilitates other pursuits and because it may be enjoyed in itself. Either way, resources share at least three features. First, they tend to subsist over a longer term. An individual's personal belongings, her state of good health, or her good reputation, can constitute resources. The avoidance of momentary irritation or affront does not. Secondly, they typically affect or are capable of affecting the quality of a person's life; the opportunities that she has for well-being. Property interests, for example, are resources just because they can help to satisfy a person's material needs and preferences. Thirdly, they have an objective dimension, in as much as the existence of a resource is ordinarily independent of the person's consciousness. A resource may be tangible or intangible (*cf.* intellectual property), but it must be something which can be impaired without the person's being aware of it at the time. Contrast, for example, defamation with offensive conduct. A person may be defamed behind his back and thus harmed, because his interest in good reputation remains an important resource; this holds even if he is unaware that his good name is being denigrated. But he cannot be offended unawares. This is an important distinction between harm (as a setback of interest) and offence, as we will see in Part III.

---

[8] *Harm to Others* 53. See also the discussion in § 7.1 below.

[9] J. Raz, 'Autonomy, Toleration, and the Harm Principle' in R. Gavison (ed.), *Issues in Contemporary Legal Philosophy* (Oxford: Clarendon Press, 1987) 313, 327. Cf. S. Perry, 'Corrective v. Distributive Justice' in J. Horder (ed.), *Oxford Essays in Jurisprudence* (4th series, Oxford: Oxford UP, 2000) 237, 256: 'The main reason that personal injury constitutes harm is that it interferes with personal autonomy. It interferes, that is to say, with the set of opportunities and options from which one is able to choose what to do in one's life.'

[10] We do not intend by this claim to exclude other kinds of living creatures from the potential scope of the Harm Principle. It is plausible that a proscription of cruelty to animals may be justified for the sake of the animals themselves, rather than for the sake of their owners or any other human beings. In this book, however, we focus on the central case of human beings.

[11] More on this below, § 3.1(a).

a. Some Examples

We have suggested that harm involves the impairment of a person's opportunities to engage in valued activities and relationships, and to pursue self-chosen goals. Most often, this occurs though the impairment of V's personal or proprietary resources. Clearly, people have interests in their property and in their physical integrity. But we also have other interests that are capable of being set back. Indeed, we can be harmed without directly being the victim; and, indeed, when there is no identifiable victim at all. Hence, on occasion, it may be appropriate to enact 'victimless' crimes. Tax evasion is rightly a crime, notwithstanding that there is no particular victim who is deprived of assets directly. Perhaps it is not the same sort of wrong as theft. But if T illegitimately reduces his tax burden, T effectively takes from, and wrongs, his fellow citizens. The money to pay for public goods must come from somewhere: if not from T, then from others. The obligation to pay tax is a collective duty, one that each person owes to his fellow citizens and not merely to the state.

Similarly, attacks on the integrity of the currency (e.g. counterfeiting) or on the operation of the judicial systems (e.g. contempt of court) matter because they undermine state-implemented regimes that exist for the benefit of us all. State intervention is warranted because members of the community in general would also suffer harm were these regimes to be undermined. Undermining the currency, for instance, would lead to losses of value stored as currency and tend to destabilise the systems that co-ordinate a nation's economic activity;[12] which, in turn, would deprive people of many opportunities for personal and social well-being. Minimising or preventing that sort of indirect, prospective harm to our interests is rightly the business of the state.

3.1   HARMS, WRONGS, AND ENTITLEMENTS

We observed in Chapter 2 that the criminal law is appropriately reserved solely for wrongful conduct. At the heart of the Harm Principle is the thought that its scope should also be restricted to conduct involving damage to another person's interests. Any harm-based account of the criminal canon requires us to identify the harm addressed by each crime, and to show that the harm is sufficiently important to outweigh counter-vailing considerations, including those of individual liberty, which militate against state intervention. Moreover, the account must not neglect to show why the defendant's conduct is wrongful. The Harm Principle provides for

---

[12] cf. *St Margaret's Trust Ltd* [1958] 2 All ER 289, 293.

protection against only those setbacks that D was not entitled to inflict on V. Suppose that D steals an old shirt from V. The shirt is worthless and of no use to V; in fact, V normally throws out his old clothing and has forgotten about the existence of the shirt.[13] Its misappropriation affects him not at all. Further, D is destitute and in great need of clothing. Yet V is wronged by D; and V wrongs no one if, later, he discovers the loss and selfishly recovers his garment from D. V's act of reclamation falls outside the scope of the Harm Principle because, although D's welfare is damaged when he is deprived of the shirt, he has lost nothing to which he had a right.

Harm, even when directly inflicted, is not always accompanied by wrong. In situations of justified self-defence, D may cause injury to the person or property of V, his attacker, but she does not wrong him.[14] Similarly, the judge who sentences P to a lengthy imprisonment for murder does not wrong P, even though she harms P in that she sets back P's interests in freedom, etc.; interests that serve P's well-being and to which P had a prior entitlement.

In § 3.2(c) below, we argue that there are also varieties of secondary, reactive harm that do not generate wrongs. Before that, however, it is important to notice a subtly different case. It might be thought that the examples of self-defence and judicial sentencing are similar to the following scenario. Suppose that Q, a business competitor of T, attracts customers away from T's store by a clever advertising campaign, in which Q makes no negative claims about T's business but simply presents his own store in an attractive light. All three examples involve the absence of a wrong. Q's case, however, is different. Even though T's prospects may be adversely affected, T is not harmed (in the sense used here), because he loses nothing to which he had a prior entitlement. The self-defence and sentencing cases disclose a prima facie wrong, a wrong that proceeds from the infliction of harm in the absence of justification.[15] The advertising case does not. This distinction illustrates the importance of *entitlements* in the

---

[13] The example is based on one discussed by Gardner and Shute, which they describe as 'the pure case of burglary' (or, more strictly, of burglarious theft): 'Suppose an estate agent who has a key to my house lets himself in while I am on holiday and takes a pile of my old clothes from the attic, passing them on to a charity shop. I had long since forgotten that the clothes were there, and I had no further use, anyway, for loon pants and kipper ties. The burglary goes forever undiscovered.' J. Gardner and S. Shute, 'The Wrongness of Rape' in J. Horder (ed.), *Oxford Essays in Jurisprudence* (4th series, Oxford: Oxford UP, 2000) 193, 201. Compare the Scottish case of *Dewar* v. *H.M. Advocate* 1945 SLT 114 (HJC). In that case, the manager of a crematorium was convicted of theft for removing, and putting to 'various lucrative uses', the lids from coffins immediately before they, and their contents, were consigned to the furnace. (Thanks to Victor Tadros for the case.)

[14] See, e.g., W. Chan and A.P. Simester, 'Duress, Necessity: How many Defences?' (2005) 16 King's College LJ 121, 123–27.

[15] These are *primary* harms: below, § 3.2(a).

Harm Principle. When we are harmed, what is set back is not just an interest, but one of *our* interests. Interests in which we have no stake, to which we have no claim or entitlement, do not qualify. This makes the allocation and recognition of entitlements just as important as the finding of wrongfulness once those entitlements are set back.[16]

a.   Post-legal Entitlements: The Example of Property Rights

The paradigmatic application of this point is in the context of proprietary wrongs. It is tempting to think that property offences are less serious than are crimes regulating injury to a person's body. This is often true in particular cases, but it is not obvious they are systemically of a different order of seriousness. If a person were forced to choose between suffering a minor assault and losing his house, for instance, it is plausible that he would prefer the former. At least from a liberal perspective, and in common with any criminal offence, the protection of property rights must itself be justified ultimately in terms of the interests of persons. Suppose a company (Enron?) collapses following some massive corporate accounting fraud. The most important concern in such cases is not the fraud *per se* but its widespread and real implications for the lives of human beings: employees who lose their jobs, shareholders and pension fund holders who lose their savings, and the like. Whether or not the crime involves property, the same questions must always be asked about its legitimacy: how is enactment of this crime justified by reference to the interests of persons? What rationale underpins the claim to state intervention on behalf of V and others, to the detriment of D?

Unlike attacks on V's physical integrity, however, it does not suffice to point to the violation of the property right *per se* as the wrongful harm that warrants state intervention. That would lead to a circularity about the application of the Harm Principle to violations of such rights because, in most modern societies, property rights are not pre-legal.[17] This is not to deny that the legal structure of property rights may, analytically and historically, be a development of pre-legal norms and rights: conduct aimed at achieving dominion over resources may exist before (or outside) any legal recognition of proprietary interests. Rather, the claim is that the

---

[16]   Note that this distinction helps to resolve the difficulty considered by Feinberg in *Harm to Others* § 3.4, where he observes (at 111) that 'We cannot know which harms may properly be prevented by the criminal law until we know which harms when inflicted indefensibly are wrongs.' Feinberg's analysis also encounters difficulties in the context of secondary (rather than primary) harms: below, § 3.2.

[17]   Thanks are due here to Bob Sullivan, co-author of 'The Nature and Rationale of Property Offences' in R.A. Duff and S. Green (eds), *Defining Crimes: Essays on the Criminal Law's Special Part* (Oxford: Oxford UP, 2005) 168, on which part of this section is based.

recognition and delineation of proprietary interests is itself a matter of legal rules, and moreover of rules that have varied considerably across different periods of social and legal development. As a formal category, property is quintessentially legal. I don't need the law to know that this arm is mine; but I do need the law to know that this is my table, or that that house is yours. Indeed, in the case of non-corporeal assets such as patents and shares, the very identification of such things as susceptible of ownership is dependent on law. Within the terms of the Harm Principle, interference with another's property rights constitutes a prima facie harm. But it constitutes a harm the existence of which depends on a determination by the state—making the state's claim to deploy criminal law apparently self-justifying. To invoke the Harm Principle successfully, therefore, we must demonstrate that the protection of property by the criminal law rests on values other than protecting property rights for their own sake.[18]

In order to do so, it is helpful to separate the question, why the state justifiably maintains an institution of property, from the question, whether that institution of property should be protected by the coercive power of the criminal law. The Harm Principle is obviously crucial to that second question. But to answer it, we need to consider the first—and in particular, the role of the institution of property in creating and protecting people's interests. There, too, the Harm Principle is in play, since it constrains other forms of state intervention besides penal legislation. Mill's parameter for state action, that 'the only purpose for which power can be rightfully exercised over any member of a civilised community, against his will, is to prevent harm to others',[19] applies also to the coercive sanctions of the civil law.[20] Hence the state ought not to give effect to a regime of property at all, even through the civil law, unless to do so is consonant with the Harm Principle.

Fortunately, it is. The law of property facilitates the creation of forms of welfare and human flourishing which would become unattainable should that institution be lost. Where this is so, the Harm Principle is brought into play by the property regime itself. The regime serves our well-being; it provides a reliable means by which we can pursue a good life, through the voluntary acquisition, use, and exchange of resources. Having such a system may promote our well-being even if the particular form of the regime is imperfect, provided that members of the community benefit by

---

[18] Compare the notorious German example of the doctrine that the crime of bigamy protects the *Rechtsgut* of monogamous marriage.

[19] *On Liberty* ch. 1.

[20] cf. the discussion in §§ 1.4, 2.3(c); also, e.g., S. Smith, 'Towards a Theory of Contract' in J. Horder (ed.), *Oxford Essays in Jurisprudence* (Fourth Series, Oxford: Oxford UP, 2000) 107.

having a predictable, reliable, set of rules with which to organise their lives.[21] Assuming minimum standards of just distribution of property, the proprietary regime is a public good.

Absent state support, however, the regime would be ineffective, and its ineffectiveness would result in lost opportunities for personal and social advancement through reliable coordinated economic activity, and for other forms of welfare and personal realisation that only the peaceful ownership and possession of property can deliver. Ensuring those opportunities justifies state intervention to enforce the institution of property. Thus even if misappropriating V's old clothes is, in itself, harmless, the Harm Principle lies in the background. No doubt V's material amenities are unaffected. But the property regime supplies V with something else: the dominion over his belongings, including the shirt. It is he, not D, who may decide when an item has outlived its usefulness for him, and how it should be disposed of. (Throw it out? Give it to charity? Tear it into cleaning rags?) This possibility of dominion is itself valuable, and enhances the well-being of owners. Hence theft of the shirt is wrongful even though the survival and functioning of the property regime is, on this occasion, unaffected by D's wrong. The connection to harm in such cases is indirect: absent some reason for treating D's case as special (e.g. in circumstances of necessity or emergency), the widespread perpetration of such conduct could ultimately damage the operation of the regime itself.[22]

By prohibiting crimes such as theft, the criminal law both protects individuals from any particular loss they may suffer, and safeguards the regime of property law more generally. Those who steal set back the dependability of proprietary entitlements; which, in turn, restricts the ability of property owners to plan their own lives, relying both on the property rights they have already and on the expectation of being able to improve their lives by formulating proprietary transactions in the future. Protecting against these outcomes is an appropriate use of the criminal law.[23] Even though the civil law provides a regime for the definition and enforcement of property rights, those rights receive extra protection and security from the criminal law. No doubt V can sue D in the civil courts for the unlawful taking of, say, his car. Sometimes, however, leaving V to civil redress alone would inadequately protect his property and, by extrapolation, the system of property rights as a whole.[24] This is partly a pragmatic

---

[21] See, e.g., J. Coleman, *Risks and Wrongs* (New York: Cambridge UP, 1992) 350–54. Much the same can be said for breach of contract, which is a wrong in virtue of being a breach of D's promise, a voluntary (and reciprocated) obligation assumed to V. Underlying this wrong is the practice of exchanging enforceable reciprocal promises. Even if this practice is imperfect, its reliability promotes our well-being.

[22] A form of remote, conjunctive harm: below, §§ 4.4(c), 5.2(d).

[23] Subject, that is, to the remote harms limitations to be discussed in Chapters 4–5.

[24] cf. *Dewar*, n. 13 above.

point: it permits V to report his loss to the police who, at least in theory, will assume the responsibility for seeking out D and the stolen property while V gets on with his own affairs. But it also symbolic: the proprietary regime is reinforced by public censure of proprietary usurpations.

As we suggested earlier, our argument accepts that violation of a property right can harm the victim directly. However, the harm is parasitic. It provides a justification for intervention only once it is accepted that the institution of property should be defended by the state.[25] Once the case for a *regime* of property rights is accepted, further more specific harms may be crystallised by the rights themselves. Those more specific harms do not justify state intervention unless and until the regime by which they are created is itself justified. They cannot stand by themselves. Suppose, in a slave-owning society, that D rejects the convention that persons may be owned, and sets out to usurp P's ownership of some slaves by helping them to escape. Although, within the terms of that civil legal system, P's interests are set back, any version of the Harm Principle rooted in liberal, inclusive values cannot justify the proscription of D's conduct. Putting the point more generally: our sketch of the functions of a property regime, as enhancing citizens' means for a good life, does not exempt particular property regimes from critical scrutiny.

However, once the case is made for establishing (and then reinforcing) a system of proprietary rights, the more specific harms crystallise and can be relied on to justify particular offences. If D steals V's car, he wrongs V because the car is V's. It is only in virtue of this legal fact that V has a right not to have his car taken by D without consent. But once that right is acknowledged, and the state has regime-based reasons for enforcing rights of that sort, V in particular can then claim to be harmed by D's theft. The existence of this harm creates the specific reason for coercive state intervention. V has lost a valuable resource, diminishing the means and opportunities with which he may enjoy a good life. While V's proprietary rights are not ends in themselves, they function not only to mark out what conduct by D counts as a wrong, but also to allocate the instrumentally valuable resources that conduce (at least in standard cases) toward V's well being.

3.2   NON-CONSTITUTIVE CRIMES AND THE BREADTH OF THE HARM PRINCIPLE

In paradigm harm-based proscriptions, the harm that the crime is designed to prevent is a *constitutive* part of the crime itself, in the sense that it is a

---

[25]   cf. the claim in § 2.3(b) that the state must create obligations (and/or entitlements) *for good reason.*

definitional element of the crime. Many very serious crimes take this form. Murder, for example, cannot be committed without causing death—the very harm that legitimates its criminalisation.

But it is uncontroversial that, even among crimes addressing harm to others, some offences are legitimately enacted notwithstanding that their defining elements do not require a consummated harm. Indeed, in differing forms such crimes pervade our criminal law. Besides murder, human life is also protected by proscriptions of attempted murder, dangerous driving, unlawful gun possession,[26] and a multiplicity of health and safety regulations. In these *non-constitutive* offences, no occurrence of the ultimate harm that justifies such crimes is required within the definition of the crime itself.[27]

In the following chapters we will explore the main varieties of non-constitutive offences and their accommodation within an extended version of the Harm Principle. Before that, however, we need to begin by distinguishing three basic types of harm.

a.   Direct, Primary Harms: The 'Easy' Wrongs

Perhaps the best-recognised cases for the Harm Principle involve what we might call *primary* forms of harm. These kinds of harm are *wrong-generating*. Typically, they involve damage to things such as our physical integrity or our property. In these cases, the wrong can be grounded in the harm. When D damages V's person or property, her conduct is prima facie a wrong, and a potential object for criminalisation, because of that very consequence—V can, and should, point to the damage itself to justify the claim that he has been wronged. That is to say, the wrong to V arises *out of* his being harmed. Imagine that D breaks V's arm. Why is that a prima facie wrong? Because it's V's arm, and it's broken (by D). We need no more. In contrast, consider a case where E causes momentary affront to Q. E's conduct involves no impairment of Q's resources. Moreover, no comparable form of wrongdoing can be derived just from the conduct's effect. In essence, E has displeased Q; but no one has the generalised obligation to refrain from displeasing others. As we shall argue in Part III, E's conduct cannot be wrong simply because it causes affront. Some further ground is required.

Straightforward candidates for prohibition under the Harm Principle are those where a primary harm to another person is brought about directly (e.g. murder), or where its occurrence is directly risked (e.g. dangerous

---

[26] Indeed, possession of a handgun is prohibited altogether within England and Wales: Firearms (Amendments) Act 1997.

[27] The term 'ultimate harm' is used by Husak, *Overcriminalization* 160; see, more generally, *ibid.*, 159–77.

driving). These are the standard cases. Of course, even in these cases it does not follow that criminalisation is justified. The Harm Principle provides for a balancing of interests, one that considers the extent and likelihood of the harm involved and weighs that against the other implications of criminalisation. Feinberg's account, for example, presents a number of factors to be taken into account at this stage:[28]

(a)   the greater the gravity of a possible harm, the less probable its occurrence need be to justify prohibition of the conduct that threatens to produce it;

(b)   the greater the probability of harm, the less grave the harm need be to justify coercion;

(c)   the greater the magnitude of the risk of harm, itself compounded out of gravity and probability, the less reasonable it is to accept the risk;

(d)   the more valuable (useful) the dangerous conduct, both to the actor and to others, the more reasonable it is to take the risk of harmful consequences, and for extremely valuable conduct it is reasonable run risks up to the point of clear and present danger;

(e)   the more reasonable a risk of harm (the danger), the weaker is the case for prohibiting the conduct that creates it.

A responsible legislator should consider the gravity and likelihood of the wrongful harm and weigh that against the social value of the conduct to be prohibited and the degree of intrusion upon citizens' lives that criminalisation would involve. The greater the gravity and likelihood of the harm, the stronger the case for criminalisation; conversely, the more valuable the conduct is, or the more the prohibition would limit liberty, the stronger the case against criminalisation. In addition, other rights that a citizen may have, for example to free speech or privacy, should be respected. These rights may militate against creating certain types of crimes, especially (as we argue in Part III) in the context of offensive behaviour.

It is a calculation of this sort that justifies the setting of speed limits.[29] In the United Kingdom, for example, it is not permitted to drive on the motorway at speeds in excess of 70 miles per hour. Is this a legitimate prohibition? The answer is, yes. On the one hand, driving at 75 miles per hour may not be inherently immoral or wrong. But the faster one drives, the higher the probability that if something goes awry, serious personal injury and property damage will result. Hence the case falls within the scope of the Harm Principle, and is amenable to criminal regulation. On the other hand, even though setting the speed limit at (say) 20 miles per hour would save more lives,[30] the social costs, in terms of reduced mobility

---

[28]   *Harm to Others* 216.

[29]   Subject to what is said in § 4.2(a), in the context of abstract-endangerment cases.

[30]   C. Grundy, R. Steinbach, P. Edwards, J. Green, B. Armstrong, and P. Wilkinson, 'Effect of 20 mph traffic speed zones on road injuries in London, 1986–2006: controlled interrupted time series analysis' [2009] British Medical Journal 339:b4469.

and inefficient transportation systems, would be too great. Decisions of this sort require a balancing of factors, such as the effect on people's mobility of setting the limit too low, against the costs, in terms of scale and likelihood of injuries, of setting the limit too high.

Resolution of that balancing process will depend on reference to standard cases. The Harm Principle is in play here because speeding *standardly* causes or creates a risk of harm, even if the actual risk varies in particular instances. Inevitably, the criminal law is a blunt instrument, regulating in terms of average cases and incapable of reflecting the myriad variations upon those cases that real life generates.

To a large extent, this is a matter of resources, and of their efficient use—it is simply uneconomic to frame and administer laws that take into account the particularities of every person's situation. Hence, criminal law tends to prohibit actions on the basis of their typical risks and consequences, leaving further refinement, if any, to the realm of exceptions. It is an offence, we have said, to drive faster on a motorway than 70 miles per hour. This is so notwithstanding that there is no intrinsic significance to that speed. (Indeed, depending on the circumstances, there may be no danger at all: a possibility we consider in the next two chapters.) None the less, specifying a precise limit is a convenient and enforceable means by which to regulate dangerous driving; and the limit itself is determined by reference to risks in standard cases.

b. Remote (Primary) Harms

The standard cases considered above become candidates for prohibition under the Harm Principle when D's action directly attacks V's interests. No one seriously suggests, however, that actions may be criminalised under the Harm Principle only when they cause or risk harm in such a manner. Many *per se* harmless wrongs also warrant criminalisation under the Harm Principle, and the Principle may come into play notwithstanding that the wrong does not cause harm even in standard situations.

One way for this to occur is when an action becomes harmful, by tending to diminish the resources that underpin well-being, not immediately but *remotely*. My selling you a handgun, for example, does not in itself harm you, but rather puts you in a position where subsequently you may harm another person. This possibility is an implicit feature of many inchoate offences, such as incitement to murder;[31] and of what are sometimes called 'substantive inchoate' offences, such as the offence of

---

[31] Though not of complete attempts, which ordinarily create a direct risk of harm. By contrast, incomplete attempts, which require further interventions by the agent, generate remote harm.

'going equipped'. It is a crime in many countries to be on the street at night when in possession of an instrument of burglary, such as a jemmy (or 'crowbar'), without lawful excuse. The justification for this offence is not that I have the jemmy, but rather that I might use it to break into a building.

We shall explore these kinds of cases in the next two chapters. For now, it suffices to sound a cautionary note about this form of justification. While it may sometimes be appropriate, very often there are difficulties about basing criminalisation on remote harms, especially those predicated on the eventual criminal choices of third persons. To invoke the Harm Principle, we have noted, an action must not only be conducive to harm—it must also be a wrong. This constraint is particularly apposite to the criminal law. Punishment, as we have mentioned, embodies by its nature an element of blame or censure; it is not obvious that D may properly be condemned for her non-harmful action, just because that action happens to be linked, through chains of complex social interaction, to the subsequent injurious behaviour of some separate and autonomous person, E. It seems unjust to impose penal censure on D, at least where D has little or no ability to control the potential harmful choices of E, and where D has not sought to assist or encourage those choices.

c.   Secondary, Reactive Harms

The last variety shares the indirect character of remote harms. Harm can also occur when people are affected by the *prospect*, rather than the actuality, of a wrongful action. One reason why the state sometimes intervenes to prevent public nuisance, for example, is not that the relevant action is harmful, but rather that avoiding it causes great inconvenience.[32] In such cases, the constraint imposed by the Harm Principle is satisfied not by the nuisance itself but by the precautions required to forestall it. This is partly, but *only* partly, to agree with the observation made by Gardner and Shute:[33]

> It is no objection under the harm principle that a harmless action was criminalized, nor even that an action with no tendency to cause harm was criminalized. It is enough to meet the demands of the harm principle that, if the action were not criminalized, *that* would be harmful.

---

[32] cf. *Chaplin & Co. v. Westminster Corporation* [1901] 2 Ch 329 (obstructing the highway).
[33] Above n. 13, at 216.

What matters, in other words, is not the question, 'is this act harmful?' but, rather, 'what if this act were always permitted?'[34] For example, the fact that I might be burgled may lead me to avoid taking lengthy holidays, take out insurance, install an alarm in my house, and so forth. These are costs that I would not otherwise need or choose to incur, in addition to the intangible harms of uncertainty and insecurity with which the prospect of being vulnerable in one's home damages one's life. On the assumption that criminalisation is at least partially effective in reducing the incidence of burglary, it therefore helps to reduce harm.

What Gardner and Shute fail to observe, however, is that reactive harm is *secondary*. The potential scope of their analysis is far too wide. It is vital to emphasise that, wherever criminalisation of an action depends for its legitimacy on reactive harm, *the wrong must be established independently of such harm*. Hence the requirement that the action be wrongful becomes especially important. It is not enough to invoke the Harm Principle that V dislikes something D does (say, D's walking her dog on V's street), and that V consequently does not leave his home in the mornings and feels obliged to erect high fences on his property in order to avoid witnessing D's behaviour. V's response has a claim, as harm, on the state's attention only if it is a justifiable reaction to D's *wrongful* conduct. Thus the wrongfulness of D's conduct must be independent of V's reaction.

Unlike primary harm, therefore, reactive harm is not wrong-constituting—as we shall see, this point is central to understanding the legitimacy of criminalising offensive behaviour. At the same time, reactive harm may go to the *character* and *seriousness* of the wrong. It just can't make conduct wrong by itself.

An example is supplied by the wrong of burglary. A typical burglary occurs when D breaks into V's home in order to commit some further crime, such as theft. Breaking into V's home is already a wrong; and we could make an argument for its criminalisation in terms of primary harm. But to do so just in those terms would be to underestimate the true nature and significance of burglary.

One aggravating consideration involves remote harm. Breaking into V's home is a significant physical step by which D commits herself to carrying out the theft, and it might warrant criminalisation as an attempt to commit a crime (theft) that itself standardly involves harm. In effect, burglary ups the stakes, making it more likely that the ulterior offence will be committed.

---

[34] This claim is consistent with Feinberg's own formulation of the principle (*Harm to Others* 26): 'It is always a good reason in support of penal legislation that it would probably be effective in preventing (eliminating, reducing) harm to persons other than the actor (the one prohibited from acting) and there is probably no other means that is equally effective at no greater cost to other values.' Feinberg's formula requires that criminalisation of an action will prevent harm, not that the action itself be harmful.

Moreover, because the activity occurs inside a building, incidental violence might ensue should D be chanced upon by someone else.[35]

But perhaps the most distinctive rationale for taking burglary so seriously is the secondary harm it generates. The trespassory entry by D not only exposes V to risk of the further crime (e.g. theft); it also, in so doing, violates V's private life.

The strongest case of this—often subject to distinctive criminalisation or sentencing provisions—is where the premises are a dwelling-house.[36] Interaction with and exposure to other members of society is integral to public life; conversely, our sense of identity and well-being as individuals depends upon our being able to reserve private space, from which other persons can be excluded. It is through controlling our private environment that we are able to have 'breathing space' from interactions with other people. Burglary compromises that space. It is hardly surprising that house burglary, in particular, causes victims great distress even if they were absent at the material time. The victim of such a burglary cannot be sure of the peaceable enjoyment even of her own home. For most people, when the integrity of their private space cannot be taken for granted, one of the foundations of their well-being is destroyed.

An analogous if less powerful claim can be made for burglary of other buildings. One of the main functions of structures such as warehouses, offices, and the like is to help safeguard people and property by establishing a physical separation from the public environment. Within that secured space, people can relax at least some of the precautions they may take when in public, by putting down their handbags, remaining late to work, and the like. Conversely, if that space is not perceived to be fully secure, such practices become disrupted. Even in these non-domestic contexts, the existence and control of a realm of quasi-private space affects the manner in which we live.[37]

The existence of secured private space also influences how we organise our property. Just as at home, goods in warehouses and offices can be arrayed or stocked without securing each individually. Thus a related harm of burglary is that it gives D unparalleled access to take (or damage) a whole range of V's goods, whether domestic or commercial, in a way that, say, pickpocketing does not.[38] Here too, the case of a domestic burglary is an aggravated one: the goods to which D has access tend to include our very personal things (underclothes, private letters, and the like) as well as

---

[35] cf. Note, 'A Rationale of the Law of Burglary' (1951) 51 Columbia LR 1009, 1026.

[36] Theft Act 1968 (UK), s. 9(3)(a); Sentencing Act 2002 (NZ), s. 9(1)(b). This was originally the only variety of burglary known to the common law. See 3 Coke Inst. 63.

[37] We assume here that a space open to the public, such as a shop floor during trading hours, should not be susceptible of burglary (e.g. by a shoplifter who enters the shop with intent to steal).

[38] Thanks to Jeremy Horder for input on this point.

things with high sentimental value—something that reinforces the sense of 'violation' experienced by burglary victims.

For all these reasons, burglary deserves its status independently as a significant crime, and not merely a form of trespass or attempted theft. Notice, though, that the most important effect is reactive. If D's mere presence in a town, or walking down the street, would lead V to fear for her safety (perhaps D is very large and wears logo-emblazoned jackets[39]), so that V sells her house and retreats to a more remote village, there is no ground for intervention under the Harm Principle—because there is no wrong.

3.3   HARM-INDEPENDENT WRONGS

Acknowledging different categories of harm allows us to reject as simplistic the attempt to shoehorn every case under the Harm Principle into a model that requires a direct attack on D's well-being. Consider Feinberg's discussion of a bare trespass:[40]

> A trespasser invades the landowner's interest in 'the exclusive enjoyment and possession of his land.' Technically that interest is violated when the trespasser takes one quiet and unobserved step on the other's land; in the somewhat special sense of harm that we have been developing, such a violation sets back an interest, and to that extent therefore harms the interest's owner, even though it does not harm any other interest, and may even be beneficial on balance.

The problem with this analysis is that it tends to collapse the distinction between harms and wrongs,[41] since individuals can always be said to have an interest in not being wronged. The very reason why bare trespass is a difficult case is that the wrongdoer's action violates the landowner's right but causes no actual harm.[42] To hold otherwise would be to make a merely formal move, modifying our conception of harm within the Harm Principle in order to include bare right-violations, and thereby disguising without dissolving the problem posed by harmless wrongdoing.

---

[39] Seemingly the fear behind the Wanganui District Council (Prohibition of Gang Insignia) Act 2009 (NZ).

[40] *Harm to Others* 107.

[41] A similar difficulty arises in Antony Duff's work: see *Intention, Agency and Criminal Liability* (Oxford: Blackwell, 1990) § 5.3; also his 'Subjectivism, Objectivism and Criminal Attempts' in A.P. Simester and A.T.H. Smith (eds), *Harm and Culpability* (Oxford: Oxford UP, 1996) 19, 37 n. 68.

[42] Hence Gardner and Shute rightly describe their burglary example (above, n. 13) as 'the case of the wrong and nothing but the wrong'. Feinberg's analysis here leaves no room for that distinction because 'interest' does double-duty here. It refers both to the right (which is violated by an act of trespass) and to the subject matter of the right (the land). The latter is the kind of resource underpinning our conception of harm—and it is not set back.

It is implicit in our analysis that some actions are wrongs prior to, and not in virtue of, any harm (whether primary or secondary) that they may cause. Indeed, there is a range of important offences where the wrong is not, in the first instance, grounded in any consequential harm. Crimes such as battery and perjury do not, conceptually speaking, specify a harm. Perjury directly criminalises the wrong, a wrong that is intrinsic rather than instrumental: it is committed even if no one is even momentarily deceived. None the less, that such crimes are (also) harmful is an important element of the case for legislative prohibition: the wrong of perjury is not criminalised merely because it is immoral.[43] As we saw in § 3.2, the seriousness of the wrong may be dependent on its consequences, e.g. for the reliability and efficacy of the legal system in general. The difference from core result-crimes such as murder is that, in battery, perjury, and the like, the harm is not the source of the wrong. They are wrongs whatever harm they cause, or risk, or otherwise may lead to. Thus the harmfulness of (say) battery takes various forms and is not distinctively, let alone conceptually or definitionally, characteristic of battery.[44] So, although harm is part of the justification of the criminalisation of battery, the crime of battery can be committed without causing that harm.

The same is true of inchoate offences. While an act of attempted murder is wrongful in virtue of the actor's motivation rather than its outcome, the grounds for its criminalisation rest, in the background, also on the fact that it conduces to harm. This is part of the worry about impossible attempts, especially about radically impossible attempts (such as attempted murder by voodoo doll): that no harm is threatened and, if the legal specification of such cases can be adequately distinguished, they should therefore not be criminalised.[45] However, there is nothing generally wrong with criminalising actions that are wrongs independently of the harm they cause.[46]

[43] Contrast Husak, *Overcriminalization*, who seems to abandon the requirement for harm (at 66) when he proposes a disjunctive 'nontrivial harm or evil' constraint, that 'Criminal liability may not be imposed unless statutes are designed to prohibit a nontrivial harm *or* evil.' (Cf. M. Moore, 'A Tale of Two Theories' (2009) 28 Criminal Justice Ethics 27, 35, 39.) Similarly, Husak defines (at 160) 'consummate' offences as those in which 'each act-token of an act-type proscribed ... produces a harm or evil.' In this book, we have preferred the phrase 'constitutive offences' to his 'consummate offences', principally in order to preserve the distinction outlined here in § 3.3.

[44] At common law, battery is a form of trespass to the person. As such, it can be constituted even by non-consensual touching: see *Simester and Sullivan* §§ 11.1, 11.3.

[45] For discussion of over-inclusion see below, § 11.4(c).

[46] Neither is there any general objection to remote-*wrong* prophylactic offences. Although the point is incidental here, it is worth noting that Antony Duff's definition of an attack is restricted to actions directed toward harming a value or interest: 'Criminalizing Endangerment' in R.A. Duff and S. Green (eds), *Defining Crimes: Essays on the Special Part of the Criminal Law* (Oxford: Oxford UP, 2005) 43, § 2. But one may also do wrong in attempting to *wrong* another, and such attempts may constitute attacks.

3.4   CONCLUSION

The requirement for wrongfulness prevents the Harm Principle from becoming a purely instrumental principle. Nonetheless, the requirement for harm *is* instrumental—the link to harm does not have to be intrinsic. Thus it is a misreading of the Harm Principle and, as we shall see in Part III, a misguided attempt to distinguish it from the Offence Principle, to tie the Harm Principle to intrinsically harmful actions. The Principle is about wrongful actions that lead to harm. But those actions need not be harmful in themselves.

It is quite possible, especially in cases of purely offensive conduct, that the victim may be wronged yet suffer no set-back to his interests. Prima facie, such a case may seem to fall outside the scope of the Harm Principle. Similarly, in the more controversial example noted by Kleinig, a temporary abduction may have no lasting effects.[47] Here too, there is a wrong—indeed, a wrong arising out of interference with a welfare interest—but no harm. However, further investigation reveals a number of ways in which the Harm Principle is capable of extending to cases where there is no immediate or necessary harm. In turn, the case for criminalising such wrongs falls within the ambit of the Harm Principle. Because the Harm Principle is capable of applying to actions that lead only indirectly to harm, and not just to actions that are intrinsically harmful, the scope of the Principle is broader than is generally recognised.

---

[47] J. Kleinig, 'Crime and the Concept of Harm' (1978) 15 American Philosophical Quarterly 27, 32; discussed by Feinberg, *Harm to Others* 52–53.

4

Remote Harms: the Need for an Extended Harm Principle

I N PRACTICE, THERE are numerous examples of criminalisation that do not sit comfortably within the standard harms analysis. Many of them are legitimate. In Parts III and IV, we shall discuss two well-known grounds for sometimes extending the reach of the criminal law, to proscribe conduct that involves offence to others or harm to the actor himself. Such extensions may be opposed by strict adherents to the Harm Principle, who would restrict prohibitions to conduct that is harmful to others. Used as a limiting principle, the Harm Principle may serve as a valuable way of keeping the scope of the criminal law modest.

However, those who aim to widen the law's scope might instead adopt a different strategy, and seek to co-opt rather than bypass the Harm Principle, by appealing to the conduct's supposed *long-term* risk of harm to others. A variety of prohibitions (for example, those relating to drug use[1]) have been defended by reference to the eventual deleterious social consequences to which the conduct leads. Extending 'harm' in this fashion has the potential to erode the usefulness of the Harm Principle as a constraint on the state's punitive power. Hence the questions for this chapter: how and why does a conventional harms analysis not suffice to deal with remote harms or risks? What additional limitations of principle should there be upon the invocation of more 'remote' forms of risk, as grounds for criminalisation?

4.1 THE PROBLEM OF 'REMOTE' HARMS

Much of the attractiveness of the Harm Principle derives from its having been applied to more immediate harms, where the standard normative constraints (e.g., concerning liberty and the imputation of fault) are readily

---

[1] See J. Kaplan, *The Hardest Drug: Heroin and Public Policy* (Chicago: Chicago UP, 1983). For more recent treatments of the drug-criminalisation debate, see D. Husak, *Legalize This! The Case for Decriminalizing Drugs* (London: Verso, 2002); D. Husak and P. de Marneffe, *The Legalization of Drugs (For and Against)* (New York: Cambridge UP, 2005).

satisfied. When applied to ordinary victimising conduct, the Harm Principle serves well as a limitation of state punitive power: ordinary citizens' freedom of action is not greatly restricted by prohibiting, say, violence or thievery. This holds also for prohibitions that concern the more immediate risks of harm: barring people from driving while intoxicated still leaves them with a wide variety of other permitted choices, not least getting drunk at home or at the corner pub.

Once this kind of standard analysis is extended to include more remote harms, however, matters change—because all sorts of seemingly innocent things we do may ultimately have deleterious consequences. It is not easy to identify conduct that confidently can be said to be without substantial risk of injury in the long run. As a result, the Harm Principle—unless suitably modified or supplemented—can lose much of its liberty-safeguarding role.[2]

When the Principle is applied to individual, victimising harms, the attribution of responsibility and fault is also relatively straightforward, because of the close links between the actor's culpable choice and the resulting harm. If I intentionally assault you, and you are injured as a result, I am to blame for the (at least, foreseeable) injury that results. This holds not only for actual injuries but for the more immediate forms of risk: when I drive recklessly, I should be accountable for the hazard my driving foreseeably creates.

When more remote risks are involved, however, holding the actor accountable for the possible injurious results becomes more problematic. Typically, what is prohibited is a present act, A, which (in the legislature's judgement) creates or helps create an unacceptable risk of some eventual harm, X. The mens rea required is merely an intent to perform the present act A, and the actor need not even be aware of its eventual deleterious consequences. In such circumstances, it is not always obvious how the actor can rightly be held to blame for those eventual consequences. And if the actor is not to blame, how can the censure of a criminal penalty be warranted?

4.2   THE STANDARD HARMS ANALYSIS

How, then, has the issue of 'remote' harm been addressed? While the subject has not received a great deal of attention, the usual mode of analysis focuses simply on the likelihood and magnitude of the risk, and on

---

[2] cf. B. Harcourt, 'The Collapse of the Harm Principle' (1999) 90 J Crim L & Criminology 105.

certain countervailing concerns and constraints. This approach is, essentially, the 'standard' analysis that we noted in § 3.2(a).[3] Stated schematically, the Standard Harms Analysis involves the following steps for deciding whether a given type of risk satisfies the requirements of the Harm Principle:

Step 1: Consider the gravity of the eventual harm, and its likelihood. The greater the gravity and likelihood, the stronger the case for criminalisation.

Step 2: Weigh against the foregoing, the social value of the conduct, and the degree of intrusion upon actors' choices that criminalisation would involve. The more valuable the conduct is, or the more the prohibition would limit liberty, the stronger the countervailing case would be.[4]

Step 3: Observe certain side-constraints that would preclude criminalisation. The prohibition should not, for example, infringe rights of privacy or free expression.

(The Standard Harms Analysis does not, of course, require that conduct automatically be criminalised whenever its criteria are met. Existing prohibitions may suffice to deal with the problem. The potential difficulties and costs of enforcement need also to be considered.[5])

The eventual harm, under the Standard Harms Analysis, should be of a kind which could properly be criminalised itself, were it to occur immediately. Claims about supposed eventual risks sometimes address bad social consequences of a non-criminal nature: John Kaplan, for example, contends that widespread drug use undermines the work ethic, leading to lowered social productivity.[6] Laziness, however, is not in itself criminal. That drug use might lead to declining work habits thus is not a valid ground for criminalisation—unless those altered work habits lead, in turn, to something else that qualifies as a harm.[7] Kaplan's argument thus would need to be revised so as to assert that drug abuse leads to laziness and lowered economic productivity; and the consequent increase in poverty is likely to lead, in turn, to (say) more theft and violence.

In the context of many immediate sorts of risks, the Standard Harms Analysis works nicely. Why, for example, might a legislature wisely

---

[3] cf. *Harm to Others* 190–93, 216.

[4] While this 'balancing' approach may seem utilitarian in its focus on the extent of injuriousness of the conduct and on the countervailing benefits, we emphasise that this does not presuppose a general utilitarian outlook. One can think that consequences, including their likelihood and gravity, matter without being a utilitarian (or even a wholehearted consequentialist).

[5] See further below, § 11.5.

[6] Above n. 1, at 131–34.

[7] See D. Husak, 'The Nature and Justifiability of Nonconsummate Offenses' (1995) 37 Arizona LR 151; Husak, *Overcriminalization* 167–68.

prohibit driving while intoxicated, while not proscribing walking in a similar state? The reason has to do with the likelihood and magnitude of the risks involved. Why should the legislature abstain from proscribing the more strenuous forms of political advocacy, even if those involve some enhanced risk of public disorder? The reason concerns the side constraint of free expression. And so forth.

Does the Analysis perform so well, however, when extended to remote risks? It has been thought so: Feinberg, for example, recommends its use, and suggests no fundamental distinction between the more immediate and remoter forms of danger.[8] Yet there are reasons for doubt.

The Standard Harm Analysis does at least recognise the issue of liberty, by making the degree of restriction of choice a counter-consideration to be weighed against the magnitude and likelihood of the harm. But liberty is treated merely as a weighing factor, which means that the greater the predicted harm, the more extensive the loss of liberty that would be permitted. It might be responded that the counter-consideration concerning 'intrusion on actors' choices' could make a difference, provided it is given sufficient weight. If little restriction of choice were tolerated, only a narrow ambit of criminalisation would be permitted. However, this only shows how sensitive the analysis is to the weight that such counter-considerations are given. Were these given reduced weight, much restriction of liberty would become permissible. Unhappily, the Standard Harms Analysis does not suggest how this critical weighting issue should be resolved: it merely says that the counter-considerations should somehow be 'balanced' against the degree and likelihood of the harm.

With regard to imputations of responsibility and fault, matters are worse: the Standard Harms Analysis provides no framework for dealing with this issue. In its concerns about the likelihood of the harm, it addresses the empirical link between the prohibited conduct and the undesired harmful result. But the normative link—why and to what extent the defendant committing a given act should be held responsible or to blame for its remote consequences or risks—is not explicitly addressed at all.

We do not mean to suggest that the Standard Harms Analysis should be jettisoned, for it has an important role to play in assessing the usefulness of prohibitions. Rather, the argument here is that the Analysis cannot stand alone. We need an Extended Harms Analysis, containing further principles, which are designed to deal with the special problems raised by remote harms.

---

[8] *Harm to Others* chs 5, 6.

4.3   WHAT ARE 'REMOTE' HARMS?

Before proceeding with our analysis, we need to illustrate what is meant by 'remote' harms. It is not literal spatio-temporal remoteness that should matter: there seems no problem, for example, in punishing the act of secreting explosives in a populous area, timed to explode months hence. We are speaking, instead, of risks that are remote in the sense that they involve certain kinds of contingencies. Let us begin by enumerating a few kinds.[9]

a.   Abstract Endangerment

Traditional criminal legislation, where concerned with risk, addresses actual danger: the prohibition is couched in terms of creating an unreasonable probability of hurting someone. (Reckless driving is the stock example.) Included may be conduct the riskiness of which depends on the existence of a contingency, but where it is not known or knowable to the actor *ex ante* whether that contingency will materialise in the particular situation. Overtaking on a blind corner endangers another only if there actually is a car behind the curve, coming in the opposite direction. But as the driver cannot know whether there is a car coming when he overtakes, this is an unreasonable risk to take.

Modern criminal statutes dealing with remoter forms of risk, however, often couch their prohibitions *abstractly*: in terms that cover instances of the conduct known to be harmless. Sometimes this is done because the behaviour ordinarily is dangerous. Consider a prohibition against driving with a high blood alcohol level (e.g., over 0.8 pro mil). Since most streets are frequented, and most persons drive badly with so much alcohol, this usually constitutes dangerous conduct. But a defendant is liable even if he knows full well that the street is empty, or that his tolerance for alcohol is especially high.[10] Typically in such legislation, the feared risk is not even included in the legal definition of the crime: the statute proscribes (say) driving with a certain blood-alcohol level. The conduct's tendency to produce accidents comes into the picture merely as the legislature's reason for the proscription.

Abstract-endangerment liability may also include, more problematically, prohibitions of conduct which ordinarily is not risky, but which is proscribed because *some* actors may endanger others. An example is

---

[9] We discuss these and other varieties in more detail in the next chapter.

[10] Of course, the driver on the empty street may endanger himself, but to criminalise that endangerment would be a paternalistic measure, outside the scope of the Harm Principle. See Part IV below.

Sweden's prohibition of driving with quite low blood alcohol levels (0.2 pro mil or more).[11] Most people at that point can still drive reasonably safely, but a minority who hold their liquor badly cannot. Many thus are barred from conduct that involves tolerably low risks, in order that the less competent few are prevented from endangering others.

b. Mediating Interventions

Legislation concerned with remote risks may also proscribe conduct which has no ill consequences in itself, but which is thought to induce or lead to further acts (by the defendant or a third person) that create or risk harm. Gun-possession is an instance: ordinarily, the danger materialises only when the gun-possessor (or another) handles or uses the weapon in certain ways.[12] The harm thus is 'remote' in the sense that it arises upon the making of an intervening choice; but the conduct is made punishable whether or not that intervention occurs. Indeed, the feared subsequent choice may occur only in a minority of cases: most people who possess guns, for example, do not misuse them.

As we shall see in the next chapter, gun control is a difficult case. Other intervening-choice claims seem even more dubious. An example noted in the previous chapter is the House of Lords' decision in *Brown*,[13] where it was suggested by Lord Jauncey that one reason for proscribing consensual sadistic/masochistic sex among adult males was that its authorisation might encourage the perpetration of similar conduct with underage boys.

The Standard Harm Analysis assigns no special status to the fact of an intervening choice. The Analysis simply addresses the magnitude and likelihood of the harm, and the applicability of the counter-considerations and side constraints. Were gun-control thought acceptable and the bad-example thesis in *Brown* rejected, it would be on account of the respective degrees of likelihood of harm involved, or the applicability of (say) the side-constraint of privacy.

---

[11] Swedish Session Laws 1990: 149.

[12] But see the further discussion of gun control, below in § 4.4(b) and more generally in Chapter 5.

[13] [1994] 1 AC 212, 246. What was directly at issue in this case was immediate harm—namely, the defendants' inflicting minor wounds on one another in the course of their sexual activities. The defendants contended, however, that since the participants were all adults and expressly had consented, the state's intrusion was an inappropriate exercise of paternalism. In arguing that the public interest called for continued proscription notwithstanding the participants' consent, Lord Jauncey adverted to the risk of eventual harm not involving valid consent: *viz.*, 'the possibility of proselytisation and corruption of young men.'

c. Conjunctive Harms

In yet other situations, the conduct does the feared injury only when combined with similar acts of others. Dumping household garbage in the river is treated as a health hazard, but the conduct actually endangers health only when numerous other persons do likewise. In such situations, however, the proscribed act is a token of the type of conduct that cumulatively does the harm: the actor cannot draw a moral distinction between his behaviour and that of the others who contribute to the injury. This is to be contrasted with intervening-choice situations, in which the conduct is harmless in itself even when cumulated, and leads to possible injury only because it supposedly induces or permits harmful choices of another kind.

4.4   REMOTE HARM AND FAIR IMPUTATION

a.   Why is Imputation Important?

As we saw in Chapter 1, an essential characteristic of the criminal sanction is that it conveys censure. The sanction is thus visited appropriately only on conduct that is in some sense reprehensible. In turn, the criminalisation of conduct calls for an explanation of why the behaviour merits the condemnation of the criminal law.

One important aspect of that explanation concerns whether responsibility for remote harms can be *imputed* to the actor. Not only should the conduct have injurious consequences, but it needs to be explained why the actor can be held accountable for those consequences. Traditionally, the Harm Principle has focused chiefly on individual, victimising harms, where such imputation is relatively straightforward: so long as the act is committed with the requisite mens rea and acceptable excuses are not present, culpable wrongdoing can usually be inferred directly from the causation of harm.

When the law is extended to include more remote harms, however, the inference from harm to wrong becomes more tenuous. Suppose the conduct to be proscribed is not immediately injurious to anyone; but it may trigger a series of actions (possibly initiated by independent agents) that eventually risk harmful consequences. It then becomes necessary to ask whether, and for what reason, those potential consequences are ones for which the defendant should fairly be held accountable.

The clearest examples of this problem of fair imputation concern mediating-intervention risks. Suppose, for example, that we were to accept Charles Murray's thesis that unregulated premarital sex, by yielding higher

rates of illegitimate births, leads to more children growing up in impover-
ished households with weakened parental control; which in its turn,
generates higher crime rates by offspring.[14] If the Standard Harm Analysis
were applied without more, there might (depending on the likelihood and
extent of the eventual harmful consequences) be a prima facie case for the
intervention of the criminal law, subject only to the applicable counter-
considerations and side constraints. Whether or not the side constraints
apply would depend on how the prohibition is couched. Direct proscription of fornication seems objectionable as a violation of privacy, but
indirect restrictions—say, a curfew on teenagers' attending discotheques
and other places deemed to encourage premarital sex—might seem less so.

A second case is the familiar one of drug prohibitions. Suppose evidence
were indeed available that widespread use of a given drug leads to lowered
social   productivity   which,   in   turn,   creates   criminogenic   social
environments.[15] The Standard Harm Analysis would then make prohibition depend in large part on estimates of the likelihood and magnitude of
such effects.[16]

In both of these cases, however, simple reliance on the Standard Harm
Analysis would overlook something fundamental: the question of fair
imputation. The harm is produced not by the actor's own behaviour, but
by the subsequent choices of third parties whom she does not control (the
offspring of fornicators, or the persons influenced by the changed social
atmosphere generated by drug use). Criminalising the conduct thus raises
the question: why is my conduct wrongful? Why should I be punished for
conduct of a kind that does no harm in itself, simply because it may
influence other persons to decide to engage in acts that are potentially
injurious? The problem is not the factual link: my behaviour may well
influence others' voluntary choices, in a variety of ways.[17] Neither is the
problem one of conventional mens rea: let us assume that the prohibited
act (say, drug possession) is intentionally committed. The problem is,

---

[14] C. Murray, *The Emerging British Underclass* (London: Institute of Economic Affairs,
1990); also C. Murray and P. Alcock, *Underclass: The Crisis Deepens* (London: Institute of
Economic Affairs, 1994). We adopt Murray's claim only as a useful hypothetical for present
purposes.

[15] See Kaplan, above n. 1, and the discussion in § 4.2 above. It is sometimes claimed that
drug use leads more immediately to harm, in that users must steal in order to pay for drugs.
That need to steal, however, appears to derive largely from the inflated price of drugs that
prohibition itself generates.

[16] Feinberg deals with intervening-choice situations in such terms. For example, with
so-called 'imitative harms' (say, the showing of a violent film which evokes actual violence on
the part of some viewers), he argues that the conduct would be covered *pro tanto* by the
Harm Principle (provided that the actor knew or should have known of the possibility of
imitations), but that countervailing concerns—particularly, interests in free expression—
militate against criminalisation. See *Harm to Others* 232–45.

[17] cf. *Harm to Others* 235–37. The point here is that X's merely having influenced Y's
voluntary action does not necessarily render X morally accountable for Y's behaviour.

rather, the imputational link: should I be held responsible for the potential ill consequences that flow from the choices of other agents, so that my original conduct is something that can be regarded as wrongful?

Under certain conditions, which we shall explore in the next chapter, an actor may properly be held responsible. The most obvious case is that of solicitation, where X requests Y to commit a crime. Another well-known case is the sale of hazardous products: the manufacturer knowingly sells a product the standard use of which creates (say) dangers to health. In these situations, however, it is not merely the actor's having influenced the subsequent choice that matters; rather, it is her having, in some manner, underwritten that subsequent choice.

On the other hand, where there has been no such involvement on the part of the defendant, he should not be held criminally accountable. The reason why not concerns the idea of personal agency in the criminal law. An actor may properly be held responsible if he brings about a harmful result himself, or if he brings it about through another person, e.g. by inducement or persuasion. But to hold him liable merely because (say) another person chooses voluntarily to follow his example, in a manner that causes or risks harm, infringes basic notions of the separateness of persons as choosing agents. It is that other person who has made the culpable choice of bringing about harm, not the original actor.

The traditional causation doctrines of the criminal law *also* contain a principle that the free intervening act of a third party ordinarily relieves the original actor of causal responsibility, on the basis that informed adults of sound mind should be treated as autonomous beings who make their own decisions about how they act, so that their free, deliberate, and informed interventions are not treated as caused by others.[18] That principle is likewise based, at least in part, on normative considerations of responsibility and fault. Does that mean that we can resolve imputation questions concerning intervening-choice liability simply by invoking traditional causation doctrines? We think not, for the context is different. The original actor, in these mediating-intervention cases, is not being held directly responsible for the eventual injury; instead, her initial conduct is proscribed as a distinct offence, on probabilistic grounds, because it is thought to contribute to the harm's eventual likelihood. Rather than trying to import traditional causation doctrines wholesale, therefore, it would be preferable to examine these doctrines (especially, the strictures concerning intervening actors) to see how they might be suggestive for developing imputation principles suited to this new context.

---

[18] *Simester and Sullivan* § 4.2(iii)(b).

Analogous objections hold where it is the original actor herself who makes the separate, subsequent choice. When harmless conduct is proscribed merely because the actor, if she perpetrates it, may then be tempted to commit further acts that are harmful, she is being treated as one might a child: as someone who lacks the insight or self-control to resist the later temptation. Assuming she is a competent actor, such treatment would fail to respect her as a moral agent, capable of deliberation and self-control.

It is not only mediating-intervention cases that raise questions of fair imputation, but abstract-endangerment liability as well. Consider the 70 mph limit imposed on UK motorways. The limit (let us assume) is well below the speeds that would be safe for the ordinary driver of a properly inspected car. Why, then, have the limit? The rationale is based, at least in part, on the statistical expectation that lower driving speeds would help reduce the number of accidents: the driver is being called upon to refrain from doing something he himself could do without undue risk, in the common interest of greater overall public safety. If driving over that limit is worthy of the criminal law's censure, that cannot rest merely upon the empirical (in this case, statistical) connection between the conduct and accidental injury. There must be a normative basis as well: that drivers have an obligation to cooperate in a safety-promoting scheme by observing certain speed limits, and that an offending driver may properly be held to blame for his refusal to cooperate in that scheme. Seeing the crime in this light, however, squarely raises the question of what limits there should be on such obligations of cooperation.[19]

The point holds also for conjunctive harms. There, the proscribed act is a token of the type that does the feared injury when accumulated. Why, however, should I refrain from conduct that in itself does no harm, merely because it becomes injurious when combined with the behaviour of others? The answer must lie, again, in an obligation of cooperation:[20] we ought to work together—by each of us forgoing some choices—for the sake of our joint interest in preventing certain harmful consequences. Such cooperative obligations, however, cannot be unlimited: I surely should not be held accountable for *everything* which might lead to harm when combined with the actions of others. At some point, the actor—when confronted with the question 'What if everyone did what you are doing?'—should be entitled to say that that is not and should not be made her business.

When speaking of such cooperative obligations, it is important to consider not only whether such obligations exist, but to whom they extend. It is one thing to assert that manufacturers, specialising in the

---

[19] Feinberg seems to imply that there should be some such limits, in his discussion of purely statistical risk-assessments as grounds for criminalisation; see *Harm to Others* 199–202.

[20] We return in detail to this discussion in the next chapter.

making of a product, should have an obligation to cooperate in a scheme of legal regulation (backed by criminal sanctions) that is designed to minimise the product's harmful environmental effects. It is quite another to say those obligations should be extended to casual users. We shall investigate these points further in the next chapter.

b. The Character of Imputation Principles

Imputability should thus be an important element in a theory of criminalisation. With respect to any criminal prohibition aimed at preventing the remoter sorts of risks, the question should be asked: *how, and why, can the supposed eventual harm fairly be imputed to the actor?* The reasons will be complex—and will vary with the specific context. But it will not do simply to disregard the question, or to assume that a purely empirical account of causality suffices.

Dealing with this question calls for a different vocabulary. It seems natural to speak of whether the actor is 'responsible' for the eventual outcome, and what is at stake certainly *is* a kind of responsibility; but we need to be careful here. Traditionally, the use of responsibility concepts in the criminal law has mainly been concerned with the character of the offender's present choice: with whether that choice is made voluntarily, with intent or foresight of consequences, without undue constraint, and so forth. The present question is different. Even if the prohibited conduct is done intentionally, and even if the conduct does empirically increase the risk of eventual bad consequences, it needs to be determined whether, and why, those consequences should be treated as the actor's responsibility in the imputational sense—the sense of being his 'business' or 'proper lookout'.[21] The term 'fair imputation' helps to convey this idea.

The issue is not necessarily one of the actor's intentions or foresight of the remote consequences. Where sound reasons for imputation exist, prohibition may be appropriate whether or not actors ordinarily can foresee the eventual harmful consequences that provide its basis (as may be true, for example, of various environmental offences[22]). Conversely, knowledge or foresight does not necessarily suffice as grounds for imputation. In the

---

[21] For different possible meanings of 'responsibility', see also H.L.A. Hart, *Punishment and Responsibility* (Oxford: Oxford UP, 1968) 210–30. One of Hart's categories is 'liability-responsibility', in which he lists several subcategories. One of these subcategories concerns 'whether some form of connexion between a person's act and some harmful outcome is sufficient according to law to make him liable.' Included in this subcategory are the criminal law's traditional causation doctrines. However, Hart does not specifically discuss imputation issues of the kind addressed here.

[22] For elaboration of this important point, see below, § 5.1(a).

Charles Murray hypothetical noted earlier,[23] for example, it should not matter whether some fornicators might consider the future social effects of their actions: as far as the criminal sanction is concerned, those outcomes should not be their lookout.

The fairness of imputation is also distinct from the question of fair warning.[24] As criminal legislation ordinarily is not well publicised, it often relies on citizens' everyday moral sense for securing compliance: not so much the legal prohibition as the ordinary person's sense of right and wrong counsels her not to assault, steal, or riot, and to pay her taxes. The more attenuated the link to the ultimate harm, the less appropriate it is for the law to expect such 'everyday' intuitions to supply fair warning to ordinary citizens. Fair warning, however, might be provided by publicising the prohibition adequately. Imputation, by contrast, does not depend upon an actor's awareness of the prohibition. Even if a prohibition has been widely publicised, it still raises imputation problems if—for the variety of reasons mentioned above—the feared harmful consequences are none of the business of the persons to whom the prohibition is addressed.

Imputation cannot be a matter of satisfying any simple general test. What is involved, rather, is constructing reasons why the (potential) ultimate harm is appropriately deemed the responsibility of the actor or actors.[25] Those reasons may, in part, be role-dependent. The extent of responsibility of a vendor, for example, depends on his social role—which provides clues about what he is implicitly representing to customers concerning his product. The responsibilities of a manufacturer or civil servant likewise will depend on their respective roles. Beyond these particular roles, every person has certain responsibilities as a citizen—for example, the obligation to contribute one's share of taxes. Such grounds for imputation cannot be drawn straightforwardly from everyday morality, because the roles involved often presuppose certain social or institutional frameworks. This makes issues of criminalisation more difficult to deal with: they are not resolved by simple general criteria of the sort provided by the Standard Harms Analysis. Yet such complexity is unavoidable if we wish to deal adequately with remote harms.

Revising the Harm Principle to include imputation doctrine offers important liberty safeguards. Consider again mediating-intervention liability. We have suggested that if a person engages in conduct that is innocuous in itself, it should not be proscribed *merely* because the conduct

---

[23]   Above, § 4.4(a).

[24]   Below, § 11.3.

[25]   Obviously, citizens' prima facie obligation to obey the law cannot supply the imputation grounds. The legislature needs valid substantive reasons (including those relating to fair imputation) for prohibiting conduct. It cannot provide those reasons, bootstrap-style, merely by prohibiting the conduct—and then pointing to citizens' duty of obedience as the justification. See further § 2.3(b).

is likely to be followed by others' taking further injurious steps. Without more, the actor has done nothing that makes her responsible (in the imputational sense) for those other persons' harmful choices. In addition, however, restricting intervening-choice liability is also important as a means of protecting personal liberty—for otherwise, virtually anything a person might do could be criminalised on grounds of potentially harmful subsequent choices.

Accommodating imputation requirements will require more attention to be paid to precisely how the conduct is linked to the eventual risks. Take the example of gun control, to which we return in the next chapter. When one inquires how gun-possession might lead to harm, various answers might be given, each carrying different responsibility-imputation implications. Is the risk mainly that of weapons' going off spontaneously?[26] This account (if factually plausible) involves no intervening choice at all: the basis for prohibition would be akin to that concerning the keeping of easily combustible substances such as nitroglycerine. Is it that guns kept in the household may become accessible to children? This still would not involve true intervening-choice liability, as the child is not a fully responsible agent. (Indeed, there may be a special basis for holding the actor answerable: namely, his duty of care toward minor offspring.) Is it the risk of guns being used in domestic or personal altercations? This does involve a mediating intervention, since the risk materialises only when a participant in the altercation resorts to the weapon. However, one is speaking here of conduct that occurs under considerable emotional pressure—namely, in the stress of a domestic fight. Might this suffice as grounds for imputation, and if so why? Is it, finally, the risk of guns being acquired by criminals? This last rationale does seem troublesome from an imputational standpoint: the ordinary person is being barred from possession because (with no encouragement on his part) that could enable others to acquire the weapons and misuse them for nefarious ends.

4.5 WHAT PRACTICAL DIFFERENCE?

Even if remote-risk prohibitions do involve the theoretical problems this chapter has raised, are they problems in practice? Some of the examples we have cited are imaginary. Much as some politicians may thunder on about family values, no one (to our knowledge) has seriously proposed that fornication be outlawed in order to forestall its supposed long-term criminogenic consequences.[27] Other cases, however, are true to life. Drug

---

[26] See *Harm to Others* 195.
[27] Charles Murray (above n. 14) advocates sharp reductions in welfare benefits for single mothers, but does not propose new criminal legislation.

prohibitions exist in most jurisdictions, and have been defended in part on grounds of the long-run social harms that use of the drugs would create. It is a crime in the United Kingdom to carry a bladed instrument in public,[28] or to possess an imitation firearm.[29] As we noted earlier, remote harm justifications lie behind drink-driving legislation.

Could not such measures, however, be disposed of straightforwardly by the Standard Harms Analysis, without need to address the admittedly more complex questions of imputation? The Standard Harms Analysis does, after all, supply a basis for challenging empirically dubious harm claims, in its requirements concerning the extent and magnitude of the eventual harm. Has the potential harm in the instances just cited—drug use, knife possession, and so forth—really been properly documented?

Perhaps not. But that is a contingent matter. Consequently, insisting on adequate evidence may not always be a sufficient safeguard. Moreover, estimates of the gravity and likelihood of harm tend to become progressively more indeterminate as the envisioned harm becomes more remote. In the context of such not-very-remote risks as those involved in driving while intoxicated, one can speak fairly definitively about the likelihood of driving impairment, the potential extensiveness of the anticipated injury, and the like.[30] But what about applying the Standard Harm Analysis to claims that drug possession should be proscribed because widespread drug use will tend to accelerate social decay, with its attendant increases in crime? Here, estimates of the magnitude and likelihood of the risk necessarily become quite speculative.

We could bar such speculative risks in applying the Standard Harm Analysis, but that strategy would encounter a further dilemma. It is not only the more debatable prohibitions which involve difficult-to-estimate risks; so do seemingly more attractive areas of intervention such as those regarding the environment. It is not easy, for example, to gauge the effects of global warming. A stringent evidential standard—one barring all but reasonably certain risks—might not only call into question the marijuana prohibition, but much environmental legislation as well. Yet loosening the standard of evidence could have the reverse disadvantage, becoming too permissive of state intervention.

The ultimate drawback of relying solely on the Standard Analysis, in the area of remote risks, is that it yields insufficient arguments of principle. Those who desire parsimony in extension of the criminal laws will be relegated to making arguments about the benefits and costs of

---

[28] Criminal Justice Act 1988 (UK), s. 139. Even a butter knife: *Booker v. DPP* [2005] EWHC 1132 (Admin).

[29] Firearms Act 1968 (UK), s. 19.

[30] See J. Jacobs, *Drunk Driving: An American Dilemma* (Chicago: Chicago UP, 1989) ch. 3.

criminalisation. That criminalisation is sometimes just plain wrong—because the potential remote outcome should not be made the actor's business—is something that cannot be contended.

Extending the Standard Harms Analysis with further restraining principles, particularly those concerning fair imputation, changes the character of the criminalisation debate. An opponent of (say) the marijuana prohibition would no longer need argue merely that the evidence of ultimate social harm is insufficient, that the countervailing costs (and difficulties of enforcement) are too great, or that (say) privacy concerns protect the user. He could raise the more fundamental objection, about whether the feared eventual result is the actor's proper lookout.

Suppose that A and B, typical users, enjoy smoking cannabis but continue to work (as so many do). Why is it their lookout that their example might induce C and D to become users, like the drug too much, and stop working, causing productivity to fall, so that E and F might lose their jobs, and decide to turn to crime?[31] The objection is not just to the factual plausibility of these links, for (who knows?) supporting evidence might be discoverable, at least in certain social settings. The real objection is to the imputation link: A and B have gone about their business, and have not abetted larceny or violence by any other person. Why, then, should E's and F's subsequent decision to offend be their proper lookout? And if not, why do A's and B's actions constitute a wrong, one warranting the imposition of criminal sanctions?

Requiring imputation will not, of course, settle debates over criminalisation. As the next chapter will illustrate, the grounds of imputability are setting-dependent, and must be constructed according to the particular activity. It will be necessary to argue why, in the marijuana example, F's and G's misconduct is not A's, B's or C's business. But, we think, it is essential to make such arguments.

None of this is to suggest that the Standard Harms Analysis should be abandoned, even in the context of remote harms. Once imputation is established, the elements of the standard analysis remain helpful in weighing up the desirability of a given prohibition—where it does matter how likely and how grave the expected harm is, how socially valuable the conduct is, and so forth. Consider the drink-driving prohibition: why should persons who drive with a blood-alcohol level over a stated limit be punished but not, say, those found with only trace amounts of alcohol? Here, the likelihood and magnitude of the prospective harm matter. The counter-considerations of the Standard Harms Analysis are

---

[31] Regarding the 'contagion' argument, see W. Bennett, *National Drug Control Strategy* (Washington, DC: Government Printing Office, 1989) 11; for the loss-of-productivity argument, see Kaplan, above n. 1, and the discussion in § 4.2.

also illuminating: it constricts citizens' options less to bar substantial alcohol consumption by drivers than to penalise even a casual sip of wine.

Rather, our claim is that the Standard Analysis does not resolve certain questions of principle. The drink-driving prohibition is a species of abstract-endangerment legislation: it covers even those who are capable of driving carefully after ingesting a proscribed level of spirits. We need to ask why and to what extent those 'safe' drinkers should have an obligation to cooperate in such a scheme of driving safety, sufficient to render them culpable wrongdoers if they violate the rule—and thus become fit subjects of the criminal sanction. This latter question, of imputation, is not answered just by assessing costs and benefits.

Ascriptions of fair imputation are not politically neutral. They can depend on matters of social and political obligation: for example, on the extent of duties of citizenship. But that's part of the point. When we debate the permissible scope of the criminal law, the relevant doctrines ultimately must rest, at least in part, on arguments about citizens' freedoms and obligations. It is best, we think, to try to make those doctrines, and their underlying assumptions, explicit. By contrast, the Standard Harms Analysis merely *seems* apolitical. Its politics are buried, only slightly, below the surface: in its normatively loaded concept of harm,[32] and in its formula that the risk of ultimate harm should be 'weighed' against the need to preserve the liberty of the subject.

Revisiting our opening paragraph, one final caveat. The issue of imputation relates to only one possible ground for criminalisation, i.e. the conduct's supposed tendency to generate remote risks. Even where this argument fails, there may be other bases for sustaining a prohibition. Consider the drug laws, once more. We have doubted loss-of-productivity arguments for criminalisation. But even supposing that doubt were accepted, there may yet be other potential grounds for criminalisation—for example, paternalistic grounds. Taking certain drugs (eg glue-sniffing) does appear to damage the health and the lives of those who take them. These effects are less remote—although, as we will see in Part IV, they raise squarely the issue of the state's entitlement to use its laws to protect persons from themselves. Either way, however, a restricted paternalism is likely to be less threatening to citizens' liberty than reliance on a broad version of the Harm Principle, not adequately hedged by imputation constraints.

So, far, we have identified the problem. We have argued that it is important to develop fair imputation principles, as part of an Extended

---

[32] cf. J. Raz, 'Autonomy, Toleration, and the Harm Principle' in R. Gavison (ed.), *Issues in Contemporary Legal Philosophy* (Oxford: Clarendon Press, 1987) 313, 328.

Harm Principle, when dealing with remote risks. But we have not sketched how they should be formulated. In the next chapter, we take some further steps toward that goal.

5

On the Imputation of Remote Harms

REMOTE-HARM CRIMES are a subset of the *non-constitutive* crimes. As we saw in § 3.2, non-constitutive crimes are those where the prospective harm that is relied upon to justify a prohibition is not specified within the crime's definition, so that the crime can be perpetrated without the harm occurring. Not all non-constitutive crimes involve remote harms. Some are harm-independent.[1] Others may involve a concrete and immediate, rather than remote, link to the underlying harm.[2] But the majority of non-constitutive offences involve remote harms.

Remote-harm offences are many and varied. The range includes most of what criminal lawyers traditionally call the 'inchoate' offences, which prohibit actors from inciting,[3] conspiring, or attempting to commit a (substantive) crime. These inchoate crimes are generic, capable of attaching to any substantive crime, whether constitutive or non-constitutive. Another type of pre-emptive offence operates by proscribing some more specific step that is typically taken toward committing a substantive crime. These 'substantive-inchoate'[4] offences include burglary (entry as a trespasser with intent to commit theft, etc.) and, indeed, the doubly inchoate offence of 'going equipped'—merely being out and about with instruments of burglary.[5] Alternatively, numerous risk-based offences safeguard against conduct that simply increases the likelihood of harm, in as much as the conduct creates various kinds of risk, or heightens those risks, that the harm will result. Dangerous driving is an example of the latter. The driving in itself is not harmful, and need not be intended to increase the risks of

---

[1] Above, § 3.3.

[2] See below, § 5.2(a).

[3] Or, in some jurisdictions, 'soliciting'.

[4] cf. P. Roberts, 'The presumption of innocence brought home? *Kebilene* deconstructed' (2002) 118 LQR 41, 48, 55–56. We use slightly different definitions in this chapter.

[5] cf. Theft Act 1968, s. 25(1): 'A person shall be guilty of an offence if, when not at his place of abode, he has with him any article for use in the course of or in connection with any burglary, theft or cheat.'

injury to others. Yet this kind of driving is criminalised primarily because it does, unreasonably, increase such risks.

As with all non-constitutive offences, remote-harm offences pose problems for criminalisation theory because they do not fit neatly within the Harm Principle. Prima facie, they generate over-criminalisation, in that they prohibit instances of conduct that are not themselves harmful. The scope of risk-based offences *includes* harmful instances of the same type of conduct; but substantive-inchoate offences don't even do that. Carrying the tools of burglary is never itself harmful. Non-constitutive offences ask us to forgo options that may be valuable and which are sometimes (or even always) harmless. Not only may I not culpably hurt you, I may not do various other things, just in case you receive an injury. Taken to extremes, such prohibitions threaten to undermine severely my liberty, since scenarios exist in which almost anything I do might ultimately affect your chances of suffering harm.

In this chapter, we explore what extensions are required to the Standard Harms Analysis to accommodate principles of imputation for remote-harm crimes. As we shall see, the relevant principles differ across the various types of these offences. But we begin their analysis with two principles that are common to all.

5.1 IN-PRINCIPLE CONSTRAINTS ON NON-CONSTITUTIVE CRIMES

a. The General Requirement of Wrongfulness

In Part I, we argued for a foundational principle of any criminalisation inquiry: that any prohibited act must be wrongful. This follows from the very nature of the criminal law as a condemnatory institution. One cannot appropriately be blamed except for doing something wrong. Any formal judgment of blame, including a criminal conviction, should be predicated upon norm-violating conduct—like all blaming verdicts, it expresses moral reproof of a person *for* that norm-violating conduct. This may sometimes be obscured by the language of mens rea: a defendant is taken to be culpable (his mens is deemed to be rea) when he intends or foresees the actus reus, or sometimes if he is negligent with respect to its occurrence. But first the conduct must be, as it were, reus.[6] The wrong comes before

---

[6] Admittedly, the conclusion that particular conduct is wrongful may itself be dependent on the actor's mens rea (for elaboration of this familiar point, see, e.g., W. Chan and A.P. Simester, 'Four Functions of Mens Rea' (2011) 70 CLJ 000). In such cases, the role of mens rea in establishing wrongfulness is none the less distinct from its role in establishing culpability, although in practice the two will overlap.

the blame. I can intend a good deed; I can be responsible for doing a good deed; but I cannot be culpable for it.

This constraint applies to non-constitutive offences too. The prohibited act, rather than any causing of the remote harm, must be wrongful. In the context of remote harms,[7] this is what underlies the problem of imputation: it needs to be shown why the prospect of some ultimate harm, perhaps brought about by an independent actor, makes it wrong for the defendant to act as she does. Sometimes, the very act of criminalisation plays a role in marking out conduct as wrongful.[8] But either way, legitimate criminalisation requires that the prohibited conduct is in some manner reprehensible, wherefore one who perpetrates the behaviour may be considered as a candidate for censure.

We emphasise that nothing in this principle requires wrongdoers to be culpable with respect to the ultimate harm.[9] While culpability requirements are essential in the criminal law,[10] the culpability must be with respect to the proscribed activity. It follows that the issue for remote-harm offences is not one of culpability, but of imputation-responsibility and, more immediately, of *wrongdoing*. The ingredients of these elements overlap, but they are not the same thing, especially in the institutional context of a legal system. One may, for instance, be culpable (i.e. morally blameworthy) for failing to prevent an event for which one is not legally responsible—being a stranger who owed no duty to intervene. Considerations affecting the legitimacy of state coercion may subtract from ordinary moral reasons. Conversely, we claim, it can add to them.

This is, in part, the familiar point made in § 2.3(b). Sometimes, the legal system may crystallise a norm as a determination of some more abstract, pre-legal wrong.[11] Driving at an unsafe speed is morally wrong; driving in excess of 70 miles per hour on a UK motorway particularises that wrong.[12] Less obviously, a regulatory regime designed to facilitate industrial safety may contain a variety of reporting and other requirements which serve the needs of that regime.

---

[7]   Other types of non-constitutive crime do not generate the same problem, either because the wrong is independent of the harm (above, § 3.3) or because the wrong is predicated on the risk of directly causing the relevant harm (e.g. an arson committed in circumstances where another person's life is endangered, contrary to s. 1(2) of the Criminal Damage Act 1971 (UK)).

[8]   See the text below in this section; also § 2.3(b).

[9]   Contrast Husak, *Overcriminalization* 174, who proposes a 'culpability principle': 'This principle withholds liability from persons who create a risk of harm unless they have some degree of culpability for the ultimate harm risked. It is not enough that the performance of the proscribed conduct just happens to make the occurrence of the ultimate harm more likely.'

[10]   Above, § 2.4.

[11]   See, e.g., J. Finnis, *Natural Law and Natural Rights* (Oxford: Clarendon Press, 1980) 284ff; A.M. Honoré, 'The Dependence of Morality on Law' (1993) 13 OJLS 1.

[12]   See further the discussion of endangerment offences, § 5.2(a) below.

Suppose that, in order to serve such remote-harm-preventing ends (and where, in accordance with § 5.2 below, those remote harms can fairly be imputed to the actor), the state justifiably enacts an offence of φing. Then we have a reason not to φ. Further, assuming D is or should be aware of the prohibition,[13] if D then intentionally φs without justification or excuse, he does so culpably. In such a case, we contend, D may legitimately be convicted of φing, notwithstanding that D was unaware of the ultimate harm lying behind the prohibition, and even if that harm would not have been apparent to an ordinary or reasonable person. (Indeed, as we argue below, this may sometimes hold even where the ultimate harm is not risked at all by D's particular act of φing.) There is no reason why D ought to be able to work out for himself exactly why certain health and safety restrictions are needed. That's the job of the regulatory authority.

Culpability judgements tend to be *ex post*, but we must investigate criminalisation questions *ex ante*. Thus the relevant question is not whether D is *culpable* for the ultimate harm.[14] It isn't even whether D is *responsible* for that harm (which, if the upstream prohibition is effective, won't actually occur); although, as we shall see below, considerations of imputation-responsibility are relevant. Rather, the key question for *ex ante* prohibition is, *why is D's conduct (in φing) wrongful?* If it is, and its permission would lead to harm, the criminal law is not yet ruled out.

Not *yet*. In § 5.2 below, we shall propose further limiting principles that constrain the legitimacy of remote-harm offences.

b.   A Direct Proscription Constraint

How far can we proceed beyond the fundamental requirement of wrong-doing? There is at least one further principle that specifically constrains the legitimacy of non-constitutive offences. This principle requires that the potential ultimate harm ought itself to meet the criteria contained in the Standard Harms Analysis for criminalisation. Specifically, *the state should not use a non-constitutive offence to proscribe conduct on the basis of its remote harmfulness unless the state would be prima facie morally justified in directly proscribing conduct that wrongfully causes the same harm.* That

---

[13] For discussion of this constraint, see D. Husak and A. von Hirsch, 'Culpability and Mistake of Law' in S. Shute, J. Gardner, and J. Horder (eds), *Action and Value in Criminal Law* (Oxford: Oxford UP, 1993) 157.

[14] In 'Convergent Ends, Divergent Means: A Response to My Critics' (2009) 28 Criminal Justice Ethics 123, 136, Douglas Husak does not consider this point, nor the possibility that the state can play a role in creating reasons, when he objects that 'I fail to see why [Simester and von Hirsch] would condemn a defendant for creating a risk of harm X even though a reasonable person in his circumstance would have been unaware that his conduct caused that risk.' As we argued in § 2.3(b), the condemnation is for φing, something (in a justified prohibition) that D ought not to do.

is to say, the ultimate harm should be of a kind and seriousness that its wrongful causation would itself qualify directly for prohibition under the Standard Harms Analysis.

In effect, the direct proscription constraint tests the case for criminalisation by suspending both the risk and imputation elements. The argument in favour of non-constitutively proscribing remote antecedent (or 'upstream') conduct cannot be stronger than the hypothetical case for a constitutive offence of wrongfully causing the harm itself. Unless the ultimate harm is of the sort that justifies criminal prohibitions, the case for upstream, non-constitutive offences cannot get off the ground. Adding imputation requirements, and discounting for any risk that the harm may not occur, can only weaken that case.

Note that the direct proscription constraint requires that the hypothetical constitutive offence involve *wrongfully* bringing about the ultimate harm.[15] This way of framing the principle helps to bring out the point that the wrongfulness of an act may depend on the manner of its doing; for example, on whether it is repeated (as in harassment),[16] or done collectively (say, by a gang[17]) rather than individually. Conceivably, it may sometimes be legitimate to proscribe conspiring with another to do an act that itself is not wrongful—or, at least, is insufficiently serious—when done by one person acting alone. Indeed, this possibility underpins the common law offence of conspiracy to defraud. Even within the terms of an Extended Harm Principle—that is, a principle making specific allowance for remote-harm offences, thus going beyond the standard harms analysis—the ultimate harm need not be the sole source of the wrong.

Neither does the direct proscription constraint rule out the possibility that the case for criminalising some particular (upstream) activity might, *all things considered,* be stronger than the case for the corresponding constitutive offence that directly proscribes the remote harm. Indeed, the case for remote-harms offences depends, in part, on its being impractical or otherwise undesirable directly to criminalise acts that cause the remote harm. In a rather more rare scenario, it may also be that a single upstream activity is linked to various risks of multiple different remote harms, so that the strength of the case for criminalisation is cumulatively stronger. Such instances are likely to be exceptional.

---

[15] In *Overcriminalization*, at 165–66, Husak proposes a somewhat different constraint in which the state must be 'permitted to proscribe conduct that *intentionally* and directly causes that same harm.' For some reservations about his version, which we think fails sufficiently to distinguish issues of culpability from wrongfulness, see A.P. Simester and A. von Hirsch, 'Remote Harms and Non-constitutive Crimes' (2009) 28 Criminal Justice Ethics 89, 91–92.

[16] See further below, § 12.2(a); also *Simester and Sullivan* § 11.8.

[17] This is part of the idea behind joint enterprise liability: see A.P. Simester, 'The Mental Element in Complicity' (2006) 122 LQR 578, 598–600.

5.2   TYPES OF REMOTE HARMS AND THEIR GOVERNING PRINCIPLES

As we foreshadowed in the previous chapter, remote harm issues arise in three broad types of non-constitutive crime. Each raises different issues of principle, which we consider in the following sections. The first type comprises what we call *endangerment* offences, where the prohibited activity, ρ, creates a risk of causing harm to others. Dangerous driving, driving on the wrong side of the road, and discharging a firearm in a public place would be instances of endangerment offences.

The second and third types are categories of what we term *prophylactic* offences: cases where the prohibited activity, σ, leads to harm only if accompanied by an autonomous act of ɸing, either by the offender or by another. By prohibiting σ, therefore, the state seeks to pre-empt the risk of that (ultimate) harm. Causally speaking, we can further distinguish between cases where σ is a cause of harm alongside ɸ (*conjunctive harm* cases) and those where the harm is caused by ɸ rather than σ (*mediating intervention* cases).

a.   Endangerment Offences

Many endangerment offences do not present remote harm problems and can be accommodated straightforwardly within the Harm Principle. That the ultimate harm does not always occur is not by itself an objection, since the Standard Harms Analysis is probabilistic.[18] Where conduct is less likely to cause a given harm to others, the case for prohibition is correspondingly weakened. Running down corridors is not criminalised, but discharging firearms is—the difference lies primarily in the level of dangerousness, in that the latter activity involves greater risk of causing serious injury to others.

The need to locate wrongful conduct can also be met. In general, risk-taking can become wrongful for either of two reasons. First, it may be unreasonable for an actor to run the risk; this is an assessment that requires the very kind of balancing exercise undertaken by the Standard Harms Analysis. (Conversely, a prohibition that criminalised reasonable risk-taking would not satisfy the Standard Analysis.) Alternatively, the risky conduct can be a wrong when it is done *in order* to harm another, at least in circumstances where the victim has a right not to be so harmed; the wrong resides here in the attack upon that right and upon the interests of

---

[18]   Above, §§ 3.2(a), 4.2.

the person who holds that right.[19] The traditional inchoate crimes are typically wrongs for this second reason. Either way, however, the wrong is not sufficient; its existence does not dispense with the requirement for harm, or at least for enough risk of sufficiently grave harm to meet the conditions of the Standard Harms Analysis. This is one reason why attempt liability is subject to a preparation threshold:[20] short of that, the ultimate harm may be too remote, too dependent on contingencies, for state intervention so intrusive as the criminal law to be justified, whether or not such preparatory conduct is directed ultimately toward harming another.

The worry, then, is that endangerment offences appear to dispense with the harm requirement, since they prohibit conduct independently of the contingencies which make that conduct dangerous. This is the concern about over-inclusiveness. When are such offences justified?

To answer that, we should begin by distinguishing two types of contingent situations. Suppose that a statute is enacted to prohibit careless driving. A driver who cuts a corner commits this offence if he cannot see the road ahead, even when there is in fact no oncoming traffic and so, for the omniscient, no risk of harm. Rightly so. From the driver's perspective, this is a contingency about which she has neither *ex ante* knowledge nor control. Such cases involve genuine risk—what we might call *concrete* endangerment. For concrete endangerment, the constraint against over-inclusion adds nothing to the standard harms analysis.[21] It requires only that there be an appropriate balance between the magnitude and gravity of the harm risked and the value of the prohibited conduct which generates that risk.

Consider, however, a rule such as the speed limit of 70 mph on UK motorways. Like the ban on careless driving, the speed limit is designed to protect people from harm. But someone who drives at 80 mph commits the offence even if the road ahead is clearly empty and no genuine risk is created. Thus the 70 mph rule involves *abstract* endangerment. It deals with conduct that generates risk only if certain contingencies are present, but the rule applies even if those contingencies are absent and the actor knows of their absence. In such cases—and unlike concrete endangerment offences—there is no genuine risk and, it may seem, no wrong by the actor.

---

[19]   cf. R.A. Duff, 'Criminalizing Endangerment' in S. Green and R.A. Duff (eds), *Defining Crimes: Essays on the Special Part of the Criminal Law* (Oxford: Oxford UP, 2005) 43, § 2. Our usage of 'endangerment' differs from that of Duff, who excludes hostile 'attacks' from its scope.

[20]   Although not the only reason: e.g., evidential uncertainty about an actor's intentions is typically greater at the point of preliminary conduct, which is likely to be ambiguous in character.

[21]   Hence, as noted in the introduction to this chapter, these cases represent a variety of non-constitutive crimes that do not involve remote harms.

Why, if at all, are abstract endangerment offences justified? Why should the genuinely safe actor be required to forgo valuable options merely because others cannot be trusted?

To some extent, this is a matter of practical necessity. Proof that conduct was in fact dangerous may impose unworkable difficulties and costs of law enforcement, and may require monitoring mechanisms that are themselves unduly intrusive. In that case, an abstract endangerment offence may better prevent harm than its concrete counterpart. Assuming that the abstract-endangerment offence being considered is the least over-inclusive formulation available,[22] the choice then becomes one between over- and under-criminalisation. While it remains a matter for assessment, the case for a concrete endangerment offence then militates in favour of the abstract endangerment version.

But the case is stronger than that, because abstract endangerment formulations can also protect against the secondary risk of mistake (about the actual levels of concrete endangerment). In particular, they may offer improved guidance to actors through specifying non-contingently what measures are appropriate to avoid the risk of harm: the injunction not to drive too fast is more easily obeyed as an enumerated limit. If, instead, concrete endangerment were required for liability, drivers would constantly be required to exercise discretionary judgement about whether the conditions of endangerment are present (e.g., what other kinds of drivers are there on the road when I drive? How much alcohol can I safely drink?). The human tendency to erroneous and self-deceptive judgements will result in drivers driving too fast, or with too much alcohol, when there actually are people on the road who would be endangered. True, the actor could then be prosecuted for crimes of actual endangerment—but by then the risk would have been incurred, and unnecessarily. Neither is that outcome in the interests of the actor, who may have been well-intentioned and just mistaken.[23] The pre-emptive, abstract-endangerment rule can help to preclude all this: saying, 'never mind trying to figure out what other drivers may be on the road, and how fast might be safe; just don't drive over the speed limit, *simpliciter*.'

In these cases, a pre-emptive, abstract-endangerment rule safeguards against concrete endangerment. Still, the rule is likely also to operate beyond that, and restrict the options of those who make accurate judgements about the risks. A 70 mph speed limit may prevent me from deciding, unwisely, that I can easily handle the vehicle at 100 mph; yet when Juan Manuel Fangio is the driver, such an assessment may be entirely

---

[22] Below, § 11.4(c).
[23] Thus abstract endangerment formulations can also advance rule-of-law values of fair warning: see *Simester and Sullivan* § 2.3; below, § 11.3.

appropriate. Are there any additional reasons for compliance that we can offer to persons such as Fangio, and to those who, say, hold a current FIA Super Licence?[24]

One possible argument rests upon obligations of cooperation among participants in mutual activity.[25] We may usefully separate abstract-endangerment rules that provide 'internal' protection—namely, protection of the members of the group whose conduct is being regulated—from those providing 'external' protection of other persons from harm. A speed limit or a drink-driving rule are examples of internal protection, in so far as it is the conduct of drivers that is being regulated and the rule is meant (*inter alia*) to protect drivers. By contrast, a prohibition relating to factory pollution is an example of externality: the factory operator is being regulated, but the beneficiaries are others, notably citizens living in the region. Of course, the factory operator might live in the area too, but then her benefit is incidental and not internal to the regulated activity. By contrast, the driver benefits *qua* driver. Internal endangerment rules constitute, in essence, a scheme of reciprocal protection: if each of us abides by the speed limit, this will not only protect others from our driving, but also protect us from others' driving at excessive speeds. In turn, the fact that the scheme provides reciprocal benefits to all participants suggests a prima facie reason why all should comply, even those of superior ability. All participants have an interest in the efficacy of the scheme, and that interest grounds responsibility in each of us for its compliance. The regime is a package deal.

If that's right, then Fangio's claim to be different, and to drive at 100 mph, is wrong because it is selfish. But perhaps that is overstated. If internality supplies a reason why an actor must give up options *whenever* she benefits from a regulatory regime, it could be very broad indeed (and suspiciously paternalistic). Moreover, it may be questioned whether selfishness is the kind of wrong that ought to attract the sanctions of the criminal law: unless bound by duties, people are generally *entitled* to be selfish and to act in their own interests. And, after all, Fangio can drive safely at 100 mph, so why should his doing so be subject to legitimate penal censure?

Yet there is another reason why Fangio's conduct is wrong, and not merely selfish. Once the standard rule is in place, it is typically no longer fully safe, even for him, to drive at 100 mph. Co-ordinating regimes such as road-traffic rules not only address the individual actor: they set the terms of interaction with other drivers (and pedestrians). Here, especially, no man is an island: others predictably and permissibly rely on those terms

---

[24] Selecting exceptions on the basis of identified qualifications helps circumvent the objection that they are *ad hoc* or a matter of self-identification—the obverse case, in effect, of restrictions imposed on those holding a provisional licence.

[25] We are grateful for discussions with Nils Jareborg that prompted this line of thought.

when themselves manoeuvring on the road. They cannot be expected to accommodate the chance that an egregiously skilled driver will not behave like the rest of us, so that what would ordinarily be a safe driving manoeuvre may suddenly be dangerous when a distant driver closes in at exceptional speed. Conversely, while Fangio can control his own car, he cannot anticipate or control the driving of others. When he drives in a manner that ordinary drivers do not expect, he therefore may generate concrete and not merely abstract risk of harm to others.

b. Prophylactic Crimes in General

What we have termed prophylactic crimes resemble endangerment crimes, in that they too proscribe conduct which increases the risk of some ultimate harm; harm, moreover, the wrongful infliction of which might legitimately be proscribed. Unlike endangerment offences, however, the risk of that harm does not arise straightforwardly from the prohibited act. It arises only after, or in conjunction with, further human interventions—either by the original actor or by others. Indeed, apart from complete attempts,[26] even the traditional inchoate offences are prophylactic: they do not lead directly to harm, and are merely steps along that path.

While prophylactic offences certainly generate problems of imputation, in our view they are legitimate under certain conditions. In what follows, we explore certain additional ingredients that may justify the imputation of such remote harms to an initially harmless act. As foreshadowed earlier, the cases fall into two main categories: mediating interventions and conjunctive harms.

c. Mediating Interventions

Most prophylactic offences prohibit conduct because of its tendency to lead to eventual harm where that harm is mediated by someone's autonomous, intervening choice. For clarity, we shall call the original actor S in such cases, and S's act σ; the later intervention, φ, may be perpetrated by S or another actor, P. In cases of this type, the prohibited conduct by S is in itself harmless, but may in some manner lead P to decide to φ, or make it easier or more tempting for S herself to decide to φ; which causes or risks the ultimate harm.

---

[26] Completed attempts might also require intervening actors; but in such cases the interventions are typically not autonomous and free (as when D lays a trap, but V must still walk into it). Even if some completed attempts still require autonomous interventions, that possibility can generally be neglected since the remaining completed-attempt cases are likely to justify criminalisation anyway on probabilistic, endangerment-based grounds.

Many of these cases present distinctive problems for criminalisation because, at least where the intervening actor is a free, autonomous agent, the intervention threatens to disrupt S's imputation-responsibility for the potential harm. If S's conduct is not itself harmful, and φ does not occur or is perpetrated autonomously by P, where is S's wrong?[27]

Sometimes, the state deals with problems like these through laws of complicity, using doctrines that impose accomplice liability upon those who aid and abet criminal behaviour by others.[28] But complicity doctrines are *ad hoc*. They do not prohibit designated activities (such as σing) in general. Rather, they attach liability to S for σing only under particular conditions. Enacting a prophylactic crime can therefore be a simpler alternative, one that better informs S of her rights and duties. Given their potential to facilitate harmful conduct by purchasers, and subject to what is said below, it might be appropriate to prohibit shopkeepers from selling certain kinds of automatic firearms and high-powered weapons (e.g. bazookas) altogether, rather than to use complicity law to regulate individual transactions. Prophylactic offences of this sort can offer more definite guidance to citizens, clarifying their legal position and leaving them better in control of their own criminal liability.[29] Such offences can also facilitate pre-emptive enforcement measures, and conviction for the prophylactic offence may on occasion better describe the nature of S's conduct than would complicity-based liability for the crime by P.[30]

The problem with this technique is that σing is not inherently wrong. Prophylactic offences thus criminalise conduct that should not, in and of itself, be criminal. S's mental state with respect to the ultimate harm might help turn σing into wrongful conduct—and this insight underpins the rationale of complicity liability[31]—but the elements of many prophylactic offences require no such connection. They stand by themselves.

In essence, the problem is that even supposing σ is correlated with and predictably followed by φ, that by itself does not make σing wrong. Further reasons must be offered why the prospect of subsequent φing is S's responsibility, so that S ought to refrain from her *per se* harmless act of σing. In any liberal conception of the state, people have a fundamental right to be treated as separate individuals, as autonomous moral agents

---

[27] In 'Convergent Ends, Divergent Means: A Response to My Critics', above n. 14, at 136, Douglas Husak misconstrues our project when he states that 'Simester and von Hirsch are seemingly interested in whether an intervention by P precludes imposing liability on S for the occurrence of [P's harmful act, φ].' Actually, our concern is with how the prospect that P might φ can possibly make S's act of σing wrongful and eligible for prohibition.

[28] Such liability need not be for P's crime. It may be for an independent offence of abetment: see, e.g., Penal Code (Singapore), s. 107; Serious Crime Act 2007 (UK), s. 44.

[29] By contrast with complicity liability, where S's liability lies partly in P's hands: see A.P. Simester, 'The Mental Element in Complicity' (2006) 122 LQR 578.

[30] A fair labelling concern: see *Simester and Sullivan* § 2.4; below, § 11.4.

[31] Simester, above n. 29.

who are distinctively responsible for the consequences of their *own* actions. The legal system should, in turn, judge its citizens according to their own actions and not according to the conduct of others. S's act does not become wrong merely because of P's freely chosen act—let alone by reason of the mere risk of P's act.

Analogous objections hold where it is S herself who makes a separate, subsequent choice. Unless or until done or attempted by S herself, the mere potential that a person might φ is an unsuitable basis for the censuring response of the criminal law.[32] When harmless conduct is proscribed merely because S is then more likely to choose (freely) to commit further acts that are harmful, citizens are being treated as one might a child: as persons who lack the insight or self-control to resist the later temptation. As we noted in § 4.4(a), such treatment fails to respect her as a moral agent, capable of deliberation and self-control.

The central question is whether we may legitimately compel S to give up options merely because she or others might later misbehave.[33] Our answer is, no. Something more than predictability or correlation is needed to make the prospect of φing S's responsibility, such that her σing becomes wrongful conduct. How should we characterise that 'something more'? The underlying idea, loosely expressed, is that S needs some form of *normative involvement* in P's subsequent choice, an involvement that makes P's act of φing the business of S. In what follows, we offer some thoughts on how this idea of normative involvement may be fleshed out.[34] Broadly, we are speaking of situations where S, through her conduct, in some sense affirms or underwrites the intervening actor's subsequent choice. But notice the 'in some sense' clause here: it allows for actions that are *like* affirmation, and which in various ways assist, encourage, or otherwise endorse wrongdoing by others. One may therefore doubt whether a general criterion exists that will capture all cases well. Still, it seems to us that a liberal conception of the criminal law requires more than a probabilistic connection between σ and φ: to pursue risk-prevention through mere conduct-profiling techniques is, essentially, illiberal.

Some Types of Normative Involvement: (i) Advocacy

What types of normative involvement might there be? Perhaps the simplest kind of case is advocacy: S urges P to φ. A standard example is the inchoate

---

[32] For some developments of this line of thought, see the collection of essays edited by G.R. Sullivan and I. Dennis, *Seeking Security: Pre-empting Criminal Harms* (Oxford: Hart Publishing, 2011).

[33] cf. R.A. Duff, above n. 19, at 64.

[34] Perhaps the most obvious example is the incomplete attempt, in which S's act of σing is directed toward S's own further act of φing (i.e., completing the attempt). As we shall see, however, such a close connection is not always required.

crime of incitement, as when I try to persuade you that the fastest route to your inheritance would be to kill Granny. While such prophylactic offences might sometimes incur free-speech objections (e.g., when I write a treatise advocating the use of force in the course of civil disobedience or a political protest), the element of normative involvement seems to be straightforwardly present: if I tell you to kill Granny, I certainly affirm such behaviour on your part. Here, the moral character of my behaviour is apparent: in urging P to φ, I *ally* myself with P's wrong. In turn, my conduct is wrongful in virtue both of my intention and of the objective nature of the behaviour itself.

(ii) Encouragement and Imitations

It is the element of communicated endorsement that distinguishes advocacy from activities which merely beget imitation. Famously, in *Brown*,[35] it was suggested that consensual sadomasochistic behaviour among adults might set a bad example, leading others to engage in such conduct with youngsters unable to give proper consent. Here, there seems no basis for holding the defendants responsible for those subsequent, hypothesised choices. If one engages in otherwise permissible self-regarding conduct, this in itself involves no affirmation that other free agents should use one's example in order to engage in harmful behaviour. Having masochistic sex with adults does not implicitly endorse or communicate that others should do the same with young adolescents.

Similarly, if less spectacularly, it is often claimed that certain fictional depictions (say, of sadistic sex) inspire some persons actually to engage in such conduct. Perhaps they might—although the onus of showing empirical likelihood is not easily discharged and, of course, the protection of fictional renderings is strengthened by norms governing freedom of expression. Even so, two further factors militate against imputing the depictor with responsibility for possible imitations so that his portrayals may legitimately be considered for restriction. The first is, crucially, that such depictions are like bad examples: the behaviour is merely presented, without suggesting that it be imitated. This objection is buttressed by the fictional nature of the depiction. In writing *Crime and Punishment,* Dostoyevski invites the reader to suspend judgement imaginatively: he does not suggest that anyone in real life should actually kill their tiresome landladies.

Certain everyday cases escape this exclusion. The bad example may be a matter of concern when, say, children are involved: perhaps Dad shouldn't drink or swear in front of Junior, because Junior might imitate such

---

[35] [1994] 1 AC 212, 246; above, § 4.3(b).

behaviour. Here, it seems intuitively plausible that avoiding that development can be Dad's responsibility. But this conclusion is based on two crucial differences. Most importantly, Junior is not yet an autonomous actor. Additionally, Dad has an obligation of care toward Junior, his dependant. These features are not present in risk-of-imitation scenarios, such as that alleged in *Brown*.

(iii) Assistance: Supply of Products used to do Harm

This is the most difficult case. Prophylactic offences are often used to prohibit activities that facilitate subsequent harmful conduct; a familiar and controversial example is the possession or supply of certain armaments. Taking product supply as a standard variety, it is clear that these offences present significant challenges for criminalisation theory. Prima facie, the very fact of facilitation constitutes a form of normative involvement. At the same time, virtually all products can be misused. On the one hand, if S sells a car to P, it is always possible that P may drive the car in such as manner as to injure others, and may even do so deliberately. Yet no one seriously suggests that car sales should therefore be prohibited. Neither should we ban the sale of computer disk drives, notwithstanding that many owners use them illegally to make pirated copies of music and film. On the other hand, almost everyone agrees with the prohibition of high street sales of bazookas or military flamethrowers. On handguns, views diverge more sharply. What, if anything, is the difference?

What follows is admittedly tentative. Assistance is not, we propose, just a matter of probabilities. As others have pointed out,[36] only a tiny percentage of handguns are put to misuse (especially contrasted with disk drives). Of course, the probabilities *also* count: imputability is necessary but not sufficient. Even were we to concede that computer manufacturers have some responsibility for the misconduct of buyers, the scale and likelihood of eventual harm must still be weighed up against the costs—in terms of valuable legitimate uses—of banning disk drives. But we should not concede that imputability; at least, not merely on the basis that disk drives happen to be useful to pirates.

Part of the difference is that cars, and disk drives, have standard legitimate uses. Cars are *meant* to be driven. Since driving is the widely understood function or *telos* of the automobile, by selling the car S implicitly affirms that it is being sold to be driven. And P has no independent legal or moral reason for desisting from use of the car: driving *per se* is neither wrongful nor harmful.

---

[36] e.g. Husak, *Overcriminalization* 172.

Contrast the sale of military flamethrowers to civilians, where the very design and function of the device is as an anti-personnel weapon. In such a case, one cannot regard the harmful use as incidental or ancillary, and unconnected to its supply. Our argument is, in effect, that to supply a tool is to condone the use of that tool for its core function. This is a sufficient normative involvement to make that use the seller's concern.

Obviously, the supply by S has the *effect* of helping P to inflict harm. But the suggestion here is that there is also a communicative element to S's conduct, such that the assistance is not merely happenstance, but something S endorses and for which S too may therefore be held responsible. The core function of a thing is ordinarily a constitutive part of our social understanding of that thing. As such, the act of supplying the thing has expressive meaning as a facilitation of its use. (Indeed, this is why, in contract law, buyers normally benefit from an implied warranty that goods are 'fit for purpose', and can rescind purchase when they are not—something buyers cannot do when the defect is incidental.) In these cases, it is not open for S to deny that the product's deleterious use has anything to do with her. Similarly, sales of police radar detectors may legitimately be considered for prohibition within the terms of an Extended Harm Principle, in as much as their core function or *telos* is illegitimate.

Clearly, any argument for normative involvement based on core functions of a product will admit of hard cases. Sometimes, these will arise because the thing has multiple standard uses, some innocent and some not (crowbars are an example[37]). In such cases, S can potentially be regarded as being prima facie normatively involved in any of the standard uses to which the thing is then put. However, the existence of standard legitimate usages, which may be foreclosed by a general prohibition, should count in the normal way as a significant weighting factor against criminalisation. (Thus in the case of crowbars, it would be inappropriate to criminalise possession or supply *tout court*.) The best option in such cases may be to include an ulterior mens rea element within the prophylactic offence, such that S offends only if actually aware that the intended use is improper;[38] or to criminalise only in specified circumstances which themselves point to non-legitimate use.

Other cases will be borderline because of uncertainty about the core nature of a thing's functions. Handguns, perhaps, are in this category. To the extent that their core use is uncertain, the case for prohibiting their supply is also borderline, and may well differ across societies. Effectively by constitutional *fiat*, the possession and use of handguns is deemed prima facie legitimate within the USA. It seems hard to claim, therefore, that their

---

[37]   And, we think, baseball bats are not, although they are certainly sometimes *misused*.
[38]   Compare the offence of 'going equipped', above n. 5.

core use is in mounting wrongful attacks on people or their property.[39] By contrast, the social understanding of handguns in the UK associates their use much more closely with violence and wrongdoing; perhaps reflecting the traditionally more crowded nature of domestic housing, which permits few opportunities for recreational use of guns.[40] In so far as this is true, their supply can be more clearly understood as associating the supplier with the wrongdoing they facilitate.

(iv) Assistance: Supply of Advice

Clearer cases are assistance by supplying advice: for example by publishing a 'recipe book' for murder. Do recipes, manuals, and other forms of advice constitute advocacy? Not quite. Recipes usually do not urge the reader to employ them, but simply describe how to do something *if* the reader wishes to. Nevertheless, the *telos* of a recipe is its use: a cookbook is made for helping people to cook. Thus the requisite normative involvement is present—making it appropriate, subject to free speech limitations, to consider them for prohibition within the terms of the Harm Principle.

What if the manual disclaims any encouragement? Consider a recipe on 'How to kill your rich Granny' which contains a statement that killing grandmothers is illegal in certain jurisdictions and not advocated, and that any user of the recipe is proceeding under his own responsibility. However, conventional advocacy is neither necessary nor sufficient here, since there may be other ways of becoming normatively involved in another's conduct. Thus the case qualifies despite the disclaimer: the *telos* of the recipe still lies in its use. Its publication can, therefore, still be wrongful.

d.   Conjunctive Harms

In these cases, the conduct to be prohibited does the feared injury only when combined with similar acts of others. Dumping domestic waste in the river is proscribed as a health hazard, but the conduct actually endangers health only when a sufficient number of other persons do likewise. In such situations, the proscribed act is a token of the type of conduct that cumulatively does the harm; ordinarily, therefore, the actor cannot draw a moral distinction between her behaviour and that of others who also contribute to the injury. By contrast, in mediating intervention situations, S's conduct is harmless even when accumulated.

---

[39] Although so-called 'Saturday Night Specials' may lie closer to that status than do many other weapons.

[40] Once in place, handgun laws may themselves help to shape differences in cultural traditions. However, while this may be a legitimate bootstrap consideration, it cannot be relied upon to justify the initial proscription.

Conjunctive harms present fewer difficulties for prophylactic criminalisation than do mediating interventions. Suppose that overboard sewage discharge poisons the river, but that the discharge from S's own facility is insufficient by itself to produce that outcome. In this case, S is a participant in bringing about the harm, since her conduct makes a causal contribution to the resulting pollution. Yet, if her contribution is neither necessary nor sufficient for the ultimate harm, S might then contend, 'if others comply, why need I?' Here, the type/token argument helps explain why compliance is also her responsibility. Granted, the harm would not occur if others desisted from the conduct and S persisted. But since her token conduct is no different in character from that of others, being an instance of the type of conduct that causes the ultimate harm, she has no reason to be exempted from responsibility for that harm. Moreover, the claim of causal insufficiency supplies no answer to the question, why should S be treated any differently?[41]

Neither is there the impediment posed by mediating interventions to finding a wrong. Indeed, our pollution example involves two kinds of wrong. Since the ultimate harm is collectively caused, the immediate wrong that causes it is a collective one. In turn, S's own contribution is individually wrong in virtue of its participating in the collective wrong.

Some Mediating Considerations

We may safely conclude that responsibility for conjunctive harm is imputable also to S. However, that conclusion does not dispose of questions about the allocation of compliance obligations, and it is worth adding something about those questions here. If my conduct alone is harmless and becomes harmful only when *we* do it, the demand that we all desist or restrict our behaviour enlists us all in a scheme of cooperation requiring joint action (or, more precisely, joint desistence). But such demands are potentially oppressive: whereas much that I might do alone is harmless, a great deal of otherwise innocent conduct may become harmful, and a candidate for proscription, should enough others do it too.

The issue is one of allocating burdens of desistance: how much need S restrict her conduct, along with others engaging in the same conduct, within a scheme for preventing possible accumulative harms? The answer may depend on reasons affecting particular classes of actor.

Consider specialists, such as those engaged in the relevant activity as a livelihood.[42] Their responsibility for the ultimate harm may seem obvious

---

[41]   This is not to deny that there may be further reasons why S should be treated differently, and we note this possibility in the discussion of mediating considerations below.

[42]   Note that in A. von Hirsch, 'Extending the Harm Principle: "Remote" Harms and Fair Imputation' in A.P. Simester and A.T.H. Smith (eds), *Harm and Culpability* (Oxford: Oxford

from a causal perspective, in as much as the specialist is likely to contribute more to the harm—the factory dumps more sludge in the river than any individual householder. But that need not be so. There need be nothing causally distinctive about the specialist: the harm could occur without him, if others continue. Thus pollution may depend on multiple factories (and multiple individual polluters) with none essential to the result. So at most, one could say that factories as a class produce more river pollution than individual householders as a class. Even that may not be true, however, depending on the numbers involved. If there are just one or two factories and many householders, the latter as a class may contribute more. Ultimately, moreover, it is not obvious why a 'stronger' causal link furnishes a stronger ground for responsibility.

What seems more significant than mere cause is the fact that the specialist puts more of his interest, time, and resources into the harm-causing activity. With such greater involvement should come greater concern. The casual user can argue that there are so many potential harms from her various possible activities, all of which compete for her attention, that this kind of harm should not be her particular concern. The specialist cannot readily make this claim: the harmful results of this activity are distinctively his business because this activity is one upon which he concentrates a greater portion of his time and attention.[43]

Conjunctive harm situations thus lend themselves naturally to the distinction that we discuss in § 11.2(d), between specialist and general prohibitions. There are, we accept, certain basic duties of cooperation which are owed by each person in his capacity as citizen, concerning such matters as the payment of taxes, the administration of justice, and so forth. These basic duties of citizenship support generally applicable prohibitions. Beyond these basic duties, however, it will often be appropriate to allocate the responsibility for cooperating to prevent remote harms on a role-related basis. The duty of cooperating to forestall a given eventual risk would seem to fall most naturally upon those most closely associated with the activity involved: i.e., upon specialists in that activity. The river-polluting factory, or the firm which manufactures aerosol sprays, *makes* the consequences of that activity its business, in a way that a mere occasional user does not. Where practicable, there is reason to prefer the regulation of conjunctive harms through specialist rather than general prohibitions. Of course, basic imputation constraints should continue to

---

UP, 1996) 259, these considerations were analysed as an imputation issue. We now think the problem is one of liberty rather than responsibility, in that burdens of compliance may interfere too greatly with S's freedom of choice.

[43] This argument is distinct from a rule-of-law claim about advance notice: that the specialist is better able to inform himself of the specific rules applicable to this activity. The notice problem could, for non-specialists, be overcome by taking measures to publicise the rule. See below, § 11.1(d).

apply: if good reasons (including reasons relating to public obligation or duties of cooperation) cannot be supplied for holding the actor accountable for the potential eventual injury, then the prohibition should fall. Thus intervening-choice risks should ordinarily be considered suspect as grounds for criminalization.

A counter-consideration for specialists is concern about extra burdens. Because the specialist does the activity as his livelihood, stringent regulation will be more burdensome on him than on the casual user. In many cases, users can readily deal with the burden of regulation as a cost of doing business. But in some cases where the activity has non-commercial value, and/or the specialist has fewer resources, the case might be otherwise: hence Maine's rule that lobster fishermen may fish for lobsters, whereas sports fishermen face greater restrictions. We cannot pursue these cases in detail here. The point is that, in conjunctive-harm cases, it does not follow from shared responsibility for the ultimate harm that the criminalisation burden should fall equally on all. The matter becomes one of degree: of how great is the burden of compliance, and of how that burden is fairly allocated.

Being a specialist is not necessarily the only connecting role that might make the ultimate harm a person's distinctive concern. A variety of other roles are possible: if I live in the neighbourhood, I should arrange my trash so it can be conveniently collected; when I use the library, I should be quiet; and so forth. The roles involved may be varied, but what they have in common is that each can invoke particular norms that apply to persons in virtue of that role—as dweller, user, etc. The content of any duty of cooperation will, in turn, partly depend on the norms each role attracts.

5.3   CONCLUSION

Nowadays, the vast majority of criminal prohibitions comprise non-constitutive offences. Any modern theory of criminalisation needs to account for such offences, spelling out when and why they are legitimate. The task is not easy. No doubt others will disagree with the analysis offered here. But what is not questionable is that one integral component of any successful theory is an account of non-constitutive offences. The challenge is to justify why individuals may, sometimes, be denied liberties for the sake of preventing remote harms.

Part III

Offence

6

Rethinking the Offence Principle

WE HAVE APPROACHED the moral limits on criminalisation in this book by separating the issues into groups. In Part II, we considered problems surrounding the nature and scope of the Harm Principle. Assuming that the state sometimes has a legitimate interest in using the criminal law to regulate conduct that brings about harm to others, under what conditions is the prospect of harm sufficient to justify that use? We have seen that there are many controversial questions here, but our concern in Parts III and IV is not with them. Rather, it lies within a second set of issues: are there any varieties of conduct that may legitimately be criminalised where the justification for doing so does not refer to harm? To this question, Joel Feinberg has answered, yes. There are instances of conduct, he says, that may rightly be made criminal even though they do not cause or risk harm to others. Indeed, they may be criminalised even though they do not cause harm at all. Feinberg accepts, advocates, and elucidates an *Offence Principle*:[1]

> It is always a good reason in support of a proposed criminal prohibition that it would probably be an effective way of preventing serious offense (as opposed to injury or harm) to persons other than the actor, and that it is probably a necessary means to that end....

If I am seated in a bus when the amorous couple across the aisle carry their affections to the point of sexual intercourse, typically I am not harmed by their conduct, at least not in the sense of harm that is thought to invoke the Harm Principle. None the less, I may be entitled to take offence, and the state might be right to criminalise the conduct on the grounds that it is offensive.

In Part III, we reconsider the Offence Principle and argue that it provides an additional basis for criminalisation, but suggest that Feinberg's account of that Principle is incomplete. In particular, we discuss whether two additional constraints ought to be met before the Offence Principle can be satisfied. First, in this chapter, we argue that offensive conduct must be a wrong; it is not sufficient that the conduct causes affront, even serious

---

[1] *Offense to Others* 1.

affront, in others. Secondly, in the chapter following, we propose that the types of offensive conduct that one should wish to criminalise also involve, ultimately, some form of harm.

This second argument supplies an opportunity to reconsider the relationship between the Offence Principle and the Harm Principle. Even though, on our view, the overlap between the two principles is extensive, there is good reason to assess the criminalisation of offensive conduct within a distinct Offence Principle and not merely as a special case of the Harm Principle. In particular, as we observe in Chapter 8, the internal structure of the two principles are different.

6.1   OFFENCE AS WRONGDOING

a.   Feinberg's Account of Offence as Affront to Sensibility

The account offered by Feinberg depends primarily on consequences. For him, offence consists essentially in an affront to people's sensibilities, i.e. in an unpleasant and disliked psychological experience.[2] Causing any such affront, in his view, constitutes grounds for invoking the criminal law, provided that enough people are sufficiently affronted and that certain other conditions are met (more on which below). In particular, he suggests that the audience's reasons for feeling affronted are irrelevant, and there is no requirement that offence be reasonably taken:[3]

> Provided that very real and intense offense is taken predictably by virtually everyone, and the offending conduct has hardly any countervailing personal or social value of its own, prohibition seems reasonable even when the protected sensibilities are not.

The main reason for disregarding the audience's reasons for taking offences is, according to Feinberg, that it is difficult to explain why one is affronted or disgusted by something; and when explanations are given, they tend to be couched in terms of infringement of conventional mores that are not, in his view, proper reasons for state intervention.

At first glance, Feinberg's case for intervention may seem to be *merely* consequentialist, in that it is driven by considerations of outcomes and numbers. A committed utilitarian, for example, could readily accept the position that offence amounts to creating an unpleasant stimulus. The conduct could thus be prohibited if the familiar utilitarian formula is satisfied—that is, if the extensiveness and intensity of such unpleasant

---

[2] Feinberg excludes certain physical discomforts (aches, nausea, etc.) and emotional states such as anxiety. See, e.g., *Harm to Others* 46.

[3] *Offense to Others* 36.

stimuli outweigh in aggregate the satisfactions generated by the conduct. This would mean that a wide variety of affronts to sensibility could be proscribed, if taboos against the conduct were broadly held.

But Feinberg does not adopt a purely aggregative approach. Instead, he offers a more sophisticated balancing test that is designed to criminalise offence more sparingly. For present purposes, the test can be summarised briefly. First, a responsible legislator should consider the impact of the conduct on its audience, by examining the magnitude of the affront to see how pervasively and intensely it is felt. As part of that examination, however, a standard of 'reasonable avoidability' is imposed: the easier it is for members of the public to avoid settings where the conduct occurs, the less serious the offence is. Pornography may cause affront to many when viewed, but the seriousness of that affront is diminished if one must specifically purchase a recording or resort to a website to see it.

Secondly, the importance of the offending conduct is examined from the actor's perspective. The more central the conduct is to an actor's way of life, the greater is the claim not to have the conduct prohibited. For this purpose, a standard of 'alternative opportunities'—the obverse of 'reasonable avoidability'—is applied: restrictions on the conduct become more acceptable if there are satisfactory alternative times and places at which the actor could perform the conduct with less offence (say by viewing pornography only at home and not more generally).[4]

The broader social impact of the conduct is also considered. The more independent general usefulness the supposedly offending conduct has, the less the claim to prohibition. For this purpose, free expression of opinion is, following Mill, deemed to have its own social value, 'in virtue of the great social utility of free expression and discussion generally.'[5]

While still involving the weighing of benefits and costs, Feinberg's test is therefore not straightforwardly aggregative. Conduct that widely offends may, for example, still be permissible when committed in settings readily avoidable by others. Overall, moreover, his test is capable of being tilted against prohibition by requiring that the balance must be strongly in favour of criminalisation;[6] conduct must widely cause great affront in order to overcome this bias.

---

[4] The full list of (six) weighting factors is set out by Feinberg, *ibid.*, 44. See also Chapter 8 below.
[5] *ibid.*
[6] cf. *Harm to Others* 9: there is a 'general presumption in favor of liberty'.

b.   The Contingent Nature of Feinberg's Account

How would Feinberg's test work in practice? In a tolerant political climate, it should generate sensible results. Behaviour would have to have been quite outrageous before it could prompt widespread and serious offence. Feinberg himself relies on this kind of calculation, suggesting that 'for most forms of unreasonable offence, the very unreasonableness of the reaction will tend to keep it from being sufficiently widespread to warrant preventive coercion.'[7] More recently, however, there seems to be a trend toward less public tolerance and more legal repression of purportedly offensive behaviour.[8] 'Incivilities' are said to have serious consequences—to cause neighbourhood decay and breed crime; and to destroy the quality of urban life for ordinary citizens.

The application of Feinberg's Offence Principle is sensitive to diminishing tolerance, since the case for criminalisation would be strengthened if greater affront were taken to a given type of behaviour. In principle, therefore, the theory could uphold prohibitions of broad scope. Activities such as begging, for example, could legitimately be proscribed if they come to cause sufficiently widespread affront. This possibility exists notwithstanding the mediating factors that are included in his analysis. Consider Feinberg's 'alternative opportunities' factor. Beggars, it may be argued, lack a range of alternative opportunities, because of the paucity of other sources of income and of places to live other than on the streets. But alternative opportunity is, on Feinberg's formula, only one factor to be weighed against the degree and intensity of the offence. In principle, if sufficient numbers of persons are sufficiently affronted by begging, the criminal law could be invoked notwithstanding the lack of adequate alternatives.

Of course, difficult cases will be unavoidable under any account of the Offence Principle, since both it and the Harm Principle are designed to mediate practical conflicts between interests such as freedom, self-expression, and the well-being of different members of society. In part, it is a strength of Feinberg's analysis that it is contingent upon such factors as the strength of the affront caused and the practical alternatives available to both actor and audience. None the less, it seems to us that his analysis of

---

[7]   *Offense to Others* 36. *Sed quaere?* History is littered with examples of popular wrongheadedness.

[8]   Hence, for example, English legislation has authorised courts to issue orders that proscribe 'anti-social behaviour', with severe criminal penalties for breach: Crime and Disorder Act 1998, ss. 1–4; Anti-Social Behaviour Act 2003. Compare, in France, *Loi pour la sécurité interieure*, No. 2003–239, 18 March 2003; in New Zealand, the Wanganui District Council (Prohibition of Gang Insignia) Act 2009. For discussion, see *Incivilities*, especially chs 7–10.

offence omits something fundamental. Moreover, the omitted factor operates as a basic conceptual requirement of offence, and not merely as something to be weighed in the balancing decision to criminalise.

c.   The Missing Element: Wrongdoing

The deficiency in Feinberg's analysis, in our view, lies in his equation of offence with affront to sensibility. If offence is defined in terms of displeasing activities (independent of any reasons why they are displeasing), its potential scope is vast. Anything you choose to do might irritate or exasperate me. A great deal depends, therefore, on how much weight is given to the various mediating principles Feinberg proposes.

As Feinberg acknowledges,[9] this is not how offensiveness is understood in ordinary moral discourse. The mere fact that V dislikes what D is doing does not by itself make D's conduct offensive. Ordinarily, when someone objects to behaviour as offensive, she can be expected to give reasons for objecting that are ulterior to the fact that she dislikes it.[10]

By way of illustration, consider the following extra-legal example. Suppose that D meets V one day when D is wearing a garish Day-Glo orange tie. V objects. Were harmful conduct at issue, V might say, 'That's *my* tie, and you've taken it without permission.' But if the issue is offence, the mere fact that V's sensibilities are affronted does not imply any similar transgression. It is insufficient for V to say, 'Day-Glo ties get on my nerves', for the tie-wearer has no general obligation to spare the viewer's aesthetic sensibilities. The objector would normally be expected to supply a further normative reason why the conduct should be considered objectionable.

It is true, as Feinberg points out, that the objector may not be able to say why he finds luminescent orange ties irritating, or other conduct disgusting. What irritates or disgusts has its roots in social conventions, and V may dislike D's tie because he has accepted certain traditional notions of proper dress. But breach of such a convention does not necessarily show that there is anything wrong with the behaviour—and charging someone with being offensive involves charging him with a kind of misconduct. Were V to say, 'It's simply not done to wear Day-Glo orange,' that would suggest merely that D is being unconventional, not that he has acted in an improper manner.

---

[9]   *Offense to Others* 1–2.
[10]   cf. R. Dworkin, 'Liberty and Moralism' in *Taking Rights Seriously* (Cambridge, MA: Harvard UP, 1977) 240, 249ff. Admittedly, in ordinary language, V may loosely describe something that is disgusting (say, a foul stench) as 'offensive'. But even in ordinary language this usage is peripheral; hence, without more, V may not describe herself as 'offended'. See further the discussion of Duff and Marshall's argument, below, § 6.4.

What is needed, therefore, is the provision of reasons why D's conduct is offensive: reasons going beyond the fact that it affronts V's sensibilities. Those reasons may be various. The objector may cite a personal relationship with the actor that demands special regard for the former's sensibilities in the circumstances. ('It's my birthday party, and you know how I hate Day-Glo orange.') Or the reason may concern the insulting character of the conduct. ('But this is the Hibernian Society Ball on St Patrick's Day!') Or there might be reasons of enforced togetherness warranting special attention to others' sensibilities. ('We're stuck together in this confounded submarine for the next three months, and many of us detest Day-Glo orange.') But if the actor is a stranger to the objector, and no such special reasons can be cited, the mere fact that the conduct causes displeasure or exasperation is insufficient.

While one must be careful when drawing parallels between extra-legal examples and criminal policy, similar reasoning holds when one is considering the legal proscription of purportedly offensive conduct.[11] It is not affronting the sensibilities of other persons (even many of them) that should justify possible state intervention, but affront *plus* valid normative reasons for objecting to the conduct. Where state intervention is involved, the range of eligible reasons could well differ from those in everyday life: for example, our birthday-party example of a special personal relationship would not provide reasons for state action. But reasons there still should be.

Feinberg explicitly disavows the need to supply such reasons.[12] Admittedly, he does restrict the scope of the Offence Principle to states of affront 'caused by the wrongful (rights-violating) conduct of others.'[13] But he then sidelines this requirement with the assertion that 'there will always be a wrong whenever an offended state [i.e. a disliked mental state] is produced in another without justification and excuse.'[14] This reasoning supposes a general, prima facie duty not to generate offended mental states in others: consequently, the separate requirement for a wrong disappears. Since people are taken to have a right not to be affronted, Feinberg slides effortlessly from affront to wrong, subsuming the latter criterion within the former. Thus it is no surprise to find that the wrongfulness requirement is disregarded in the rest of the book.[15] Absent further considerations, 'we don't like it' suffices. If enough people find Day-Glo ties upsetting, there would be a case for prohibition.

---

[11]   Compare *Brooker* v. *Police* [2007] 3 NZLR 91, [55] (Blanchard J): 'Behaviour which is offensive in a public place must be capable of wounding feelings or arousing real anger, resentment, disgust or outrage in the mind of a *reasonable* person of the kind actually subjected to it in the circumstances in which it occurs.' (Emphasis added.)

[12]   cf. *Offense to Others* 36 (no requirement that the affront be reasonably felt).

[13]   *ibid.*, 1–2.

[14]   *ibid.*, 2. Compare *Harm to Others* 105–109.

[15]   See, in particular, the difficulties outlined in *Offense to Others* 27ff.

By withdrawing the normative element from V's objection, the justification of prohibition rests, ultimately, merely on conventional sensibilities. As Feinberg intends, this avoids rendering the Offence Principle into one version of legal moralism—but only at the risk of permitting a type of aesthetic majoritarianism. Perhaps it is true that whenever D's φing causes displeasure to V, or affront to V's sensibilities, there is in every case a prima facie *reason* (as opposed to duty) for D not to φ. But, even if this be conceded, assuming D is a private citizen, her reasons not to φ are not quite the point. What matters is *whether the state has a prima facie reason to prohibit D from φing.* On the latter question, our objection, in short, is that Feinberg's portals to the Offence Principle are too wide. Affront to sensibility, by itself, should never suffice to invoke the Offence Principle and therefore qualify for the sort of weighing exercise that both Harm and Offence Principles must then conduct.

Another strand of argument supports this analysis: one concerning the censuring role of the criminal law. We are speaking, here, of condemning offensive conduct through its proscription, and of treating offenders as having done wrong. This being the case, as we argued in Chapter 2 the criminalisation of conduct should require a plausible claim of wrongdoing. With conduct that supposedly is offensive, one must thus ask why the actor has done anything to deserve censure. If the gravamen of offence is merely that the conduct displeases many people, then it is not clear that wrongdoing has occurred at all. Better reasons need to be provided why and in what respects there is something reprehensible about the behaviour that properly may attract a censuring response.

6.2 WHAT WRONGS MIGHT INVOKE THE OFFENCE PRINCIPLE?

Our argument points up a need for further inquiry, into what sorts of wrongs might satisfy this element of the Offence Principle. Fully discharging that task lies beyond the scope of this book. However, it is worth noting some of the standard *exempla* of offence—that is, of conduct that may involve both (with Feinberg) affront to people's sensibilities and (beyond Feinberg) an element of wrongdoing.

a. Insulting Conduct

One reason why conduct might be offensive is its insulting or demeaning character. Indeed, insults are a paradigm way of giving offence. Insult involves, by its very nature, disrespectful treatment. It is social convention, of course, that gives various words, gestures, or acts an insulting meaning. But expressions of contempt are wrongful for reasons that go beyond mere convention. People have a prima facie claim, grounded in human dignity, against intentional demeaning treatment.[16] Conduct is insulting not simply in virtue of the effect (of causing affront) that it may have on its audience, but rather because of what it expresses. Thus it does not suffice to violate that prima facie claim that another person might happen to feel insulted (anything might do that). Rather, the conduct must *be* insulting—for example, because it is, and is intended to be, grossly derogatory. Such conduct becomes offensive even if the discomfort it produces is relatively fleeting, and no longer-term interests of the person are compromised.[17]

b. Exhibitionism

Another type of offensive conduct is exhibitionism. Suppose that D is sitting peaceably in the park, but cannot concentrate on his newspaper because E and F are copulating noisily on the grass nearby. D may rightly complain. One way of thinking about the wrongfulness of exhibitionism is as a type of reverse-privacy violation. Ordinarily, privacy involves the exclusion of others from one's personal domain. But there is also an interest in not being involuntarily *included* in the personal domains of others—particularly, in being spared certain private (especially, intimate) activities of others. Intuitively, this point is readily made: there is something plainly obnoxious about a couple's having sexual intercourse in public, or even about their arguing in a crowded train compartment over the clinical details of their deteriorating romance. Others, in such settings, seem to have a legitimate claim not to have such matters forced upon them. This may be singularly in point in locations like parks, which we value, *inter alia*, as places to interact with other persons who are not intimates, and where, consequently, such offensive activities are likely to be particularly intrusive and discomforting. However, it is important to note that offensive exhibitionism can also occur in private spaces. If my host, uninvited, exposes himself at a dinner party, I am entitled to take offence even though he has done so in the privacy of his own home.

c. Infringements of Anonymity in Public Spaces

People are entitled, when moving about in public space, to be left essentially alone. That general entitlement of anonymity—which is based on notions of privacy and autonomy—involves being free to go about one's

---

[16] Sometimes, there may also be a claim predicated on harm (below, § 7.2). We are concerned for now with the core case.

[17] Which is not to deny that on occasion they may be compromised, as we shall see in the next chapter.

business without certain forms of substantial interference: with no more than momentary and casual scrutiny by others; and with no more than fleeting unsolicited requests from others for one's attention or assistance. One might briefly be asked by a stranger for directions, but if one does not wish to respond, he or she is not entitled to pursue the matter insistently. Being asked by a stranger for monetary assistance is similar: a brief, polite request is not intrusive, but insistently or aggressively demanding funds offends against one's entitlement to anonymity in public places—one's right to be left alone. Sometimes the impact can be quite direct: on reflection, it should be no surprise if Venetian shopkeepers discourage inquiries from tourists for directions, since such inquiries can be so numerous as to significantly impede those merchants' daily work. But it is worth noting that the right to anonymity is broader, and covers a range of overlapping freedoms. It also underpins a concern about excessive CCTV surveillance: that one is subject to constant scrutiny, and is *exposed*, in public, to persistent examination. Imagine a line of security guards standing nearby, watching our every move, not only at a supermarket checkout but everywhere we move outside the house.[18] As with exhibitionism, the underlying idea seems to lie in a trade-off between public and private, a trade-off that generates obligations of mutual restraint in the context of social interaction.[19] We retain a right to certain levels of privacy in public, and well as private, spaces.

6.3   THE MULTIFARIOUS, YET UNIFIED, AND CONVENTIONAL GROUNDS OF OFFENCE

It may be concluded from the preceding examples that there is no one particular explanation why conduct is offensive. Moreover, the explanations differ in type: insult directly expresses disrespect and tends to be targeted at individual victims or groups; exhibitionist conduct is frequently not targeted at all, and its wrongfulness depends in part on negotiated social conventions. Certain cases, especially of infringement of anonymity, may sometimes become offensive only in virtue of repetition. These variations suggest that different types of offensive conduct may warrant different forms of legal and non-legal regulation. But, wherever criminalisation is contemplated, specific reasons need to be generated, and to be

---

[18] cf. A. von Hirsch, 'The Ethics of Public Television Surveillance' in A. von Hirsch, D. Garland and A. Wakefield (eds), *Ethical and Social Perspectives on Situational Crime Prevention* (Oxford: Hart Publishing, 2000); also B. von Silva Tarouca Larsen, *Setting the Watch; Privacy and the Ethics of CCTV Surveillance* (Oxford: Hart Publishing, 2011).

[19] See further below, § 6.3(b).

subjected to critical scrutiny, before conduct is deemed offensive. It is not enough that the conduct be widely disapproved of, or that it infringes traditional taboos.

Even so, a unifying feature of these various types of wrong is that each involves a failure to treat others with due consideration and respect, a failure to accord the victim full moral standing as a person. Indeed, it is this failure, rather than the resulting affront, that is an indispensable facet of offence: V may laugh off an insult, without being distressed by it in any way, yet the insult would still be offensive. Of course, the depth and breadth of affront caused by D's conduct is rightly, as Feinberg asserts, a consideration within the Offence Principle—but, while affront is a neces- sary condition of that Principle, it is neither a necessary nor a sufficient condition of offensive acts.

In a sense, the analysis offered here proceeds in the opposite direction to Feinberg's. Instead of beginning with the effects of someone's action, the wrong originates in the action itself: in the disrespect that it displays for others. As such, the action may be wrong, and offensive, whether or not it generates affront. *Pace* Feinberg, the wrong does not derive from that affront. In turn, the normative power of the Offence Principle arises not from Feinberg's posited 'right' not to be affronted, but from the right that we each have to be treated with consideration and respect. Rather than requiring that persons subordinate their behaviour to the fickle sensibilities of others, it helps to articulate the idea that each individual is valuable and should be treated as such.

a.   Difficulties about Identifying Offensive Wrongs

Let us stipulate, for the sake of argument, that insult, exhibitionism, and anonymity-invasions wrong their victims. Even then, the extent to which their prohibition is desirable will be debatable.[20] Various mediating con- straints must first be considered,[21] and it may be that few, if any, insults would qualify for criminalisation once those constraints are addressed. In a frictional, pluralistic, society we expect persons to have a certain thickness of skin. Conflict must be tolerated; indeed, it may quite often be desirable, if differing, valuable, but contradictory ways of life are to be upheld where

---

[20]   As it happens, existing treatments of insult vary within Western Europe. Germany and Sweden both have general criminal prohibitions of insult (although the proceeding must ordinarily be initiated by private prosecution); England's provision on the subject is somewhat less sweeping. Compare the German Penal Code, s. 185, and Swedish Penal Code, ch. 5, s. 3, with the Public Order Act 1986 (UK), ss. 4A and 5.

[21]   See Chapters 8 and 11. Wrongs of these sorts will, for instance, raise problems of definition, since not every intentionally demeaning act is a wrongful insult. It may be difficult for the law accurately to specify the criteria of insult in a workable form.

it is a feature of some of those ways of life that certain other valuable ways of life must be opposed.[22] None the less, *in principle at least*, insult might be a portal to the Offence Principle. This is especially likely in respect of victims who belong to more vulnerable groups within society, for whom insults may have greater resonance than for the majority of citizens.[23]

Similarly, what constitutes an unduly self-revelatory conversation in a train or restaurant is no doubt too variable a matter to be the subject of criminal legislation. Despite this, some clearer varieties of 'public indecency' might properly be proscribed as exhibitionism, including indecent exposure, public urination or defecation, sexual congress in public, or the like.[24]

Conclusions about the significance of particular conventions, and the rightness of criminalising specific forms of behaviour, will scarcely be beyond debate. One might argue that we would be better off if few or no obligations of mutual reticence were recognised, or that any such obligations are overridden by the need for mutual tolerance of diverging lifestyles. This shows that the way forward is contentious, since the ethical norms underpinning a particular claim of offensiveness may themselves be disputable. But it does not lead us back to Feinberg's claim that the normative basis for taking offence should not matter.

b. Respect and (Valuable) Social Convention

A notable feature of the varieties of offensiveness noted in § 6.2 is that they all depend, in one way or another, on social convention. Moreover, the contours of such conventions vary with time and place. In many countries, it is no longer indecent for a woman to display her bare legs in public. The display of genitalia is still considered indecent, but is acceptable in some continental European countries when it occurs in specified public bathing areas. A further challenge, therefore, is to prevent our analysis from becoming simply a vehicle to enact conventional mores through the criminal law. We think it does not, although the reasons for our view can only be sketched here. In the account we have presented, the importance of convention is intermediate, rather than directly constitutive of the wrong in offensive actions. This intermediate role is, indeed, typical. Much, if not all, of our interaction with others is shaped by conventions. Often the very

---

[22] For example, commitment to a particular religion may entail opposition to other religious ways of life.

[23] cf., e.g., *Collin v. Smith* 578 F 2d 1197 (1978); *R v. Keegstra* (1990) 3 SCR 697. We revisit insult in § 7.2(b).

[24] In German law, for example, this conduct would be punishable under StGB §§ 183 (exhibitionist behaviour) and 183a (exhibitionism leading to public outrage). See also the Swedish Penal Code, ch. 16, s. 16.

meaning of actions (e.g. waving goodbye by moving one's arm) is straight-forwardly a matter of shared conventions. On other occasions, the relationship is more complex. Ordinarily, one wears dark colours to a funeral, because this indicates that one approaches the occasion with due gravity and respect; failure to do so may be offensive because it signals to others that the occasion is not respected in this way. In turn, it also communicates a lack of respect for the other participants to whom the occasion is important.[25]

Suppose a convention exists that one does not expose oneself, uninvited, to strangers. While breach of that social convention may convey a lack of respect for others, it is not the breach itself that makes one's behaviour offensive; because the convention primarily is of instrumental rather than intrinsic value. It is a co-ordination rule,[26] one that helps to delineate the boundaries between personal and public, something that necessarily involves limits on what kinds of access people may have to the lives of others. Lying behind it are the interests of *people*, especially in our having some degree of control over the terms of our interaction with others. D's respect for V may call for him to observe the terms under which they (usually, by convention) interact. This holds independently of the particular terms of the convention. When D exposes himself, uninvited, to V, he both violates the applicable social convention and, further, wrongs V by failing to respect the terms under which she interacts with others. Conversely, where the applicable convention is not violated, the identical behaviour toward V may disclose no lack of respect. Thus nudity on a public bus is different from nudity on a public nudist beach, even though, for some persons, it may produce the same level of affront in either case; and even if D knows this.

The interplay between offence and convention is no surprise, since the wrongfulness of offence is closely connected to the expressive vice of incivility. Offence communicates basic moral attitudes of disrespect, intolerance, and inconsiderateness; this communication operates by reference to

---

[25] This conclusion might be defeasible. Suppose that D has recently arrived from another country where the relevant convention was different; D has no knowledge and, let us assume, no reason to know that his conduct infringes a social convention. Even though his behaviour may cause affront, no wrong is committed. This is not merely a claim that D lacks culpability. Integral to the offensive wrong is the lack of respect communicated by means of violating the social precept. The mere fact of non-conformity does not establish offensiveness; it depends on how and why the unconventional behaviour occurred.

[26] In principle, such a convention should be susceptible of derogation between consenting parties, typically in private contexts where strangers will be unaffected. See also below, §§ 9.4(b), 11.1.

socially conventional rules for the expression of respect, tolerance, and the like.[27] Hence, offence is tied to social conventions in a way that many moral values are not.[28]

There are deep waters here, which cannot be resolved within the scope of this book. Prior to a relevant social convention, the difference between exposing legs and exposing genitalia may not be obvious. Yet even if the content of a convention be arbitrary, that convention may create reasons for action once it comes into existence, in virtue of the function it performs. On this view, exhibitionism is a wrong not because of the inherent content of the exhibit, but because D's act treats V disrespectfully by violating a convention, about reticence and restraint in self-disclosure, that helps to maintain mutual respect.[29] As we saw in § 2.3(b), rules often create reasons in this way: it may be a random matter whether, in a given society, one drives on the left-hand or the right-hand side of a road—but the rule, once adopted, crystallises reasons for driving on one side or the other. Similarly, violation of a seemingly arbitrary convention may be wrong in virtue of the underlying purpose that convention serves. What makes infringement of exposure conventions offensive is thus something beyond the mere existence of the convention: the convention itself articulates a right of reverse-privacy, that guards one from being confronted with certain intimate disclosures concerning others. It is through encroachment upon this right that exhibitionism treats others without consideration.

A caveat is appropriate. Our remarks here concern the relationship between valuable conventions and wrongs. They presuppose that the relevant social convention, underpinning the finding of an offensive wrong, is justified. It may be that a particular convention is itself objectionable because of the behaviour it requires or prohibits, notwithstanding that the convention might have instrumental value. Where this is so, that ground for a finding of wrongdoing will fall away. One example of this might be a convention that contravenes the human rights of some members of the community. Suppose, for example, that there still were a convention in Alabama that persons of different races should not have any physical

---

[27] A point seen clearly by David Hume: 'Many of the forms of breeding are arbitrary and casual; but the thing expressed by them is still the same. A Spaniard goes out of his own house before his guest, to signify that he leaves him master of all. In other countries, the landlord walks out last, as a common mark of deference and regard.' D. Hume, *Enquiries Concerning Human Understanding and Concerning the Principles of Morals* (3rd ed. with notes, ed. L. Selby-Bigge and revd. P. Nidditch, Oxford: Oxford UP, 1975) 262.

[28] For valuable discussion of the differences between expressive and other virtues (and vices), see C. Calhoun, 'The Virtue of Civility' (2000) 29 Philosophy and Public Affairs 251; also S. Buss, 'Appearing Respectful: The Moral Significance of Manners' (1999) 109 Ethics 795. As Calhoun observes, communicating moral attitudes is not the same thing as having those attitudes; it matters, for example, not just that V *is* respected but also that he is made to *feel* respected.

[29] cf. T. Nagel, 'Concealment and Exposure' (1998) 27 Philosophy and Public Affairs 3.

contact in public. If an interracial couple hold hands in the park, they breach that convention but it does not follow that their behaviour is offensive—even though it may cause widespread affront amongst others in the park.

6.4   DISTINGUISHING OFFENCE FROM NUISANCE

It seems, however, that affront is not always conventional. Thus Antony Duff and Sandra Marshall identify a distinction between 'mediated' and 'immediate' offence. Whereas mediately offensive conduct is offensive only when it violates a social convention or standard, the wrongfulness of *immediately* offensive conduct derives, they say, from the sensory affront it causes:[30]

> We can take noise as a good example of this: noise that offends not because of its meaning (as racist hate speech offends), but simply in virtue of its character as noise—its particular sound (as when a finger scratches a slate), or its volume or intrusiveness.

Suppose that my cesspit makes a pungent assault on my neighbour's senses. The smell, Duff and Marshall would say, is 'offensive' in virtue of its immediate sensory unpleasantness and the visceral response it elicits, not in virtue of any disrespect it may (or may not) manifest. Any lack of respect I show by maintaining the cesspit is a derivative wrong, whereas the case for criminalisation arises directly from the noxiousness of the cesspit itself. Similarly, where I disturb my neighbours by regularly playing loud music, they assert that the wrong rests in the noise *per se*: 'the basic wrong, which gives us reason in principle to criminalise my conduct and only given which does my persistence display a lack of respect, is the persistent making of such offensive noise.'[31]

We concur with Duff and Marshall that affront may sometimes be caused via the senses rather than, as on other occasions, via our normative sensibilities. But even here, more is required to establish a wrong.[32] First, as Douglas Husak has pointed out,[33] disgust is not a natural category; it is, rather, an acculturated, learned, response. Conversely, one can develop a tolerance even to immediately offensive phenomena. In turn, whether a given sensory experience causes affront is likely to depend on time and place: on whether exposed sewers, for instance, are a feature of the main

---

[30]   R.A. Duff and S. Marshall, 'How Offensive Can You Get?' in *Incivilities* 57, 59–61.
[31]   *ibid.*, text in n. 52.
[32]   Duff and Marshall accept that not all immediately offensive events need be wrongful: the offensiveness must impose a burden on its audience that they should not be expected to tolerate. None the less, on their analysis such events are wrongful *in virtue of* their immediate offensiveness.
[33]   D. Husak, 'Disgust: Metaphysical and Empirical Speculations' in *Incivilities* 91.

streets. This is not to reject the distinction drawn by Duff and Marshall. But it is to suggest that even immediate offence is normatively sensitive and, as such, is not the negative of mediated offence. Given that responses of immediate affront are acculturated, the affront itself depends upon embedded normative standards and beliefs. We may say, therefore, that there *are* reasons—reasons, moreover, that are amenable to normative review—why a person is immediately offended.[34]

Secondly, even where a smell or noise is typically experienced as disgusting or affronting, it does not follow that it is wrongful. Gangrene may smell worse than flatulence, but only the latter is capable of being wrongfully offensive—and even that case depends on how and why it occurs. If I am woken at midnight by my neighbours' (intentionally) causing loud bangs and flashes on their premises, this does not establish offensiveness without further specification concerning whether their conduct is inconsiderate in the circumstances: is it, for example, Guy Fawkes Night (or the Fourth of July)?

None the less, the discussion of immediate offence draws our attention to an important aspect of direct sensory affront. While such affront may, without misuse of language, be characterised as 'offensive',[35] its 'offensiveness' derives from the affront whereas, in ordinary (mediated) offence, the affront is a product of the wrong. As such, the regulation of direct sensory affront is likely to be a matter for the Harm Principle, rather than the Offence Principle.[36] Sometimes, as the law of nuisance recognises, unpleasant stimuli may interfere with the quiet enjoyment of our homes or other resources. A glue factory, like the cesspit, might (in modern contexts) seriously affect the habitability and quality of life in nearby houses. But these are cases where the reason why we then may complain is because of the *effect* such things have on our lives; because they set back our interests and make our lives go worse. In other words, any claim of wrongfulness in such cases is grounded in their harmful consequences. The case for their proscription falls, in turn, to be evaluated within the scope of the Harm Principle.

a. Pre-emptive Public Behaviour

Nuisance can be public as well as private. Consider conduct which is not exhibitionist but obtrusive, sufficiently so that it pre-empts others' normal use of public space. Suppose, in the days before Walkmans and iPods, that someone is playing a large portable stereo ('boom-box') at top volume on

---

[34] Compare Duff and Marshall, above n. 30, at 60 n. 7.
[35] See n. 10 above.
[36] We discuss further the overlap between harm and offence in the next chapter.

public transport facilities. In this situation, the bare fact that other passengers are affronted or irritated does not capture why or how such behaviour is problematic. What makes it wrongful, and profoundly inconsiderate of others, is that the loud radio-playing is so intrusive.

In one sense, pre-emptive behaviour resembles exhibitionism, in that both are forms of inconsiderate conduct which deny to others the peaceable use of public space. But in exhibitionism, the conduct does not pre-empt common space in the same direct fashion as loud radio-playing. Something needs to be added concerning why exhibitionism is objectionable—why it treats others inconsiderately, so that the affront it causes is justified.

By contrast, in pre-emptive behaviour, the reason why the conduct is wrongful is that the actor makes use of the space for his preferred activity in a manner that leaves reduced scope for others there to pursue their preferences in peace. The inconsiderate nature of the conduct derives from its direct effect. It is difficult to concentrate on reading one's newspaper, or to carry on a normal conversation with a friend, if someone else is making a terrific din nearby on his boom-box.[37]

In these situations, whether the intrusion is wrongful is mediated by norms of cooperation, norms which govern the give-and-take of social interaction. The relevant norm here is that of mutual consideration in the use and enjoyment of shared public space. Someone wishing to play his radio ought to show consideration to the newspaper reader, by not playing it too loudly. The newspaper reader, on the other hand, may not insist on complete silence, as he could in a library; this leaves others (including the radio-player) sufficient scope for their preferred activities. What makes the loud playing of the boom-box wrongful is the infringement of such norms of mutual use and enjoyment.

6.5   CONCLUSION

Doubtless, insult, exhibitionism, and anonymity invasions do not exhaust the grounds for considering conduct offensive in the context of the criminal law. Reflection on other types of obnoxious conduct may suggest different reasons. But such reasons should be made explicit why each type of putatively 'offensive' conduct is inconsiderate or disrespectful. Some of those reasons will need considerable elucidation, and some are likely to be controversial. But the very demand for reasons limits significantly the scope of offence. It is not enough that the conduct displeases; grounds must be provided why that conduct is wrongful, in the sense of treating others in

---

[37] Or, in France, the accordion player on the metro: tolerable for a short while, but not when performing in the same carriage throughout an hour-long journey.

a manner that is grossly inconsiderate or disrespectful. It is this lack of respect or consideration, rather than the affront to sensibility itself, that establishes the wrongfulness of the conduct—without which element the censuring sanction of the criminal law should not be invoked.

A requirement of wrongdoing substantially restricts the scope of the Offence Principle. Recall our example of public begging.[38] Since begging can generate much public resentment, a purely subjective standard of offensiveness could support a broad prohibition of begging, such as exists currently in England.[39] Our proposed analysis, however, would not support a prohibition that would include peaceable, non-aggressive solicitation—because of the lack of convincing reasons why this treats others disrespectfully or inconsiderately. It is only aggressive begging that is thus intrusive and so may fall within the ambit of the Offence Principle. The wrongdoing requirement calls upon the proponent of criminalisation to put forward reasons *why* the conduct is a wrong—namely, under our proposed account, why the conduct treats others with a gross lack of consideration or respect. Indeed, providing adequate reasons is crucial to our model, in order to avoid circularity. Suppose that a given species of conduct is widely disliked. It should not be permissible to argue simply that the conduct makes public spaces less enjoyable for others, and is (for that sole reason) inconsiderate. Were this mode of argument permissible, our suggested model would collapse into Feinberg's subjective standard. We need independent normative arguments why certain kinds of conduct are inconsiderate or disrespectful, and hence potentially offensive.

[38] Above, §§ 6.1(b), 6.2(c).
[39] Vagrancy Act 1824, s. 3; made a recordable (hence imprisonable) crime in 2003. For advocacy of a sweeping prohibition of peaceable begging, see R. Ellickson, 'Controlling Chronic Misconduct in Public Spaces: of Panhandlers, Skid Rows and Public Zoning' (1996) 105 Yale LJ 1165; contrast A. von Hirsch and C. Shearing, 'Exclusion from Public Space' in A. von Hirsch, D. Garland and A. Wakefield (eds), *Ethical and Social Perspectives on Situational Crime Prevention* (Oxford: Hart Publishing, 2000).

7

The Distinctiveness of the Offence Principle

IN ANGLO-AMERICAN criminal law theory, the Harm Principle is the principal basis for assessing the legitimacy of criminalisation. It serves as a protection of personal freedom: to justify interfering with the actor's liberty through criminal prohibition, it must be shown why his conduct is injurious or potentially injurious to others. By contrast, offensive behaviour such as exhibitionism is not in any obvious way injurious. Is the Offence Principle therefore separate? Or can offence prohibitions be rationalised in terms of their potential harmful consequences to others?

Intuitively, it seems clear that there is a difference between offensive and harmful behaviour. But even if harm and offence are distinct, it does not follow that liberals need to subscribe independently to the Offence Principle. In § 7.2, we discuss ways in which some offensive actions may invoke both the Harm and the Offence Principles. Ultimately, in our view, these are the only offensive actions for which criminalisation is justified; a conclusion that raises questions about the need for a separate Offence Principle. We shall address those questions in § 7.3 before turning, in Chapter 8, to the distinctive mediating principles associated with criminalising offensive behaviour. Even if the Offence Principle is modified along the lines for which we argue in this Part, there remain structural differences between the Harm and Offence Principles. It is only within the latter Principle, for instance, that mediating considerations of reasonable avoidability play a role.[1] These differences suggest that while the Principles may overlap in their application to particular actions, they have separate logics and paradigmatically apply to different types of actions.

7.1 HARMFUL VERSUS OFFENSIVE ACTIONS

What distinctions are there between harmful and offensive actions, such that criminalisation of the former is thought to lie within the scope of the

---

[1] Above, § 6.1(a); below, § 8.1(b).

Harm Principle and criminalisation of the latter is not? The main difference lies in their generic consequences. As we saw in Chapter 3, harm involves a setback to a person's interests, where a person's interests comprise the things to which he has a claim and that make his life go well. When we are harmed our prospects are changed for the worse. In particular, harm involves the impairment of a person's opportunities to engage in valued activities and relationships, and to pursue self-chosen goals. In this sense, harm is prospective rather than backward-looking: it involves a diminution of one's opportunities to enjoy or pursue a good life. Characteristically, harm is brought about though the impairment of V's personal or proprietary resources. However, as Feinberg observes, what makes such impairment harmful is not the impairment *per se,* but its implication for V's well-being:[2]

> A broken arm is an impaired arm, one which has (temporarily) lost its capacity to serve a person's needs effectively, and in virtue of that impairment, its possessor's welfare interest is harmed.

Similarly, of interference with another's proprietary resources, Joseph Raz observes that 'any harm to a person by denying him the use of the value of his property is a harm to him precisely because it diminishes his opportunities.'[3] Here, Raz acknowledges that the justification for recognising property rights requires, ultimately, an account that gives priority to persons. D's proprietary rights are not ends in themselves: before the state may legitimately intervene, there must be harm to D (or to others).[4]

By contrast, at least paradigmatically, offensive behaviour does not in itself reduce a person's opportunities or frustrate his goals. Rather, it tends to cause the victim distress without affecting the sorts of interests that are the concern of the Harm Principle. Offence, we have seen, is marked by the fact that it involves a (wrongful) causing of affront to another person. In this sense, offence is experiential rather than forward-looking: the affront suffered by V need not, though it may, survive the cessation of the offensive conduct. Hence offended states are not in themselves a harm,[5] since they do not necessarily imply any prospective loss of resources on the victim's part: 'They come to us, are suffered for a time, and then go, leaving us as whole and undamaged as we were before.'[6] They do not, in other words,

---

[2] *Harm to Others*, 53. Cf. John Kleinig's claim that, in the case of a temporary hurt or an abduction that has no lasting effects upon its victim, there may be interference with a welfare interest but no harm: 'Crime and the Concept of Harm' (1978) 15 American Philosophical Quarterly 27, 32; *Harm to Others* 52–53.

[3] 'Autonomy, Toleration, and the Harm Principle' in R. Gavison (ed.), *Issues in Contemporary Legal Philosophy* (Oxford: Clarendon Press, 1987) 313, 327.

[4] See above, § 3.1(a).

[5] cf. *Offense to Others* 3.

[6] *Harm to Others* 45.

set back our interests.[7] Ordinarily, the causing of offence is not a matter of harm, of interference with the victim's means and capacities for enjoying a good life. There are, of course, exceptions to this proposition: but they fall to be dealt with below as exceptions, and not as characteristic of offensive behaviour.

a.   The Need for a Wrong

We argued in the previous chapter that offence requires a wrong. However, while the specific character of that wrong may be distinctive (a point to which we return below), offence cannot be differentiated from harm merely in virtue of being wrongful; because, as we saw in Chapter 3, criminalisation generally, whether under the Harm Principle or otherwise, also requires a wrong. Even though D's action may adversely impact upon V's well-being, it does not follow that V has lost anything to which he had an entitlement.[8] In such cases, D may have a prima facie reason not to do the action (because of its effect on V), but the state does not yet have a reason coercively to prevent D from performing it. The interests of different members of a society frequently conflict; and the requirement for a wrong supplies one means by which those interests are mediated, as well as a basis for criminal censure.

b.   The Experiential Nature of the Wrong

Offensive behaviour, then, involves conduct that constitutes a wrong, but which does not intrinsically set back the victim's interests and well-being. On this view, offence differs from harm in that it need involve no effect apart from the affronted mental state that is typically caused to the victim.

We can say something further about that consequence of affront. Underlying both offensive and harmful actions is the agent's distinctive contribution: her physical conduct. Disregarding telekinesis, it seems reasonable to assert that physical conduct is an indispensable means of bringing about both offence and harm. Typically, however, the agent's

[7]   This is so even though, according to Feinberg, people have an 'interest' in being treated with due consideration and respect, an interest that is violated (rather than set back) when a person is offended by the conduct of another: 'All offenses (like all hurts) are harms, inasmuch as all men have an interest in not being offended or hurt . . .. [O]ffensiveness as such is strictly speaking a kind of harm, but harm of such a trivial kind that it cannot by itself ever counterbalance the direct and immediate harm caused by coercion.' (J. Feinberg, *Social Philosophy* (Engelwood Cliffs, NJ: Prentice Hall, 1973) 28.) But 'interest', in this passage, has a different meaning from that upon which the Harm Principle depends. Consequently, the passage tends to conflate harm with wrong. See also above, § 3.3.
[8]   Above, § 3.1.

conduct brings about harm and offence through differentiable routes. Harms (property damage, physical injury, etc.) normally are brought about by an agent in a straightforward causal manner. By contrast, offence normally involves causation of a certain sort of mental reaction through some form of communication from the wrongdoer to the victim, and in particular through conduct that manifests a lack of consideration or respect for the victim. As we argued in § 6.3, it is this manifestation of disrespect that constitutes the wrong in offensive conduct. In turn, this underpins the essentially *experiential* character of offence; why, unlike harm, offence cannot occur unless V is aware of D's behaviour, and why 'bare knowledge' offence seems, in this respect, to resemble moralism.[9] Of course, harms too can be caused by communicative means; think of Holmes's example of gratuitously shouting 'fire' in a crowded theatre. Therefore this characteristic cannot suffice by itself to distinguish harm from offence. But it seems at least to be a facet of offensive actions.[10]

7.2   CRIMINALISATION OF OFFENCE UNDER THE HARM PRINCIPLE

We have argued that there is no conceptual link between offensive actions and harm. In particular, offence is unlike harm in two ways. It need not, and ordinarily does not, affect someone's longer-term interests, and may be of only momentary consequence for the person affected. Secondly, offence is experiential, and so is dependent on the person's awareness of another's behaviour. Nonetheless, and as a contingent matter, it is possible for offensive actions to fall within the scope of the Harm Principle.

a.   The Breadth of the Harm Principle

The possibility arises because the Harm Principle is capable of applying to actions that lead only indirectly to harm, and not just to actions that are intrinsically harmful. Earlier, in Chapter 3, we saw that wrongdoing can lead to harm in a variety of ways. Paradigm cases for prohibition under the Harm Principle arise when D's action directly sets back or risks setting back V's interests. Alternatively, conduct may also be eligible for prohibition when it leads to harm remotely, provided there are grounds to impute the risk of such remote harms to D's original action. Further, sometimes the harm may be secondary, and constituted by the reaction of others to D's

---

[9]   As when other persons are offended 'at the very idea' that the relevant conduct occurs, even in private: see *Offense to Others* 58.
[10]   We return to this point in § 7.3.

wrongful conduct. In such cases, we argued,[11] the secondary harm may satisfy the requirement in the Harm Principle for harm, but cannot be relied on to establish wrongfulness; to be eligible for criminalisation, D's conduct must be independently wrong.

There is no reason why, as a contingent matter, offensive wrongs cannot similarly lead to harmful consequences. As we saw in Part II, the Harm Principle's requirement for harm is instrumental—the link from wrongful conduct to harm does not have to be intrinsic. Thus it is a misreading of the Harm Principle, and a misguided attempt to distinguish it from the Offence Principle, to tie its application to intrinsically harmful actions. The Harm Principle is about wrongful actions that lead to harm; hence it can be invoked in favour of criminalising some action without the need to show that the action is directly harmful *per se*. There is a variety of ways in which wrongdoing may lead to harm. As such, even though the Offence Principle contemplates the criminalisation of wrongful actions that lack harmful consequences, the distinction between the Harm Principle and the Offence Principle does not track the distinction between directly harmful and offensive actions.

b.   The Potential Harmfulness of Offensive Conduct

It follows that the Harm Principle is sometimes capable of applying to offensive behaviour. Indeed, in our view offensive conduct can involve harm in each of the divers ways that we identified in Chapter 3. This is not to say that all offensive conduct falls within the ambit of the Harm Principle. But many of the more serious forms of offence do so. (It is a further question, considered in § 7.3, how strong is the argument in favour of criminalising the remaining cases of offence.)

Offence as Psychological Harm

First, and most obviously, conduct that is prima facie offensive can lead to physical or psychological harm analogous to that suffered in a physical attack: as when victims of racist insult, for example, suffer consequent mental breakdowns or hypertensive illnesses.[12] Similarly, insult may become like defamation if it affects a person's social or professional standing. These are straightforward examples. However, the application of this reasoning is sometimes exaggerated. For example, a generalised thesis of offence as psychological harm has been advanced by Louis B.

---

[11]   Above, § 3.2(c).
[12]   cf. R. Delgado, 'Words that Wound: A Tort Action for Racial Insults, Epithets and Name Calling' (1982) 17 Harvard Civil Rights-Civil Liberties LR 133, 137–79.

Schwartz.[13] Offensive behaviour, he argues, may do no physical harm, but nevertheless visits *psychic* harm on the members of its unwilling audience. When ordinary persons see someone exposing himself in a public bus, the dismay, distress, and shock they feel constitutes psychological harm. This injurious character permits a direct appeal to the Harm Principle—so that offensive conduct may be prohibited on the same basis as physically harmful conduct.

Should offence thus be assimilated generally to harm? We doubt it. Psychological harm is something that does exist, and on occasion it may be caused by offensive conduct,[14] but it is not constituted merely by affront. Harm involves more than generating distress: it involves a set-back to something more substantial—the impairment of a person's interests, an interference with her longer-term means or capabilities. When harm is so understood, this can help explain the link between harming and wrong-doing: if D damages a resource belonging to P, and does so with intent or negligence, this is prima facie a culpable wrong—and, thus, legitimately a potential object for the censuring response of the criminal law. In this case, D's conduct is wrong in virtue of the consequential harm. By contrast, consider the case where E causes momentary affront to Q. Her conduct involves no impairment of Q's resources. Moreover, were the idea of harm extended to include such cases, it is not clear why any comparable form of wrongdoing is involved. In essence, E has displeased and upset Q; but, as we argued in the previous chapter, no one has the generalised obligation to refrain from displeasing others.[15] E's conduct cannot be wrong simply because it causes affront. In turn, absent wrongdoing, the imposition of a criminal sanction is inappropriate.

The concept of psychological harm, as actually used in ordinary language, reflects this understanding: it consists of more than the state of being affronted. The psychologically harmed person's personal resources or coping mechanisms need to be impaired in some way; for example, through his having been traumatised, or his having difficulty in concentrating on work or in conducting normal social relations. These are not the standard effects of offensive conduct: diminution of one's cognitive or evaluative powers, for example, does not ordinarily follow from experiencing obnoxious behaviour. The normal person may be irritated or disgusted

---

[13]   L.B. Schwartz, 'Morals Offenses and the Model Penal Code' (1963) 63 Columbia LR 669.

[14]   Something long recognised in the law of tort: *Wilkinson* v. *Downton* [1897] 2 QB 57. More recently, the House of Lords confirmed that psychiatric injury amounting to a clinical condition may constitute bodily harm for the purposes of crimes against the person: *Burstow* [1998] AC 147.

[15]   cf. J.J. Thomson, *The Realm of Rights* (Cambridge, MA: Harvard UP, 1990) 254–55, emphasising the variable and subjective nature of individual sensibilities.

when seeing someone exposing himself on the bus, but he or she is unlikely to suffer such impairments. Mere affront, in our view, is not a species of psychological harm.

Other Effects on Well-being

Apart from psychological harm, offensive conduct may attack well-being in more complex ways. This consequence is often claimed for racial insults: that such insults are liable to lessen the self-confidence or self-esteem of persons who are the targets of such insults, and may damage their sense of identity and membership of society. There is a limited analogy that may be drawn here with rape, a wrong that everyone agrees falls within the Harm Principle. Rape victims may suffer great trauma, lose their sense of self-worth, lose their confidence in their social or physical environment, or be in other ways profoundly affected by their experience.[16] To diminish a person's actual or prospective quality of life in this sort of way is to harm that person. If similar consequences arise from offensive wrongs, such as racist insults, those wrongs are rightly also characterised as harmful.

Remote Harms

A third version of the offence-as-harm thesis relies on connecting offence to remote harms, by claiming that offensive conduct has a tendency to cause harmful results in the long term. This version recognises that harm involves a setback of interest, and that offensive conduct is not ordinarily harmful *per se*. But incivilities left unchecked, it is contended, lead ultimately to a higher incidence of actually harmful (and criminal) behaviour. A paradigm instance of this argument is the 'broken windows' thesis of the American criminologists James Q. Wilson and George Kelling, who argue that permitting incivilities in a neighbourhood (graffiti, unruly behaviour by young people, and so forth) will cause the locality's decay, the departure of its more respectable residents, and thus an environment that fosters higher rates of theft and violence.[17]

As it happens, empirical support for the Wilson-Kelling thesis has been sparse.[18] For present purposes, however, the thesis raises a more important and non-contingent issue about justifying the criminalisation of offence on

---

[16] See, e.g., J. Temkin, *Rape and the Legal Process* (Oxford: Oxford UP, 1987) 1–6.

[17] J. Wilson and G. Kelling, 'Broken Windows: The Police and Neighborhood Safety' (1982) Atlantic Monthly (March) 29; see further G. Kelling and C. Coles, Fixing Broken Windows: Restoring Order and Reducing Crime in Our Communities (New York: Simon & Schuster, 1997).

[18] See R. Taylor, 'Crime, Grime and Responses to Crime' in S. Lab (ed.), *Crime Prevention at a Crossroads* (Cincinnati, OH: Anderson, 1997); also R. Sampson and S. Raudenbush, *Disorder in Urban Neighborhoods: Does it Lead to Crime?* (Washington, DC: National Institute of Justice, 2001).

the basis of claimed 'remote' harms. Those who engage in offensive behaviour do no harm themselves, but merely help generate social conditions in which *other persons* might choose to do harm. The resulting harm, in other words, depends upon intervening choices by others. The indecent exposer directly injures no one; it is just that his conduct might help induce respectable people to leave the neighbourhood, creating the potential for a 'criminal element' to move in—and it is the latter who may decide to hurt people. As was argued in Chapter 4, ordinarily such remote harm, when caused by others acting autonomously, does not supply a reason why the original act is wrong and therefore does not supply a ground for criminalisation.

Offensive behaviour (in the sense outlined in Chapter 6) is, however, independently wrong; hence, in principle, the remote harms need only satisfy the Harm Principle's consequential aspect. So understood, harmful offence might even be regarded as a paradigm case for the criminalisation of remote harms. The strength of this analysis, however, is also its weakness: that the wrongfulness of the conduct is unrelated to its harmfulness. These intervening-choice scenarios raise problems of fair imputation: it is doubtful whether the harmful choices of later actors should be treated as being, even in part, the moral responsibility of the initial actor. Unless the initial actor, through his conduct, gives implicit support or endorsement to others' subsequent harmful choices,[19] or is in some other way responsible for those choices,[20] criminalising his conduct infringes basic ideas of the separateness of persons as moral agents. As we shall see in § 7.3, this disjunction in part underpins our argument that, normally, the criminalisation of harmful offence is best justified under a separate Offence Principle, and not simply on the basis of harm.

Not all cases of remote harm suffer from the difficulty we have identified with respect to the Wilson-Kelling argument. For example, a different argument sometimes made in favour of criminalising racist insult is that such conduct can have the effect of inducing third parties to value the victim(s) less, thereby undermining the victim's membership of the community and his environment and opportunities more generally. Lawrence observes that racist speech delivers a message not only to the victim, but also to society at large, that the relevant minority is unworthy of full

---

[19] See the principles discussed earlier, in Chapter 5.

[20] For instance, there may be cases of *conjunctive* harm or offence, in which any one person's conduct is not by itself so harmful or offensive as to justify criminalisation, but where, if enough others did the same, there would be sufficient harm or offence. (Environmental harms, such as pollution, are often accumulative in this way: see above, §§ 4.3(c), 5.2(d).) A version of this possibility figured in *Chief Constable of Lancashire* v. *Potter* [2003] EWHC 2272 (Admin): in deciding whether there were grounds to make an Anti-Social Behaviour Order against a prostitute, a court may consider the anti-social effects of her behaviour not merely alone, but in conjunction with that of other prostitutes in the area.

participation in the affairs of that society.[21] By working upon the larger audience, Lawrence argues, such speech can actually diminish the victim's participation in society, by depriving his voice of persuasive power *in the ears of others*.[22] This is a variety of remote harm; harm, moreover, that is intimately related to the wrongness of the offence and, hence, is rightly imputable to the initial wrongful activity. Here, therefore, the Harm Principle is brought within range.

Reactive Harms

Finally, and most importantly, we argued in § 3.2(c) that (secondary) harm can also occur when people are affected by the prospect, rather than the actuality, of wrongful action. To the extent that such precautionary responses are reasonable, they are relevant to the case for criminalisation. However, unlike imputable remote harms, they cannot help to *constitute* the initial wrong—that is, they do not supply the reason why the initial activity is wrongful. Paradigmatically, it is this type of harm that the criminalisation of offensive action forestalls.

To illustrate, recall the example with which we began the previous chapter. If I am seated in a bus when the amorous couple across the aisle carry their affections to the point of sexual intercourse, typically—we said—I am not harmed directly by their conduct. But the conduct surely is offensive and, if I know that taking a bus is likely to involve experiences of this sort, I might no longer want to take the bus. As such, my interests are set back. I lose access to an important and valuable public resource; the availability of which, for many people, matters to their well-being. Of course, that loss of access is also my own choice, so it cannot be invoked to establish that exhibitionism on the bus is wrong. The wrongdoing is supplied by the immediate offensiveness of the exhibitionism itself. But the extent of reactive harm, which arises as a reasonable response to the manner in which exhibitionist behaviour detracts from the quality of public facilities, helps to measure the seriousness of the wrong, and hence the strength of the case for prohibition. It reflects the impact of that wrong on people's lives.

---

[21]   C. Lawrence, 'If He Hollers Let Him Go: Regulating Racist Speech on Campus' [1990] Duke LJ 431, 439.

[22]   *ibid.*, 470: 'An obvious example of this type of devaluation would be that black political candidate whose ideas go unheard or are rejected by white voters, although voters would embrace the same ideas if they were championed by a white candidate.'

7.3 A SEPARATE OFFENCE PRINCIPLE?

So far, we have argued that the Offence Principle requires a wrong, and not merely that D's conduct causes affront. We have also argued that offensive conduct is capable of causing harm in a variety of ways. Our discussion in this section concerns two questions. First: is harm, as well as wrong, a prerequisite of the Offence Principle? Or, in the terms with which we began Part III, are there cases of offensive conduct that may legitimately be criminalised where the justification for doing so does not refer also to harm? Secondly: if harm is also involved in offensive conduct, why is the Offence Principle—rightly, in our view—acknowledged independently of the Harm Principle? Why, in other words, should not the criminalisation of offensive conduct simply be left to be justified within the terms of the Harm Principle?

a. Criminalising Offence Without Harm?

Our first concern is with those types of offensive conduct that do not lead, either directly or indirectly, to harm. For convenience, we term such cases *mere offence*. Here, it seems that criminalisation must be justified, if at all, by reference to the fact that the conduct manifests a lack of consideration or respect for other persons and that consequently it affronts those others: it is wrong, and it is disliked, but it does not damage other people's lives.

Mere offence differs from mere immorality (and, indeed, from paternalism). The requirement for a wrong, outlined in the previous chapter, is not a requirement just that D's behaviour be wrongful. It is, further, a requirement that D's behaviour wrongs *someone*—characteristically, that the behaviour violates V's right to be treated with due consideration and respect. This difference between offence and immorality creates normative space for arguments in favour of criminalising mere offence, where those arguments do not rely just on the immorality of the conduct but respond to the fact that D has attacked V's right to be treated as an equal qua self-determined, morally responsible, human being.

The point is that, unlike the sorts of cases that legal moralism distinctively addresses, D's conduct is not merely wrongful *in abstracto*: it is other-affecting. D's wrongdoing generates a tension between V's right to be treated with respect and D's interest in being able to express herself freely. That tension is not an abstract one: typically, D's attack has real, unpleasant, effects in virtue of the affront it causes to V. Moreover, where there is tension between individuals in a community, regulating the terms of their engagement is exactly the sort of function that the state exists to perform. At least where that tension is sufficiently serious, the state has a prima facie reason to intervene, in virtue of its supervisory role in co-ordinating social interaction.

So the case for regulating mere offence is different from, and stronger than, the case for regulating mere immorality. The argument for intervention still gives priority to the interests of people and not simply to morality. Hence, it contains and does not eschew the central advantage that the Harm and Offence Principles have over legal moralism.

But is that difference ever likely to be sufficient, in the absence of harm? Two considerations militate against that conclusion. First, criminalisation is an intrusive and condemnatory form of coercion. Accepting the general case for criminalising mere offence will, inevitably, lead to restrictions of individuals' autonomy, especially because the criminal law is so coarse-grained. For practical reasons, its prohibitions are framed in general terms, ruling out both valuable and valueless instances of a proscribed activity. For some persons, the very existence of the prohibition will mean that their lives go less well. The strongest cases for depriving people of opportunities in this way arise where the D's activity is likely to damage the capacities that *others* have to live good lives. In these cases, a condition of D's well-being (her autonomy) is weighed against a condition of V's well-being: a real trade-off of competing welfare interests needs to be made. But in these very cases, the character of D's conduct is by definition harmful. Where, by contrast, the conduct is merely offensive, it is not clear that the grounds for intervention are sufficiently weighty to defeat the strong prima facie reasons that always exist not to criminalise. For this reason, and because of the distinctive considerations associated with criminalising (even harmful) offensive conduct that are outlined in the next section, it seems to us that mere offence is, by itself, insufficient for criminalisation.

This analysis fits with our conception of the state in § 2.3(c), as an entity concerned with advancing the welfare of its subjects. On that view, the state's use of coercive power should be restricted to conduct that affects people's means and capacities for pursuing a good life. The same conclusion is buttressed by an inductive argument. As we have seen, the kinds of offensive conduct for which criminalisation seems most plausible are those that also involve harm. Consider insult: the strongest case for its prohibition concerns racial insult. Yet the latter conduct not only conveys contempt but also has the potential adversely to affect V's access to community life—which is a matter of harm. Similarly, consider exhibitionism: indecent exposure in public spaces, such as streets or parks, not only shows a lack of consideration and respect but may also restrict others' access to and enjoyment of these public facilities—again, a matter of harm. From a liberal perspective, it is difficult to think of an attractive case for criminalising offence where, either directly or indirectly, no form of harm is involved.

b.   Do we Need a Separate Offence Principle?

If the kinds of offensive behaviour that liberals should wish to criminalise so often, and plausibly always, also involve harm, what remaining role is there for the Offence Principle? Why not decide whether to criminalise offensive conduct, like other wrongs, simply by reference to the Harm Principle? We think, however, that there remain good reasons why the criminalisation of offensive conduct should be determined under a separate Offence Principle.

The Dependence of Criminalisation upon Offensiveness

The first step in our reasoning involves a subsidiary question. Since we are concerned with cases of harmful offence, why not disregard the offensive character of the conduct altogether and decide whether to criminalise it (within the terms of Harm Principle) simply on the basis of its harmfulness? This is really a question about the Harm Principle, but we must dispose of it before proceeding. In our view, the question misunderstands the nature of the Harm Principle. It neglects the requirement for a wrong. In § 7.2(b), we observed that the harmful consequences of offence can be remote and contingent. The exclusionary social effects of racial insult, for example, may depend on the decisions and reactions of other independent actors—perhaps D's racial insult restricts V's opportunities because it induces third parties to think worse of V, so that they become less willing to offer him employment or to interact with him socially. As we noted there,[23] criminalising actions by reason of such remote harms is ordinarily problematic because D exercises little or no control over the choices of the eventual harm-doers. Those choices do not make D's own conduct wrong. In racial-insult cases, however, there is more than an eventual harm mediated through others' choices; there is also a wrong by D himself. It is via *this* act of treating V with gross disrespect that D becomes eligible for penal censure. Hence it may be legitimate to criminalise racial insult yet, at the same time, illegitimate to criminalise other varieties of conduct that also reinforce adverse racial stereotypes but which involve no immediate wrong by the actor.

In other respects, too, the criminalisation of harmful offence involves different considerations from those that are involved in the criminalisation of other harmful wrongs. If the structure of the offence-criminalisation decision differs from the structure of the Harm Principle, it follows that the Offence Principle has independent status. We believe this to be the case, for two reasons.

---

[23]   See also Chapter 4.

First, it seems to us that the shapes of the Harm and Offence Principles differ, reflecting a difference in the balance of work done by harm and wrong. In the Harm Principle, harm, its gravity and likelihood, is the driving force behind the decision to criminalise. Conversely, in the Offence Principle it is the conduct's offensiveness that provides the initial impetus toward criminalisation—which is why one might take seriously the possibility of criminalising mere offence, while simultaneously rejecting the possibility of criminalising behaviour that is purely a moral wrong. What is noxious about insult, for example, is primarily its offensive character, rather than any consequences it may generate: that it treats those targeted with gross disrespect. As such, the significance of harm within the Offence Principle seems to lie in counteracting the mediating factors that otherwise militate against criminalisation, such as the restraining principles regarding free expression and the toleration concerns requiring a degree of resilience in a diverse, rough-and-tumble, society (more on which below). These restraining principles militate against prohibiting bare insult. With racial slurs, however, elements of harm enter the picture—this particular species of insult may adversely affect the ability of people from minority groups fully to participate in the community's social, political, and economic life. Within the Offence Principle, those prospective harms work to defeat the mediating factors: the policy concern for resilience has less force, for example, when the conduct damages people's social and economic opportunities.

The Distinctive Considerations Associated with Offensive Conduct

The second difference is one of particular content. While both the Harm and Offence Principles require wrongdoing, the wrong required by the Harm Principle has no special *marque*, and tends to vary according to the harm involved. By contrast, the wrong of offence is independently a communicative wrong, one that does not arise in virtue of any further consequence. In § 6.3, we noted that offensive conduct is characteristically a form of expressive action, something that communicates to V, the person experiencing the conduct, a lack of respect and consideration. This feature is distinctive of the Offence Principle. In turn, because of the expressive nature of the wrong being assessed for criminalisation, the internal structure of the Offence Principle differs from that of the Harm Principle. Hence the Principles exist separately.

Why is this expressive character so important? Even though D's offensive conduct may not be valuable when viewed in isolation, nonetheless it can be valuable as a constituent expression of D's chosen way of life—a way of life that on the whole may be valuable, even if this element in isolation is not. The over-amorous couple on a public bus may offend, but their activity may, for them, be an important expression of their intimate relationship—something from which they derive fulfilment. We may say to the couple that they should conduct their relationship differently, at least in public, without meaning to attack that relationship. But if the offensive conduct is, for that couple,[24] an integral element of their relationship, then in attacking that element we necessarily attack the whole. And when we criminalise that element, we suppress an aspect of that particular, valuable, way of life.

Prohibition of such activity may yet be justified. It is a commonplace that criminalisation removes options. Its doing so is a price we sometimes must pay, for example if significant harm is to be prevented. But, where the conduct is an act of communicative expression, there is especial reason to be cautious. For most of us, our lives involve, and are in part defined by, the interaction and relationships we have with other members of our society. A successful life normally requires that there be conciliation between the individual's way of life and the society in which she lives, something that depends, in turn, on the individual's being permitted to express her own values and chosen way of life in a tolerant environment. It is only through such interaction that her participation in and membership of the society is affirmed, in the eyes both of the individual herself and of her audience.[25] Imagine that D, E, and F are old friends, and that F is homosexual. Suspecting this, D and E say to F, 'If you are homosexual, that's okay—so long as you don't tell us or manifest any such tendencies in our presence.' This is not a tolerant response.[26] It denies P full membership of the friendship, and denies her full status as a person. The prohibition of communicative acts, including offensive ones, tends not only to censure and preclude the particular act that is proscribed, and the way of life to which that act gives expression, but also to undermine D's participation in the society itself.

The consideration outlined here is buttressed by other lines of argument in favour of a right to free expression, such as arguments that link the right to our collective interests in having a democratic government, one that operates under the rule of law.[27] Collectively, they skew the Offence Principle, in particular, against criminalising even harmful offence. Moreover, the inherently communicative wrong of offensive conduct warrants other, structural, differences between an Offence Principle and the Harm Principle. In particular, the avoidability of the offence, and the alternatives

---

[24] As Raz observes, 'we cannot deny them sovereignty over defining for themselves what their way of life is, and what is integral to it.' J. Raz, 'Free Expression and Personal Identification' in *Ethics in the Public Domain* (revd. ed., Oxford: Oxford UP, 1995) 146, 162.

[25] cf. Raz, *ibid.*, 153ff.

[26] Similarly, the so-called 'don't ask, don't tell' policy for the US military, introduced into 10 USC § 654 by Public Law No. 103–160 (1993), was fundamentally illiberal.

[27] We do not explore these arguments here, mainly because the existing literature is so extensive.

available to the actor, play a key role under the Offence Principle in mediating the attempt to reconcile interaction between different ways of life. It is no answer to the argument for criminalising assaults on 15th Street that one can walk safely down 14th or 16th Streets—that 15th Street is avoidable. By contrast, indecent exposure, or portrayals thereof, may be permitted at designated beaches and in licensed cinemas. D is thereby left some freedom to express himself. But V does not have to pay attention.

To some extent, the argument made here also militates *against* D, since D's offensive action may itself be inimical to V's way of life. In such cases, however, the attack is ordinarily private; it lacks the authoritative voice of the state and does not put in question his full membership of the community.[28] By contrast, criminalisation condemns D's expressive conduct on behalf of the community. Here, too, the possibility of avoidance is important in ensuring that D's attack on V is not representative of the environment as a whole.[29] One of the objections to racial insults directed against minorities, for example, is that frequently it is not isolated but widespread; conversely, racial slurs against someone of the majority race in a community are unlikely to be so damaging. Where insult is widespread and unavoidable, the force of each insult is, in part, that it is no longer private; the victim comes into conflict not only with a particular wrongdoer but with the community of which he is a member.

In sum, there is a conceptual link between offence and expression. It follows that there is a conceptual link between the justification of the Offence Principle and freedom of expression arguments. The need to accommodate diverse and sometimes inconsistent styles of life, which may depend for their success on being socially accepted, militates in favour of a 'thick skin' approach to the regulation of expressive acts, even where those acts are offensive to others. Friction is a characteristic of social interaction, at least in a pluralistic society. Such societies require of their members a certain robustness of sensibility, so that incivility is sometimes tolerated for the sake of social discourse. But this, it seems to us, is no bad thing.

---

[28] There may be exceptions to this, e.g. where D has representative standing. We cannot pursue such possibilities here.

[29] See further § 8.1 below.

8

Mediating Principles for Offensive Conduct

WE HAVE ARGUED in Part III for a narrow version of the Offence Principle, one restricted to behaviour that treats others without consideration or respect. Even so, the conclusion that particular conduct is offensive does not suffice to establish that it should be criminalised. Amongst other things, the consequences also count: affront must be serious and widespread, as Feinberg insists. Indeed, we have argued in the previous chapter that the conduct standardly should also involve harm. Beyond those requirements, moreover, there are additional mediating factors that need to be taken into account.

Some of these mediating concerns take the form of supervening constraints, such as freedom of speech. In political discourse, for example, it may be necessary to tolerate insulting utterances for the sake of having free public debate. Other mediating concerns constitute pragmatic criminal-policy and social-policy considerations. Consider insult. Having a general criminal prohibition against insult might make more sense in a highly ordered society with well-established patterns of deference and civility than in a more loosely-organised, rough-and-tumble, society. Given that most developed Western countries have been evolving in the latter direction, it seems preferable to eliminate or narrow the scope of such general prohibitions of insulting conduct as now exist. However, this still leaves open the possibility that certain grave forms of insult—such as demeaning references to minority groups—should be presumptive candidates for criminalisation.[1] We return to these considerations in § 8.1(a).

If such mediating factors are still involved in decisions to criminalise, how does our analysis go beyond Feinberg's account—which we criticised in Chapter 6 for depending too heavily on weighing factors? The answer is that, on our account, these factors will operate differently and with narrower scope. Given that our initial threshold for establishing offence is

---

[1] cf. StGB § 130(1), which contains such prohibitions; also, in the UK, the Public Order Act 1986, s. 19.

more stringent than Feinberg's, mediating principles are no longer all that stands between the majority's attitudes and criminalisation.

In Feinberg's theory, conduct is prima facie offensive whenever it is experienced as unpleasant. Much of his analysis then involves a balancing exercise, comparing the factors for and against criminalisation. Feinberg's mediating principles are necessarily designed to accommodate a broad, subjectivist definition of offence.[2] Ultimately, the conclusion is very much dependent on how intensely and how widely the conduct is disliked. Within our approach, however, upsetting behaviour is not even presumptively offensive: reasons must be given why the behaviour is insulting, exhibitionist, or the like. Consequently, some of the considerations that Feinberg treats as weighing factors have a different status in our analysis. On his view, the 'reasonable avoidability' of the conduct weighs against criminalisation. It ordinarily militates against criminalising purportedly offensive behaviour conducted in private. But it is no absolute bar to criminalising such conduct; if sufficient numbers were upset by 'the very thought' of the behaviour occurring behind closed doors, Feinberg admits, it could be prohibited.[3] On our analysis, the presence of an audience would be no mere weighing factor, but a necessary part of the reasons that make conduct offensive in the first place. Exhibitionist conduct, for example, involves compelling others to witness certain intimate behaviour. It cannot occur unwitnessed.[4]

In what follows, we outline some further principles by which the criminalisation of offence may be mediated.

8.1   WEIGHTING FACTORS AND MEDIATING PRINCIPLES

At the outset, we should not neglect the various weighting factors that are common to all criminalisation decisions. As in the Standard Harms

---

[2] Requiring, for example, that the affront to sensibility must be serious and widespread, albeit not universal: see *Offense to Others* 27–36.

[3] *ibid.*, 64–67.

[4] Kurt Baier would disagree: '[W]here there are standards that are widely and deeply embedded, witnessing is not necessary to cause offence. Of course, if I draw my blinds whenever I eat human flesh for dinner or have sexual intercourse with my goat or with my devoted sister, then no one's sensibilities can be affronted by witnessing what I am doing. But if I tell others or invite them to parties and ask them to bring their own favourite corpse or goat or relative, the case is different. The fact that they need not come or participate is not necessarily sufficient to make my behaviour inoffensive.... A neon sign on my house proclaiming "*Cannibalism, Bestiality, Incest.* Tickets $5.00. Meals $25. Close relatives half price" would be even more offensive to those who accept the relevant standards of sensibility.' K. Baier, 'The Liberal Approach to Pornography' (1979) 40 U Pittsburgh LR 619, 621–22. But here the experienced communication occurs via the invitation and/or neon sign, which may themselves be offensive. The actual perpetration of the advertised conduct should stand or fall for criminalisation on its own terms. Arguments that others may be offended by reports of the conduct also violate the immediacy requirement, discussed below in § 8.1(c).

Analysis, we should consider the importance of the relevant conduct to those who will be subject to the prohibition, as well as its social value more generally, and the extent and seriousness of the affront caused to others. There will also be pragmatic considerations, of the kind to be discussed in Chapter 11. When evaluating possible insult prohibitions, for example, a significant criminal-policy concern would be the limited effectiveness and high financial costs of such measures. Compelling angry male adolescents (or, for that matter, exasperated drivers generally) in urban traffic jams to refrain from rude gestures is difficult to achieve through criminal sanctions, and very likely futile, while resort to the criminal courts for the purpose would be expensive and time-consuming. It would also be necessary to consider whether more effective restriction might be achieved by other regulatory mechanisms, or even through civil tort remedies.

Beyond those familiar factors, however, there are certain further considerations that are particularly apposite to the assessment of offensive conduct, and which operate as distinctive constraints upon its criminalisation.

a.   Social Tolerance

In the previous chapter, we noted that offensive conduct is characteristically expressive. As such, by contrast with directly harmful behaviour, it tends to have much more to do with presentation of self in public space. Even if offence upsets others, and sometimes can adversely affect their lives, its regulation is likely to be considerably more restrictive of personal self-expression. Styles of self-presentation may, and frequently do, conflict: behaviour that you consider a matter of your personal style (e.g. 'naked rambling'[5]) may be intrusive upon my peaceable enjoyment of shared spaces. But a plural society is not just a present social fact—that people have different lifestyles—which needs to be 'managed'. It is also a normative matter—we *ought* to facilitate varying and sometimes even conflicting lifestyles.[6] Two lifestyles can be valuable even if they contain elements that conflict; indeed, even if they contain elements that are themselves objectionable.[7] If we take the idea of a plural society seriously,

---

[5] The so-called 'Naked Rambler', Stephen Gough, made a series of widely reported journeys around Britain in 2003–04 and 2005–06. His unclothed walks were frequently interrupted by officials: see, e.g., 'Rambler stripped of his freedom again', *The Times*, 10 September 2005.

[6] See, especially, J. Raz, 'Free Expression and Personal Identification' in *Ethics in the Public Domain* (revd. ed., Oxford: Oxford UP, 1995) 162f.

[7] This point is nicely seen in Molière's play, *Le Misanthrope*. The principal character, Alceste, is flagrantly and deliberately rude and tactless to others, because he wishes to reject the prevailing culture of insincerity, and present an 'honest' picture of his views and feelings

therefore, we should be especially concerned about the effects of prohibiting unconventional behaviour on the lives of those regulated. As such, this argument suggests the desirability of sparing use of offence prohibitions.

The case for sparing use is reinforced by the character of offensive behaviour, in that it does not, in itself, affect others' longer-term interests in the manner that harmful behaviour does. Granted, offended persons suffer a wrong, in virtue of the disrespectful or inconsiderate manner with which they are treated. But the absence of direct setbacks to their interests tends to give the wrongdoing a less serious character, and thus leaves more scope for countervailing concerns such as the importance of self-presentation. This argument generates a mediating principle of *social tolerance*: that a significant margin of tolerance should be granted even to conduct that is disrespectful or inconsiderate. So far as offence prohibitions are concerned, it is legitimate to call upon citizens to be reasonably thick-skinned, so that only the more egregious forms of offensive behaviour should be proscribed. The principle of social tolerance should, for example, significantly curtail the criminalisation of insult: as we noted earlier, in a lively, plural, society it does not seem appropriate to criminalise routine insults, such as the use of certain well-known rude words or gestures—even though these certainly involve disrespectful treatment. Only grave forms of insult (for example, demeaning references to minority groups) should be candidates at all for criminalisation.[8] In our formulation of the Offence Principle, we have thus required that there needs to be a *gross* lack of consideration or respect. What matters is not only the extensiveness and intensity of affront caused but also the degree of lack of consideration or respect shown by the conduct. Merely using an insulting name or gesture should not suffice for criminalisation, because the disrespect involved is insufficiently serious.

This argument is supported by a second line of thought. Harms generally have a verifiable character, which tends to make compliance with their prohibitory norms more straightforward than for offence: one need only refrain from attacking someone, burgling his house; snatching her purse, etc. Offensive conduct, however, tends to be constituted by more complex norms of mutual consideration that characteristically allow persons to pursue their own preferences in shared space, while allowing sufficient scope for others to do likewise. Observing these cooperative norms

---

to the world. The play does not convey positive approval of his behaviour—it portrays clearly how wounding is the conduct to others' feelings. None the less, there is considerable sympathy for Alceste, because his conduct attempts to reflect an unconventional way of living that emphasises personal sincerity.

[8] Contrast English criminal law, which has traditionally contained no general criminal prohibition of insult, to § 185 of the German Penal Code, which proscribes insult generally. In England, ss. 4A and 5 of the Public Order Act 1986 now prohibit a range of insulting conduct.

involves interpreting clues about what would interfere with others' pre-ferred activities, and responding to those clues appropriately in the light of what seems a 'reasonable' use of public space. In traditional societies, observing these norms might still be relatively straightforward, in as much as they are widely understood and shared. A pluralistic conception of permissible lifestyles, however, makes such social interaction more complex. If some modes of self-presentation presuppose a greater degree of reticence, and others a lesser degree, it becomes more difficult for people to pick up, interpret, and respond to clues about where the boundaries of acceptable behaviour lie (e.g., about how much noisy self-expression or physical self-exposure is appropriate). Consequently, when people appear to overstep the bounds of reasonable interaction, a substantial degree of leeway should be allowed for such missteps in order to accommodate the potential for genuine misunderstanding.[9] This leeway is especially appro-priate because many of those charged with offensive behaviour are likely to be under-privileged individuals, having reduced opportunity to develop skills of social interaction—in particular, of interaction with others having differing lifestyles and outlooks than their own.

Harm

It will readily be seen, therefore, why—as we argued in the previous chapter—harm should play a significant role even in the context of offensive conduct. It supplies an important further reason for withdrawing social tolerance and criminalising behaviour; namely, when the behaviour in question is conducive to significant adverse social effects. Racial insult, for example, tends to engender an atmosphere of bigotry that may lead to a variety of eventual harms, ranging from unfair job discrimination to actual violence. As we argued in Chapter 4, the mere risk of such harms would not by itself justify proscribing the behaviour *directly* under the Harm Principle, because of concerns about fair imputation: the causal chain leading to the ill consequences is mediated through choices of numerous independent actors. Nevertheless, in situations such as these, the immediate offensiveness of the conduct can properly be combined with the concern about its remotely harmful consequences in order to justify criminalisation. Racial insult is manifestly offensive. Should it nonetheless be tolerated? One reason why not is supplied by the conduct's long-term social side-effects—its potential for exclusionary social consequences. Invoking such effects would not be subject to the objection concerning fair imputation, because the justificatory work in establishing wrongdoing is

---

[9] A similar argument buttresses the requirement for *grossly* inconsiderate treatment of others, given the possibility of good-faith interpretive error: we can be more confident that such behaviour is genuinely a wrong.

done by the immediate offensiveness (in our sense) of the behaviour. The adverse social consequences are being invoked as a supplemental ground in order to help overcome our reluctance, for the sake of permitting varying styles of self-presentation, to criminalise even disrespectful or inconsiderate conduct.[10]

In gauging the conduct's longer-term effects, their frequency, severity, and pervasiveness should be considered. In deciding whether to criminalise intrusive begging, for example, it would be proper to take into account the extent of its adverse impact on the use of public space. As we shall emphasise below, shared access to public space is particularly important in the context of the Offence Principle. Under the Harm Principle, conduct that does substantial harm to its victims may be prohibited even if the conduct occurs relatively infrequently and has few social side-effects, because the protection of the individual's vital interests is so important. Within the Offence Principle, by contrast, the direct impact on individuals who are affronted plays a smaller role, because there is no immediate intrusion into the victims' longer-term interests. Concerns about the pervasiveness and scale of its side-effects therefore have a more significant role to play.

Of course, the Harm Principle allows for indirect effects too. If we may thus consider eventual harmful consequences, what is gained through the separate adoption of an Offence Principle? Why not base penalising the behaviour directly on the conduct's (indirectly) injurious effects, as would advocates of the 'Broken Windows' thesis?[11] The answer is that the conduct's being immediately offensive, in our suggested sense, remains essential for its criminalisation. Conduct that does not qualify as grossly inconsiderate or disrespectful, such as peaceable begging, should not be criminalised, even if it were to have adverse indirect effects on others' enjoyment of public space.

b. A Constraint of 'Ready Avoidability'

One mediating principle suggested by Joel Feinberg, although he does not spell out its rationale, is a notion of 'avoidability': that it speaks against criminalising offensive conduct that others could readily avoid witnessing or being confronted by it. As we noted earlier,[12] the Offence Principle is distinct in this respect from the Harm Principle, where ordinarily no

[10] Note that the contrast implicitly drawn here with mere or ordinary insult rests on an assumption that, in modern societies, a person's interest in maintaining his standing vis-à-vis strangers in a public setting does not have the degree of importance that it did in traditional societies, emphasising personal honour.
[11] Discussed earlier, § 7.2(b) (Remote Harms).
[12] Above, § 7.3(b).

avoidance principle applies. It is no reason for tolerating assaults on 14th Street that those wishing not to be assaulted may safely use 15th Street instead.

On Feinberg's suggestion, showing pornographic images would not be sufficiently offensive to justify prohibition if the images were available only on DVDs or by internet subscription, which those who object need not view. Notice, however, that this example is a polar case of avoidability, since it characteristically involves conduct done in private that occurs unwitnessed from the public domain, and which one must volunteer to witness. As such, it is hard to see how, under our analysis, it is offensive behaviour at all. The reason for not criminalising 'offensive' conduct that is wholly segregated from public view is not that it is avoidable, but that, since offence is a communicative wrong, there is no offensive wrong—no wrong to another.

Conversely, were someone to show pornography on a large screen in the park or marketplace, the case is straightforward and its avoidability has no practical role to play; the pornography is, in effect, unavoidable. It is between these extremes, where conduct is at least partially in the public domain, that avoidability has a place as a mediating principle.

An illustration of this role is provided by the well-established practice of nude bathing in certain continental European countries. In Germany, for instance, the public display of genitalia is legally permissible, provided it occurs in designated public bathing areas. Here, the segregation from view may be only partial: the nude bathing area may be simply a portion of the riverbank, which is visible to others from the opposite side of the river. What appears to be at work here is a notion of reciprocity: certain areas are segregated, albeit partially, from general public view. This gives those wishing to bathe nude more scope to engage in that conduct, while providing clues to others that if they do not wish to witness it, they might direct their attention elsewhere. Such reciprocal arrangements give greater scope to varying, otherwise potentially colliding, lifestyles.[13] Thus we propose, for offensive wrongs in public spaces, an explicit, additional, constraint of 'ready avoidability': that the conduct is a candidate for prohibition within the Offence Principle only if others cannot *readily* (that is, without undue restriction of their own range of options) avoid being confronted by the behaviour. Doing so would, in effect, introduce a threshold standard of avoidability as a *limiting* rather than strictly mediating principle. Even then, however, once that threshold is crossed, and potentially offensive conduct cannot readily be avoided (so that the limitation is not engaged), the degree to which it is avoidable, and the

---

[13] In the case of nude bathing areas, such arrangements might be established by local regulation, but that need not be a prerequisite: an established common practice should suffice.

extent to which its avoidance intrudes upon the liberties of others, remain operative as secondary weighting factors when assessing the case for prohibition.

c. The Requirement for Immediacy

A further principle restricting criminalisation concerns immediacy, or proximity: the prohibited conduct should be offensive in itself, and not merely make it possible or likely that the actor (or someone else) engage in *further* behaviour that is offensive. The gathering by teenagers on a street corner is, by itself, not a candidate for proscription under the Offence Principle; no matter that their behaviour may later deteriorate.

What is the rationale for this immediacy principle? The concern about immediacy derives, in the first instance, from the idea that there must be wrongdoing involved in the offence; there is nothing wrong with conduct, such as gathering on a street or entering a park, that *might* induce an intervening choice (by the actor or someone else) to engage in subsequent conduct that is offensive.

Still, might there be grounds for overcoming the intervening-choice objection, as there are for the Harm Principle,[14] when the initial actor's conduct implicitly endorses the subsequent offensive choices? It is not so easy, in the context of offensive conduct, to think of instances where this might be the case—in part because of significant structural differences between the Harm and Offence Principles. In the Harm Principle, the wrongdoing is typically focused on the ill consequences or risks of the conduct, since it is generally prima facie wrong to cause harm to others. Thus, where the fair-imputation issue can be overcome, it may be permissible to criminalise conduct that creates a risk of remote harms without itself being harmful. In the Offence Principle, however, the wrongdoing is constituted by the disrespectful, or inconsiderate, expressive character of the conduct itself. As such, it is less straightforward to overcome imputation concerns and justify the criminalisation of conduct that—even though it may raise the likelihood that others, or the actor himself, will commit further acts that are offensive—in itself lacks any characteristic of wrongfulness.[15]

Beyond these difficulties concerning the structure of the Offence Principle, there is an important additional consideration: the effect of a prohibition on liberty and, particularly, on freedom of movement. An immediacy

---

[14] Above, chs 4–5.
[15] Many cases of aggregative offence, discussed in Chapter 7 at n. 20, will satisfy the requirement of immediacy, since they typically involve conduct that is immediately and wrongfully offensive, albeit sufficiently so for criminalisation only when part of a similar pattern of behaviour by others.

requirement is of particular importance for the criminalisation of offence because of the implications for access to public space. If the requirement is not insisted upon, so that conduct may be proscribed merely because it may lead to subsequent offensive choices, this will tend to permit the exclusion of people from public space because of concerns about what they may subsequently do when there. Examples might include barring beggars altogether from public spaces, on the grounds that they may engage in intrusive begging, and prohibiting youths from congregating in certain public spaces, because they may then behave offensively toward passers-by. Prohibitions of this kind, were they to become extensive, would tend to create a two-class scheme of access to public facilities: unrestricted access to a preferred class of conventional citizens; and restricted access for individuals deemed to have the potential for engaging in offensive conduct if permitted entry. This contravenes a fundamental principle of modern free society: namely, that its public spaces should be available for unrestricted access by all.

Unfortunately, the possibility of criminalisation on the basis of 'remote' offence is, these days, very real. As we shall see when discussing two-step prohibitions, English courts now have extensive powers to make personal orders to regulate the future behaviour of those who commit 'anti-social' acts.[16] Such orders can, and frequently do, operate as a form of pre-emption,[17] by prohibiting D from entering a locality, such as an estate or shopping precinct, in case D might then behave in an unruly fashion. In such cases, what is prohibited under the order is, in itself, entirely innocent behaviour, and not wrongful at all.

Of course, all criminal prohibitions restrict liberty. Even though legislators should be cautious before creating new crimes, it is, as we have seen, sometimes entirely justified to prohibit D from exposing himself in public or otherwise behaving in a grossly inconsiderate manner. But it goes a great deal further to take away freedoms because the actor *might* behave offensively. Anti-social behaviour orders of this type violate the principle of immediacy.

---

[16] Anti-Social Behaviour Act 2003; below, Chapter 12.

[17] In the criminological literature, they are a type of situational crime prevention. For general discussion, see A. von Hirsch, D. Garland and A. Wakefield (eds), *Ethical and Social Perspectives on Situational Crime Prevention* (Oxford: Hart Publishing, 2000), especially ch. 5.

d. The Importance of the Public Sphere

Could it be, *pace* Feinberg, that we have not gone far enough?[18] Tatjana Hörnle has criticised our analysis of offence for being overbroad, because the notion of disrespectful or inconsiderate behaviour could embrace much *private* incivility: included would be such everyday wrongs as keeping someone waiting or making tactless remarks at a private wedding reception about the groom's (or bride's) previous romances.[19] Because of the supposed inability of our approach to exclude private incivilities, Hörnle rejects it.[20]

Perhaps in the past we encouraged this criticism,[21] by not emphasising the special importance of affront in the public sphere. Our account took for granted that legal offence is concerned primarily (though not exclusively) with public settings, and focused on certain additional requirements of wrongfulness and indirect harm. But the importance of the public sphere needs to be spelled out more fully.

First, however, a comment on the example. We take it as a virtue of our account that the tactless wedding speech can qualify as offensive conduct. Depending on the extremity of the content,[22] it is. Of course, this is not to say that such speech should be prohibited by law—*even when it occurs in public space*. But the reasons for non-prohibition lie in a variety of mediating factors rather than a lack of wrongfulness: especially, the lack of sufficiently widespread and serious affront; the importance of free speech and social toleration; and the impracticality of prohibiting offensive speeches without over-inclusion.

At the same time, it also militates against criminalisation that the behaviour occurs in private or quasi-private space. The case for criminalisation is, we think, generally stronger when offensive conduct takes place in the public sphere, such that it has an adverse effect on the attractiveness and availability of public environments for general use. Where offence occurs in public, an important reason for the state's intervention is to preserve the quality of life in such settings. It is in the public interest to

---

[18] '[It does not seem] helpful', asserts Hörnle, 'to have a very wide standard such as . . . lack of respect as a "wide entrance" for debates about criminalisation and then to require a set of [mediating] principles "to keep the ghost one has called in the bottle". Why start with [such] an extensive standard in favour of criminalisation if the majority of cases in the end have to be sorted by resorting to mediating principles?' T. Hörnle, 'Legal Regulation of Offence' in *Incivilities* 134, 145.

[19] See Hörnle, *ibid.*, 144f.

[20] Her own alternative proposal is discussed below, in § 8.2.

[21] Hörnle's critique is directed particularly to our essay, 'Rethinking the Offense Principle' (2002) 8 Legal Theory 269.

[22] One of us recalls hearing about an undergraduate wedding dinner at which, in his speech, the best man vouched personally for the sexual prowess of the bride *and* of the groom.

help maintain a pleasant environment on streets, parks, and in public transport facilities, so that citizens can make comfortable use of these facilities. Offensive conduct detracts from such an environment. In such settings, moreover, informal social control has reduced effectiveness, *because the interaction occurs among strangers.* If the noisy or obstreperous passenger on the bus is willing to ignore the irritated stares of his neighbours, there is not much further remedy they can provide on their own.[23]

In private settings, however, the warrant for state intervention diminishes. The interaction is among persons who choose to associate with one another. Those involved are therefore in a better position to preserve the civility of such interactions themselves; the rude or tactless guest can be excluded from that social circle in future. Hence the concern to safeguard the quality of people's lives in social interaction environments has reduced urgency. Even where conduct is disrespectful or inconsiderate, criminalisation would ordinarily not be appropriate.

Concerns about personal privacy add to the case against state intervention. Unwelcome as affronting behaviour among social acquaintances can be, those concerned should have the widest scope to decide whom they wish to associate with, and how they should deal with breaches of decorum. In private contexts, the participants are and should be able to set their own terms of interaction. Having the state intervene with its penal powers would introduce an undue element of intrusion and coercion into what should be voluntary social dealings. Bad as the tactless wedding guest's behaviour may be, it would be much more worrisome were such social occasions policed by state authorities for inappropriate behaviour.

A comparable step, of limiting the scope of the Harm Principle in private settings, is less persuasive. Harm in private settings—for example, a wedding guest's assaulting the groom or making off with the silver—directly sets back important interests of those affected. Such behaviour is also less easily addressed informally: leaving dealing with such occurrences to the private initiatives of those present could leave victims helpless, or else prompt retaliatory responses on the part of the offender. However, the public nature of the conduct is important but not always decisive even in the context of offence. Just as some publicly offensive behaviour, like mere insult, should not be criminalised, sufficiently serious affronting behaviour of a non-public character, such as a guest's exposing himself at a private dinner party, remains within the potential scope of the Offence Principle. The public/ private distinction thus operates here as a mediating consideration, rather

---

[23] Hörnle also notes the difficulty of invoking informal social remedies in such public environments: above n. 18, 144f.

than as a limiting constraint. It greatly strengthens the case for prohibition when offensive conduct occurs in a public setting.

8.2   PROTECTING A CONSTITUTIONALLY-DERIVED INTEREST?

Another interesting suggestion by Hörnle is that the criminalisation of offensive behaviour should be explained via a different line of argument, namely by invoking the (German) constitution's catalogue of rights.[24] Offensive behaviour may properly be criminalised, she argues, when it intrudes upon interests that have constitutional significance. Emphasis is given, for example, to the constitutional guarantees of *Menschenwürde* (human dignity) and *allgemeine Persönlichkeitsrecht* (protection of personality). No separate Offence Principle, of the kind we advocate, is needed.

Clearly, a practical limitation of her approach derives from its dependence upon positive legal norms. Important and impressive as the German constitution's catalogue of rights are, they remain enactments: at a higher level of authority than ordinary legislation, true, but still norms adopted by a particular legal order. Her analysis of offence does not hold for liberal legal orders having less ambitious constitutional documents than Germany's. Thus some countries' constitutional laws, such as those of the USA, contain a Bill of Rights enumerating particular entitlements such as free speech and limitations on search and seizure, but lack general substantive principles guaranteeing liberty or dignity that are comparable to Germany's *Menschenwürde* and *Persönlichkeitsrecht* guarantees. Still other constitutional orders, such as Sweden's, have various specific protections which are mostly defeasible by legislative enactment. One European state, the United Kingdom, lacks a modern Bill of Rights, although it has effectively incorporated the European Convention on Human Rights by statute.[25] Yet a theory of offence should be capable also of explaining (and restricting) the scope of offence prohibitions in those jurisdictions.

Furthermore, even in the German context, there may be objections to deriving a normative theory of offence from an appeal to constitutional standards. Constitutional civil-liberties guarantees have as their primary function the protection of individuals from state intrusions. While there may sometimes be secondary obligations falling on the state, to protect citizens from intrusions by other individuals, using such guarantees as the standard basis of criminalising conduct inverts their primary function. It increases the individual's exposure to coercive state intervention. In certain

---

[24]   T. Hörnle, *Grob Anstössiges Verhalten: Strafrechtlicher Schutz von Moral, Gehfühlen und Tabus* (Frankfurt a.M.: Klostermann, 2005) ch. 6.
[25]   Human Rights Act 1998.

situations this would manifestly be problematic: one noted example is that of the German Supreme Administrative Court's decision to outlaw 'peep-shows',[26] a paternalistic prohibition that was purportedly justified on grounds of protecting the actors' human dignity. The difficulty with such an approach is that it allows the invocation of a constitutional right to short-circuit ordinary principles of criminalisation—in that case, principles restricting paternalistic interventions.[27] It is not clear that human-dignity norms, notwithstanding their constitutional status, should be applied to restrict the self-determination of the persons involved. Likewise with offence prohibitions. Their justification is a complex matter, requiring explanation why behaviour can be wrongful, albeit not harmful; and involving the negotiation of various prima facie constraints on the censuring response of the criminal sanction. One thus needs nuanced criminalisation norms, rather than appeal to their potential constitutional status, to help account for offence prohibitions.[28]

Reference to constitutionally protected rights seems to generate unproblematic outcomes at the high end of the spectrum of offensive behaviour. Consider *Volksverhetzung*, or racial abuse. Such conduct, Hörnle argues persuasively, calls into question the status of the persons targeted as citizens deserving of equal respect (*gleichberechtige Bürger*). The constitutional, human-dignity guarantee thus provides reason for proscribing such conduct[29]—at least, for countries such as Germany that have such forms of guarantee.

For less grievous forms of offence, such as common insult (prohibited by § 185 of the German Criminal Code), Hörnle appeals to another constitutionally identified right: the *allgemeine Persönlichkeitsrecht*, which protects the personal identity and self-definition of individuals. Personal insult infringes such an entitlement, she argues: to be denounced to one's face as a fool, poltroon, or fraud denies the mutual recognition of self that is the basis for tolerable social interaction.[30] She is cautious, however, about over-extending this analysis and so is critical of existing German doctrine that extends the reach of the insult prohibition in § 185 to casual rude words or gestures among strangers in public places. The driver who

---

[26] BVerwGE 64, 274. For discussion, see N. Hörster, 'Zur Bedeutung des Prinzips der Menschenwuerde' *Juristische Schulung 1983*, §§ 93–96.

[27] Below, Part IV.

[28] Hörnle herself is strongly critical of the peep-show decision, and makes it clear that she opposes an uncritical grounding of criminal prohibitions (or other intrusions on liberty) on constitutional human-dignity guarantees (above n. 24, at § 119). Instead, she offers a sophisticated examination of various offence prohibitions in the German Criminal Code, and analyses why and to what extent these are supportable by values derived from constitutional norms. Our doubt, however, is whether those value-based arguments should be dependent on their reflecting constitutional norms.

[29] *ibid.*, § 120f.

[30] *ibid.*, § 135f.

responds to an adjacent driver's clumsy or aggressive driving style by making an obscene gesture may show his exasperation in an inappropriate way; but his conduct, she concludes, does not amount to a denial of mutual recognition.[31]

Yet this is a matter of degree. There is surely an element of denial of respect in such insults. And, of course, the spectrum is continuous. Consider the following case. A young couple enter a tavern and sit near D, an individual who apparently has had several drinks and is trying to engage others in conversation. He gives an inappropriate compliment to the young woman, and is politely reprimanded by her partner. D responds angrily, subjecting the partner to an abusive tirade of several minutes; but leaves when ordered to do so by the owner of the establishment. Some time later, the victim initiates a prosecution under § 185. Should this kind of middle-range offensive behaviour be criminalised?

In our view, all these cases, including the last, involve offensive behaviour. But, notwithstanding the constitutional interest allegedly in play, the wrong in the driver's rude-gesture case is too minor—the lack of respect is insufficiently serious. In the tavern case, on the other hand, such kinds of sustained abuse clearly do involve gross disrespect to the person affected. Whether they should be criminalised, however, depends on the scope of the mediating principle of social tolerance.[32] The social-tolerance principle calls for a modicum of 'thick-skinnedness' in public interactions, in order to give a margin of allowance to varying lifestyles in a plural society. A somewhat enhanced margin of tolerance might especially be warranted in this kind of setting, i.e. in a drinking establishment, where a certain rough-and-tumble style of interaction would not be unexpected. Our theory does not, of course, compel decriminalisation of the conduct. Much depends on how permissive ought to be the countervailing norm of tolerance that facilitates differing styles of self-presentation.

By contrast, a constitutional approach such as Hörnle advocates tends to pre-empt a differentiated assessment of the normative merits. If the conduct significantly denigrates the person, on her analysis, then its criminal prohibition becomes appropriate. But this approach over-emphasises the right being protected, placing the prohibition more beyond question than is desirable. When the constitutional status of norms is taken to supply reason for the prohibition, that constricts the moral space within which to account for mediating factors that should constrain the criminalisation decision.

Recall that offensive behaviour does not, in itself, affect others' longer-term interests and resources in the manner as does harmful behaviour.

---

[31] *ibid.*, § 140f.
[32] Above, § 8.1(a).

Granted, the offended person is wronged, in virtue of the disrespectful or inconsiderate manner with which she is treated; and the behaviour, if permitted to become pervasive, could adversely affect the quality of public environments. It is these features of the conduct which, on our analysis, provide prima facie grounds for criminalisation. But the absence of setbacks to the affected persons' interests tends to give such wrongdoing a less serious character—and so leaves greater scope for countervailing concerns, such as those relating to self-presentation.[33] Our basic reservation about Hörnle's analysis is that, by tying offence prohibitions to central constitutional values concerning individual dignity and equal resepct, she unduly narrows the scope of mediating principles that can mitigate the case for prohibition. If the fact that the particular wrong has constitutional significance is to make a difference in her analysis, it restricts the potential for such countervailing concerns to prevail.

8.3 CONCLUDING THOUGHTS

In Part III, we have suggested that the concept of offensive behaviour can better be elucidated through an Offence Principle that is distinct from the Harm Principle. That Offence Principle, moreover, should not concern itself merely with the affront that a person's conduct causes to others' sensibilities; it should also provide an account of when, and why, causing that affront constitutes a wrong. We have suggested a general standard of when the offence becomes a wrong, one that relates to the conduct's showing a manifest lack of respect or consideration for others; and we have suggested, through a number of illustrative cases, when and why that may be the case. Additionally, we have sketched a number of mediating principles that would restrain criminalisation even of conduct qualifying as offensive under our definition. These principles include an expectation of social tolerance for offensiveness, grounded in respect for varying styles of self-presentation; a principle of 'ready avoidability', restricting criminalisation of conduct that others easily can avoid; and an 'immediacy' requirement, mandating that the conduct be offensive (on our definition) in itself, and not merely likely to lead to offensive behaviour in the future. The principle of social tolerance, in particular, shows why mere offence should not in itself qualify ordinarily for proscription, and why the case for criminalisation needs to be buttressed by showing an eventual adverse impact on the interests of others. More generally, our proposed wrongfulness requirement for offence, and our suggested mediating principles, are aimed at keeping criminal offence prohibitions suitably constrained in scope.

---

[33] Above, § 7.3(b).

These two bases for criminalisation, harm and offence, overlap in important ways. Both are concerned with the protection of other persons and their lives; and both seek to ground the wrongfulness of the conduct in normative claims those persons have not to be treated badly. Thus, ultimately, both Principles broadly depend upon the imperative to treat individuals with respect for their dignity and humanity. The Harm Principle and the Offence Principle are united in being thereby distinct from legal moralism. Nevertheless, we think the analysis can be undertaken in a more differentiated fashion if a distinction is observed between conduct that sets back persons' interests and resources, where the Harm Principle comes into play, and offensive conduct that does not itself diminish the person's resources but nevertheless treats them, in certain ways, without the consideration and respect that should be due to them as fellow citizens.

Part IV

Paternalism

9

Reflections on Paternalistic Prohibitions

L ET US RECAP for a moment. In Chapter 2, we argued that criminal prohibitions should apply only to morally wrongful actions. According to the Necessity Thesis, the wrong is an indispensible requirement of justified criminalisation; and where there are harm-based constraints on state intervention to regulate wrongs, they are complementary in nature.

The Necessity Thesis holds that criminalisation of φing can be justified only when φing is morally wrongful. At the same time, we argued that wrongfulness is *insufficient*. The Non-qualifying Thesis claims that wrongfulness by itself does not establish even a pro tanto case for criminalisation. Only certain kinds of wrongful conduct qualify. The Non-qualifying thesis thus stands opposed to Patrick Devlin's famous assertion that 'it is not possible to set theoretical limits to the power of the State to legislate against immorality ... or to define inflexibly areas of morality into which the law is in no circumstances allowed to enter.'[1]

For those of us who reject Devlin's conclusion, the challenge is to identify what else is needed, to justify the additional criteria that state intervention requires. Most responses to that challenge are consequential, holding that conduct is eligible for criminalisation only when it involves further effects.[2] Depending on the version, qualifying effects may be restricted to those adversely affecting people and their lives, or might be extended to other kinds of victims, such as other sentient creatures. This should be no surprise, since (secular) authority does not exist, and is not granted, for its own sake—it exists for instrumental reasons, as a means to promote the quality of people's lives, or perhaps the lives of other creatures, etc.[3] According to the Harm Principle, for example, what counts

---

[1] P. Devlin, *The Enforcement of Morals* (Oxford: Oxford UP, 1965) 12–13.

[2] Hence, for Mill, 'the only purpose for which power can rightfully be exercised over any member of a civilised community against his will is to prevent harm to others.' *On Liberty* ch. 1, para. 9: above, § 2.2.

[3] Thus is it possible for an otherwise valid reason to be outside the scope of authority of an actor such as the state. Cf. below, n. 12.

in the justification of state intervention is the potential impact of conduct upon other human lives. Conduct becomes eligible for prohibition when it adversely affects the interests that serve another person's well-being, the opportunities that she has (or may have) to pursue and enjoy a good life in a politically organised society.[4]

How much constraint does the Harm Principle add? Certainly, as we saw in Part II, the Principle is nowhere near as restrictive as it might seem. Conduct may prima facie qualify for proscription without actually harming people, either directly or necessarily. Certain more remote connections will do.[5] Even indirectly, though, there must be an element of harm—some negative effect on people and their lives.

Yet this, too, seems a tenuous constraint, since in at least one sense the effect need not be negative. Seemingly, it is permissible within most versions of the Harm Principle for the state to enact coercive laws for the sake of *improving* people's lives.[6] Securing benefits finds its best known expression in the criminal law through the law of omissions, which sometimes imposes positive duties to act for the sake of others, e.g. by rescuing someone who has fallen into danger,[7] or by sending one's child to school.[8] Such cases are controversial because of their potential onerousness,[9] but not because of their *ineligibility* under the Harm Principle. If my child does not attend school, he will be worse off (in the long run). He will lack an adequate preparation for adult life in a developed economy, being denied many of the employment and other opportunities to advance his welfare that others will typically have.

So there is nothing in the Harm Principle, or in the requirement of wrongfulness, that draws a sharp line between the promotion of value and the prevention of disvalue. Sometimes, even frequently, there may be associated differences in the kinds of interests affected by acts and omissions,[10] but those differences enter the criminalisation analysis later, affecting the strength of the case for regulation rather than its eligibility. Sometimes, one may be morally obliged to act for the benefit of another,

---

[4] See, e.g., J. Raz, 'Autonomy, Toleration, and the Harm Principle' in R. Gavison (ed.), *Issues in Contemporary Legal Philosophy* (Oxford: Oxford UP, 1987) 313.

[5] Above, § 3.2.

[6] This is especially common in the civil law. Standard examples include the enforcement of regimes of property rights and contract, for the sake of facilitating forms of welfare that would otherwise be unattainable: above, § 3.1(a).

[7] By contrast with English law, many Continental jurisdictions require bystanders to an accident to effect rescue: see, e.g., StGB § 323c. For discussion of the rationale underpinning the German rule, see A. von Hirsch, 'Criminalising Failure to Rescue: A Matter of "Solidarity" or Altruism?' in M. Reiff, M. Kramer and R. Cruft (eds), *Crime, Punishment and Responsibility* (Oxford: Oxford UP, 2011).

[8] cf. Education Act 1996 (UK), s. 444 (obligation imposed on the parent).

[9] See A.P. Simester, 'Why Omissions are Special' (1995) 1 Legal Theory 311.

[10] cf. A.M. Honoré, 'Are Omissions Less Culpable' in P. Cane and J. Stapleton (eds), *Essays for Patrick Atiyah* (Oxford: Oxford UP, 1991) 31.

sometimes to refrain from acting to another's detriment. Neither the Necessity Thesis nor the Harm Principle precludes this.

What, then, is the point of the Harm Principle? In what way does it flesh out the Non-qualifying Thesis? What constraint does it add? In fact, it supplies two constraints. The conduct must (i) adversely affect one or more people's lives; and they must be (ii) *other* people, not the actor himself. We have considered the former constraint in Parts II and III. It is the latter constraint that rules out paternalism, as Mill intended it to. But was Mill right? Is this second constraint always justified?

9.1 THREE ABSOLUTIST OBJECTIONS TO PATERNALISTIC INTERVENTION (CIVIL AND CRIMINAL)

The second constraint is certainly important. Without it, there would be a wide scope for paternalistic intervention. Yet it is not obvious that Mill's absolute rejection of paternalism is correct.

To see this more clearly, we need first to take a backward step, and revisit a point made in § 3.1(a). Mill's endorsement of the Harm Principle as the sole basis for state intervention is not specific to the criminal law: it applies to any exercise by the state of coercive power over its citizens. As Mill conceived it, the Harm Principle applies both to civil and criminal law, to contract or tort as much as crime. Similarly, many of the standard objections to paternalism would rule it out for all forms of state intervention. In our view, that conclusion is too strong. There are, as we shall see, good reasons for objecting to certain forms of paternalism, especially in the criminal law. But there are different ways of intervening, some more invasive than others, and different kinds of reasons for doing so. And there is no knock-down general objection that rules out legal paternalism altogether. Some interventions are legitimate, others not.

The lack of straightforward moral arguments against legal paternalism in general should be unsurprising. Like any intervener, the state should act morally, i.e. for good reasons. Assuming one is not a thoroughgoing moral sceptic (and criminal lawyers cannot be), that something is morally good supplies a prima facie reason to promote its realisation. Conversely, that something is bad supplies a prima facie reason to avoid its occurrence.[11] This isn't controversial; or, at any rate, it shouldn't be, since it is inherent in the very idea of morality. *Any* agent ought to do good and avoid bad,

---

11 The claim here is only that there is *some* reason, not that it is sufficient or even that the actor has standing to act upon it (in which case it is, as Raz would say, excluded). No doubt one should not intervene when one sees a friend's daughter about to embark on a relationship that will be very bad for her. But that doesn't mean there is no reason in play here *at all*.

and the state is an agent too.[12] To be sure, it is a fallible agent, as are we all. And sometimes—frequently—it should not intervene. But this does not mean that it should never act at all.

So it is quite plausible that prima facie reasons can exist to avert conduct that harms the actor herself. As we shall see in § 9.1(c), it does not follow that the state is entitled to do so by passing coercive laws, let alone criminal ones. But, leaving the legal system to one side for a moment, one can readily imagine individual situations where, all things considered, paternalistic intervention is morally desirable. Someone who sees another pedestrian about to step off the kerb in front of an oncoming car should physically restrain that person.[13] Suppose that D proposes to kill or maim himself without having sufficient reason to justify so doing.[14] He ought not to do it.[15] It follows that, in appropriate circumstances, anyone in a position to help D to avoid that event can have a prima facie reason to act.[16] Indeed, it is this possibility that creates the moral space for justifying *any* form of paternalistic intervention, including the limited varieties that we endorse below.

Moreover, in practice, intervention even by the state for our own good is pervasive. All sorts of health and safety rules exist to save us from harm, whether we want them or not. We cannot buy cheaper cars by forgoing airbags. In the United Kingdom, most charity stores no longer accept donations of second-hand electrical equipment. Children's playgrounds must be closed if the local council cannot afford the latest standards of equipment. Regulations abound concerning the wearing of seat belts, helmets, and the like. Perhaps some of these restrictions are over-zealous. But few people reject them all *in principle*. Of course, justifying interventions of this nature involves a complex evaluation, one that takes account of such matters as the seriousness of the harm and the scale of the

---

[12] This claim is consistent with state-neutrality theories that see a range of reasons, especially controversial ones, as being excluded in the hands of the state. The arguments for state neutrality (which are themselves not straightforward) are moral arguments. They do not, or at least should not, exempt the state from the constraints of morality. In any event, they cut across and do not rule out all kinds of paternalism. See also above, § 2.3(a).

[13] 'There is nothing wrong with coercion used to stop one from stepping into the road and under a car.' J. Raz, *The Morality of Freedom* (Oxford: Oxford UP, 1986) 378. More: it would be wrong not to.

[14] D is not, for instance, a trapped mountain climber, needing to amputate his hand to escape: A. Ralston, *Between a Rock and a Hard Place* (London: Simon & Schuster, 2004). A more controversial example is Body Integrity Identity Disorder.

[15] Arguably, D may have a duty not to do it, in so far as we owe duties to ourselves: on this familiar and controversial possibility see, e.g., J. Raz, 'Liberating Duties' in *Ethics in the Public Domain* (Oxford: Oxford UP, 1994) § 5; and of course I. Kant, *Grundlegung zur Metaphysik der Sitten* (1785). Our argument is open on this point.

[16] We emphasise prima facie. The act must also be appropriate, all things considered—and we consider the considerable restrictions on justifying various forms of intervention across the rest of this chapter. For a note on the generality of reasons, see above, § 2.3(a).

sanctions involved. But that's the point. The need to allow for conflicting considerations means that it is not ruled out *tout court*.

a. Choosing One's Own Life

What arguments might be given, then, for restricting interventions to cases where the agent harms others? Doing good for anyone's life seems an admirable goal. But one worry about it is whether a person's life *can* go better for being successful in the pursuit of values and goals that she does not choose herself. Ronald Dworkin raises this concern when he suggests that it is a condition of something's being valuable for D that D himself desires it: 'The misanthrope's life is not made better by the friendship he thinks is pointless.'[17] Kant too observes that 'I cannot do good to anyone according to *my* conception of happiness (except to young children and the insane), but only according to that of the one I intend to benefit.'[18] The worry, in other words, is that success in pursuing a goal can contribute to the quality of a person's life only if that person endorses the goal.

This type of concern is important. It is hard to imagine fulfilment being achieved in a person's life through successful pursuit of goals that he himself *rejects*. A life lived for reasons that D finds alien, and which are external to him, seems a recipe for a failed life.[19]

Yet its importance should not be overstated. The alternatives 'self-chosen' and 'rejected', while mutually exclusive, do not exhaust the variety of possible relationships that individuals have with their values. It does not follow from the extreme case of consistently rejected values that one's goals and values must always be self-chosen. One may come to embrace values that one has not consciously chosen. Certainly, a person can, over time, come to accept choices that initially were imposed upon him. More pervasively, the unchosen acquisition of values and goals is an integral feature of any upbringing within family and cultural environments. Most of our character is moulded before we have a chance to choose it. In practice, we don't often choose—or even much think about—our values, except at the margins. The important thing is that, chosen or no, the values *are* ours—that we are reconciled to them, identify with them, and do not reject them—rather than *how* they came to be ours. In this sense, the test is

---

[17] R. Dworkin, *Foundations of Liberal Equality* (*Tanner Lectures on Human Values*, vol. 11, Salt Lake City, UT: University of Utah Press, 1990) 77. See too Feinberg's discussion of moral harm in *Harm to Others*, 65ff.

[18] *Doctrine of Virtue*, vi 453.

[19] In our own experience, we sometimes encounter students who are pursuing a career in law only because their parents want them to, and who have themselves no liking for the subject matter. The outcome is rarely positive.

a negative one, requiring merely that the values or goals be not rejected by D. The suggestion that goals and values must be self-chosen therefore seems too strong.

b.   Choosing Virtues?

A related and more plausible worry, however, is whether agents *can* be made to exhibit virtues. An action is virtuous, we take it, when one is motivated to perform it by the fact that it serves a particular value; that is, a value corresponding to the virtue being exhibited. One exhibits the virtue of fidelity, for example, when one keeps a promise *because one made the promise*. One fails to exhibit fidelity when one keeps the promise only because it is profitable or economically efficient to do so. Obviously and dramatically, when one keeps a promise because of coercive threats, fidelity is missing. One's action is prudent rather than faithful. To the extent that the state creates instrumental reasons for action, therefore, it risks undermining the possibility of virtuous conduct.

This is a particular worry for *moral paternalism*, according to which it can be in a person's interests to be a morally better person. On this view, being a morally better person is good for one: it improves one's well-being, makes one's life go better. That is to say, one's life is not just more valuable: it flourishes better. Moral paternalists hold that the moral goodness of our values and of the lives we lead can contribute to our well-being; and when it does, the state has reason to intervene and improve people's moral characters because doing so is in that person's interests.

Moral paternalism is a subcategory of paternalism. Of course, one might question whether being virtuous necessarily makes one's life go better. (There seems to be no conceptual reason why one cannot derive fulfilment from a vice—why one cannot have a successful life that rests in part on an imperfect moral character or on pursuit of a morally inappropriate goal. If so, the potential exists for living a fulfilling life by unvirtuous means.) None the less, it seems possible that one may benefit from a virtue, and that moral improvements may benefit one's quality of life. Perhaps, for example, one may tend to have better friendships,[20] and typically more opportunities, when one is a better person. And, to the extent that virtues are correlated, exhibiting a virtue may have beneficial effects on one's other values and interests. This is largely an empirical matter (and of course the state normally must deal in empirically typical cases), but even Feinberg accepts that most forms of moral excellence tend to promote one's interests

---

[20] This may be especially likely where some virtue is linked to mutually beneficial experiences, e.g. in friendship. For useful discussion, see G. Dworkin, 'Moral Paternalism' (2005) 24 Law and Philosophy 305.

and well-being.[21] So a paternalist might conceivably embrace selective moral paternalism, at least in cases where promoting a virtue happens to make the agent better off.

Even if we grant that possibility, however, the more fundamental worry remains that virtues cannot be coerced, that any attempt to induce people into virtuous action is bound to fail.

There is force in this objection, but it too should not be overstated. Its scope is confined by two considerations. The first draws on a distinction between action and character. We have noted that actions exhibit a virtue when their performances are motivated by the corresponding value. As such, it does indeed seem unlikely that the state can create (say, prudential) reasons to *act for the sake of a value* without those reasons being ulterior to the value itself. That said, we have seen already that there is no reason why one's *values* must always be self-chosen. If so, then it is logically possible for the state to play a role in forming individual character, as those with experience of educational systems can testify. Once the character is formed, virtuous action becomes possible. So moral paternalism remains feasible, at least in principle.

A second consideration relies on the distinction between virtuous and valuable action. Virtue is exhibited through acting for the sake of value, but the obverse does not apply: value does not always depend on virtue.[22] At least some actions can be valuable even though performed for unvirtuous reasons. Suppose that D is a particularly callous doctor. One day, when off-duty, she encounters P, who has just been injured in an accident and is in need of treatment to save his life. Ordinarily, D would not intervene but would walk by and allow P to die (as the common law permits her to do). However, on this occasion she recognises that P is the enemy of T, whom D hates. So she saves P's life, acting solely in order to frustrate and annoy T. D's act is not virtuous; but it is beneficial. And it would be so even if done solely because the law had imposed a duty to intervene. A reason to save P exists even if D does not acknowledge it. In turn, the value embedded in that reason is served just by saving P, whatever the motive. Thus one may perform good actions, and live a good life, without exhibiting the corresponding virtues. To the extent that reasons can derive from the effects of an action, the objection that virtues cannot be coerced does not refute the possibility of paternalism.

---

[21] *Harm to Others* 68.

[22] Although sometimes it does so depend; as when the value of an action is partly constituted by one's motives for doing it.

c. Ends and Means: The Use of Coercion

A more promising objection, in our view, depends on the *means* of paternalistic intervention. In Parts II and III, we have argued that state intervention should be designed to protect and improve the quality of people's lives, to promote the goods of human welfare. As we have noted, that end is compatible with many kinds of (non-penal) intervention to improve welfare. There is widespread state-implemented support for all sorts of activities seen as having public value, including high culture, sport, social and medical support systems, and the like. These interventions are all predicated on value judgements about what is in people's interests and advances their well-being.

Doubtless, social engineering is often a good thing, at least when it is done through the creation of options.[23] But some kinds of engineering, most notably in the criminal law, operate by quite different means—by coercively eliminating options. Even if the remaining options are beneficial, they are imposed rather than voluntary. Moreover, the interventions are recurrent in nature: this feature is characteristic of criminal laws, which rule out options permanently rather than occasionally. In this respect, criminal prohibitions are quite unlike intervening to restrain someone about to step in front of an oncoming car.[24] On that specific occasion, intervention may be the right thing to do. But crimes are not concerned with one-off scenarios. They regulate activities systematically.

There are two points at work here. First, the distinction between *ad hoc* and rule-based interventions, a distinction that is bound up with the authoritative nature of legal rules, primarily raises concerns about over-inclusion. As we noted in § 9.1, this generates reason for caution rather than an absolute bar. Just as Mill observed, paternalistic intervention is quite likely to get it wrong, ruling out valuable as well as harmful options;[25] and this is especially true when the person being harmed is the actor himself, who is often better placed than the state to make nuanced judgements about the effects of a contemplated action in the particular circumstances.

Suppose, then, that the state were to consider proscribing certain self-injurious conduct, and could avoid substantial over-inclusion when doing so.[26] In these kinds of case, the first worry, about the generality of a

---

[23] Even here, there may be an indirect element of compulsion, in that the funding of such options is likely to be through compulsory taxation regimes. Because our focus is ultimately on criminal law and the coercive methods it uses, we will not pursue that further issue here.

[24] Above, § 9.1.

[25] All the more so where the political system becomes dominated by interest and lobby groups.

[26] Compare the discussion in § 10.7 below, of criminalising the consensual infliction of serious bodily injury. The occasional instances where such activity really is good for the defendant might be accommodated by way of medical defences.

prohibition, would be no barrier. Even so, we would be left with the second concern: that intervention is by coercion. Agents are being required to forgo options because doing so will serve their interests. This is a concern about means rather than ends: while the end may be valuable, there are also norms about how we treat people in the pursuit of those ends. Perhaps we can agree that the state is entitled to foster beneficial rather than valueless options; but to what extent can we infringe citizens' self-determination for the sake of promoting those options? Are not citizens, in virtue of their autonomy, entitled to decide upon, and indeed waive, their own interests? A meaningful right of self-determination must include a right to make bad decisions, at least when those decisions do not adversely affect the interests of others. Yet, as we have noted, there is nothing wrong with stopping the pedestrian from stepping in front of the car. Our theory of criminalisation must reconcile these propositions.

9.2   DIRECT AND INDIRECT COERCION

We cannot hope, in what follows, fully to discharge that obligation. Yet, as we have suggested, occasionally paternalistic coercion does seem to be appropriate, albeit rarely in the criminal law; and the remainder of Part IV will pursue some of these possibilities in greater detail. To help that investigation, we begin with some definitions, including a distinction that traces back to the work of Gerald Dworkin.[27]

a.   Direct Paternalism

In what follows, we will restrict our discussion of paternalism to interventions that compulsorily deprive a person of certain behavioural options, where the justification for removing those options is that they are (potentially) harmful to the person from whom they are removed; hence, the intervention is 'for the benefit' of that same person. Such interventions can be direct or indirect. By 'direct' legal paternalism, we refer to the (civil or criminal) *coercion, for their own benefit, of those who would harm or risk harm to themselves*. Some objections to direct paternalism will be explored below. Broadly speaking, however, there seem to be two main types of cases in which direct paternalism may potentially be legitimate.

The first ground involves various types of what we might loosely call 'error', or better perhaps, 'misalignment'.[28] A central feature of the pedestrian example is his mistake—it is not a step that he would take were

---

[27]   G. Dworkin, 'Paternalism' (1972) 56 *Monist* 64, § 3.
[28]   cf. J. Kleinig, *Paternalism* (Totowa, NJ: Rowman & Allanheld, 1984).

he aware of its implications. He has simply overlooked the risk of the oncoming vehicle and has no wish to be run over, as a matter of either first- or second-order preference. Rather more complex extensions of this kind of idea involve a misalignment of a person's immediate choices with her own second-order preferences. In everyday life, people frequently make decisions that are not aligned with their longer-term interests and goals. This is typically true of seat belt laws—most of us really don't want the grave injuries at risk and, rationally, would choose to wear a seat belt had we thought the matter through properly. We shall suggest below that legal paternalism in such cases can sometimes be justified, although the issues involved are difficult. Intervention in such cases is not simply a form of 'soft' paternalism, because there is no suggestion that the agent lacks the capacity to understand the implications of his actions. Yet neither is it fully 'hard' paternalism, in that it is not overruling a fully considered and informed exercise of those capacities.[29]

The second and more controversial ground for intervention aims to develop, foster, or protect the *capacity* for morally responsible personhood; including the capacities to reflect upon, endorse, and decide for oneself between competing values, options, and forms of life. These kinds of capacities are, in a sense, value-neutral, in that they are preconditions of our abilities to pursue good lives without actually committing us to do so. Arguably it may, as Mill contemplated, be appropriate for the state to prevent us from selling ourselves voluntarily into slavery. Generally speaking, however, intervention on this ground should be restricted to agents who are not fully competent actors, such as children. Thus we might distinguish compulsory child schooling from compulsory career choices, with the former a permissible intervention to foster capacity:[30] the latter is not.

Beyond these two varieties, other cases of direct paternalism tend to contravene a right closely associated with autonomy, i.e. a right to be treated as a self-determining being. This is a moral right of human dignity. And it is violated by coercive measures, such as direct paternalism. There is an attack on D's right to choose *whenever* intervention is made contingent on the choice's being made for good reasons. At the level of principle, of

---

[29]   The terms 'soft' and 'hard' paternalism are coined by Feinberg in *Harm to Self*, ch. 20. Briefly summarised, the term 'soft paternalism' refers to interventions to prevent self-harm where the actor (e.g., a child) lacks sufficient capacity for exercising choice. 'Hard paternalism' refers to coercion to prevent self-harm by a person who is an adult, fully informed, *compos mentis,* and suffering from no disabilities that would impede his capacity for rational choice. As the example in the text shows, these criteria generate a spectrum rather than a binomial. In order to avoid confusion, therefore, we shall not rely on them here.

[30]   However, while intervention through the civil law is frequently less objectionable in such cases, many of the concerns that will be expressed in § 9.4, about direct paternalistic intervention via the *criminal* law, apply to non-competent actors as well.

course, violations of another's right may be open to the possibility of justification. But the justifying aim would have to be compatible with the aspiration to fully responsible agency.

b. Indirect Paternalism

On the other hand, the force of this worry about direct paternalism does not apply in the same way to *indirect* paternalistic prohibitions: that is, to measures that do not coerce the very persons they are designed to benefit. The foregoing argument doesn't show that the state should promote or protect bad choices; it merely denies that the state should coerce the beneficiary to avoid them. So we need a different reason for objecting to indirect paternalism.

As has been noted, instances of indirect paternalism are in practice widespread, such as the requirement that car manufacturers include airbags in their products. Similarly, physical injuries that may lawfully be self-inflicted are more likely to be proscribed when inflicted by others, even with the putative consent of the 'victim'.[31] None the less, it seems to us that indirect paternalism is also problematic, and has the potential to undermine D's right to be treated as a self-determining creature. But here, there seem to be two classes of case.

In the first kind of case, involving airbag-type prohibitions, there are (as with direct paternalism) grounds for worry about the *means* of intervention. This time, however, the beneficiary is more manipulated—stage-managed—than coerced outright. The self-harming option is eliminated rather than criminalised. State intervention of this variety is, in effect, a form of situational engineering, of prophylactic harm-prevention.[32] Indirect paternalism in these cases operates to pre-empt D's choice by coercing the preconditions of its exercise. Thus consumers are prevented from forgoing an airbag, buying the same car more cheaply, and spending the difference on other goods. This is accomplished simply by the state's eliminating the possibility of choice, through coercion of the manufacturer.

For most interventions of this first type, any justification for pre-empting the option will depend, in parallel with direct paternalism, on the proposition that consumers would tend to make poor decisions if given the option of buying a cheaper car. The second type of indirect paternalism, however, cannot be justified on this ground. Proscriptions of killing on request differ

---

[31] The regulation of such consensual harms is a matter of indirect paternalism, to be considered in Chapter 10.

[32] An even more indirect variant of situational crime prevention: cf. A. von Hirsch, D. Garland, and A. Wakefield (eds), *Ethical and Social Issues in Situational Crime Prevention* (Oxford: Hart Publishing, 2000).

from compulsory airbag rules, because the central case does not involve misalignment. Admittedly, as will be seen,[33] the possibility of error may be a factor meriting temporary interventions to restrain would-be suicides. It may also warrant over-inclusive prohibitions, to protect vulnerable persons from being unduly influenced to request killing. Subject to those qualifications, however, any outright prohibition of requested killings requires a separate justification. In this second type of indirect paternalism, the worry is straightforwardly about the end: should the state be in the business of removing such important options from its citizens—and is its doing so compatible with the right to self-determination? Any in-principle case for pre-emptively withdrawing considered, desired options would seemingly have to be built on the ground, identified earlier, of protecting the capacities of persons to direct the course and aims of their own lives. Successful justifications of this sort would surely be rare.

However, we shall defer these concerns about indirect paternalism until Chapter 10. For now, the concentration is upon direct paternalism.

9.3   DIRECT PATERNALISM IN THE CIVIL LAW

Paradigmatically, direct paternalistic interventions in law have two salient characteristics. First, the aim of the intervention is to prevent harm to the actor herself.[34] Secondly, the intervention involves compulsion: the actor may not refuse the proffered assistance. As have seen, it is this second characteristic—compulsion—that distinguishes paternalistic interventions from other forms of state social assistance. One might therefore be sceptical about coercive, paternalistic interventions, even while favouring an extensive scheme of social welfare supports.

In the specific context of the criminal law, direct legal paternalism refers to the use of criminal sanctions to penalise those who harm or attempt to harm themselves. This requires us to divide the issues into two main types. The first concerns direct paternalism generally: the legitimacy of employing any form of coercion to prevent a person from inflicting self-injury. The second question, to which we come in § 9.4, relates to the appropriateness of using *criminal* law for this purpose.

---

[33]   Below, § 9.4.

[34]   We focus on this as the central and strongest case: the discussion applies *a fortiori* to other coercive interventions made for the sake of the affected actor.

a. Kleinig and Dworkin on Limited Direct Paternalism

The starting point is, we think, a presumption against paternalistic interventions. Coercion always stands in need of justification: unless one is an out-and-out consequentialist, the problem here is that beneficial ends do not necessarily justify the coercive means. Ordinarily, the state should not employ its compulsory powers to prevent an individual from injuring herself. This presumption rests on an idea of autonomy: paternalistic interventions infringe the actor's entitlement to decide matters concerning her own life. But autonomy in how rich a sense?

Conceivably, autonomy could be understood for present purposes in terms of 'deep' self-determination, namely someone's acting according to a coherent set of goals of his own considered choice. On that view, a person could engage in apparently self-destructive activities, but only if these were part of a fuller life-conception or plan of his own. An example would be the writer or poet who drinks heavily because a life involving alcohol consumption inspires his work. (Dylan Thomas? Brendan Behan?) That approach would, however, allow for extensive substitution of judgement. The state could intervene whenever the person apparently is not acting according to well-defined, long-range goals; as when, for example, his self-injurious behaviour is at odds with his own stated aims, or when he fails adequately to reflect upon the longer-term effects of his behaviour.

Such a perspective seems manifestly problematic. The scope of intervention would be extremely wide, well beyond the scope of 'misalignment' identified in § 9.2(a). It would allow the state to intercede against self-injurious behaviour whenever it is not based on a coherent set of personal goals. Self-damaging actions, when not reflective of considered, long-term preferences, would no longer be matters for self-determination, with the result that many people could no longer direct the course of their own lives. The approach fails also to give recognition to the individual's *capacity* for deliberation concerning his own interests. Even someone with an apparently chaotic lifestyle may be capable of choosing to live otherwise. The person who takes excessive risks because he (mistakenly) believes that he is unusually skilful or lucky could still, unless he suffers from significant mental incapacity, be capable of reconsidering such beliefs and choosing to act with a greater degree of reflection and prudence. The conception of a person as rational agent involves precisely such capacities for reconsideration, and coercive intervention would bypass that capacity for agency. It would fail adequately to respect the individual as a deliberating moral agent—albeit someone who does not always get it right. Thus a presumption against paternalistic intervention should not rest upon, or apply only to, such a rich conception of autonomy.

Instead, the presumption should rest, as Feinberg suggests, on simple sovereignty of choice:[35] for competent actors, it should be the person himself who decides upon his self-regarding behaviour. Prima facie, this starting point casts doubt upon all direct paternalism. However, while such an approach respects each person's capacity for choice, it does so at considerable personal cost. Humans are fallible, and may be tempted in moments of stress to take actions that lead to drastic and irreversible consequences. In such situations, a refusal ever to intervene could indeed frustrate the achievement of the person's own longer-term goals.

To deal with these situations, John Kleinig and Gerald Dworkin have suggested limited versions of direct paternalism.[36] The starting-point, on their versions, is simple self-determination: each person decides upon his own conduct, and substitution of judgement is ordinarily impermissible. In certain situations, however, a person's own longer-term goals could be used as grounds for intervention. When someone, whose life hitherto suggests a commitment to various continuing projects, attempts suicide or other self-injury after a personal setback (for example, the collapse of his marriage or career), temporary intervention may be appropriate in order to secure time for reflection and reconsideration. The person's apparent long-range preferences would thus be positively relied upon to justify the intervention. Such intervention would, however, be exceptional: it could not be used, for example, against those whose longer-range commitments cannot thus be identified. Furthermore, intervention of a prolonged character would not be permissible.

This approach differs substantially from the 'deep' understanding of self-determination referred to above. There, a choice to commit self-injury would be recognised as autonomous only if it accords with the person's explicit longer-term preferences; so that those lacking in well-defined long-term goals could be subjected to extensive restraint. In the account of limited paternalism just described, the presumption is reversed. Ordinarily, the person would be free to act. It is *only* if the person has identifiable long-term goals, *and* the immediate act would apparently frustrate those goals, that temporary restraint could be invoked.

Admittedly, the presumption does not guarantee that intervention always comports with a person's actual long-term preferences, since mistakes may be made in identifying the person's aims—especially when state agencies attempt such judgements. The person who appears to have been strongly committed to his job and family, but who tries nevertheless to end his life after a serious personal setback, may truly have come to a definitive judgement that his existence is no longer worth living. Thus, if he

---

[35] *Harm to Self*, ch. 19.
[36] Kleinig, above n. 28; Dworkin, above n. 27.

attempts suicide by taking an overdose of sleeping pills, pumping out his stomach and holding him for observation for a few days would frustrate his considered personal choices. But the law must deal with standard cases, and in most such cases the person may well be acting out of immediate desperation. Moreover, on this limited version of paternalism, agents would eventually be permitted to attempt suicide without further interference, with a mechanism available to establish that this is their considered wish.

Even so, the grounds for intervention remain narrow. Thus Kleinig concedes that the state and its agencies would seldom have enough insight into the character of someone's longer-term plans to make coercive state intervention feasible or desirable. He himself would therefore restrict the permissibility of this kind of paternalism chiefly to interpersonal situations, as when a person hides his despondent friend's barbiturates.[37]

The account offered by Gerald Dworkin is somewhat more sympathetic to state intercession.[38] Intervention is permissible, he asserts, when (1) the self-harm is potentially grave and irreversible (for example, death or serious injury); (2) the person appears to be acting under unusual stress; (3) the duration of the intervention is limited; and, we would add (4) there are restrictions on repeated interventions.[39] It is arguable that, in many—typical—instances of self-harm, the agent responds to the stress of the moment and inconsistently with his long-range preferences. None the less, ultimately he will be free to terminate his life should he still so wish.

It should be emphasised that, for all their restricted character, Kleinig's and Dworkin's schemes of intervention authorise a significant limitation upon the autonomy of mature agents. Self-determination involves, *stricto sensu*, disposing of one's interests as one *now* chooses, notwithstanding the supposed longer-range preferences one has developed previously. The argument in favour of these schemes seeks not to deny that the intervention is paternalistic. It simply claims that temporary paternalistic intervention is sometimes justified, at least when it supports the subject's own longer-range preferences and priorities.

---

[37] *ibid.*

[38] *ibid.*; see also G. Dworkin, 'Paternalism: Some Second Thoughts' in R. Sartorius (ed.), *Paternalism* (Minneapolis, MN: University of Minnesota Press, 1983) 105. In effect, Dworkin's approach permits the kind of presumption that the law often must make when it works with standard cases.

[39] This additional criterion is a natural extension of Dworkin's condition (3). We make it explicit because, otherwise, the state might intrude (albeit temporarily) to prevent D from harming himself *each time* he seeks to do so; thereby permanently forestalling D's realisation of his wishes.

9.4   THE DISTINCTIVELY PROBLEMATIC CHARACTER OF PATERNALISTIC CRIMES

The limited paternalism just discussed provides warrant only for coercive intervention of some kind; it does not purport to justify intervention specifically by means of the *criminal* law. There are special objections to invoking criminal sanctions, even where a limited-paternalism model might justify limited state intervention in another form. In simple cases, such as attempted suicide, the point seems obvious. Perhaps it is appropriate, as § 9.3 contemplates, for the state to interfere under certain circumstances with suicide attempts, say by holding the would-be suicide for a limited period to allow him to reflect and reconsider. It is a quite different matter, however, to *punish* his attempt at suicide. Indeed, the latter crime has been removed from most modern statute books.[40]

The leading European criminal-law systems, in Germany and the United Kingdom, both generally avoid direct paternalism in their criminal law. Deliberate self-injury is no crime—although there are certain apparent exceptions, notably those interdicting the acquisition and possession of drugs.[41] Perhaps surprisingly, there has been little discussion in Germany of *why* directly paternalistic criminal prohibitions should be eschewed. The leading criminal-law commentator, Claus Roxin, asserts that self-damaging behaviour should be seen as part of the person's self-determination and hence is not a proper subject of criminal sanctions; but his thesis has not been debated extensively by German scholars.[42] Anglo-American debates about paternalism go back so far as the mid-nineteenth century;[43] yet there has been relatively little attention to the possibility of principled differences between paternalistic criminal prohibitions and other forms of coercive state intervention aimed at preventing self-damaging conduct, for example in civil or administrative law.

<hr/>

[40]   Though not all—see, e.g., the Singaporean Penal Code, s. 309. Retention of the crime in Singapore appears to be a reflection of Confucian ethics: compare the *White Paper on Shared Values* Cmd. 1 of 1991 (Singapore: National Printers, 1991).

[41]   See, e.g., *Betäubungsmittelgesetz* (BtMG) § 29 (Germany); Misuse of Drugs Act 1971 (UK). For critical discussion of a paternalistic rationale for drug-possession prohibitions, see D. Husak, *Drugs and Rights* (Cambridge: Cambridge UP, 1992) ch. 2.

[42]   Roxin, *Strafrecht AT*, vol. 1, 23–25.

[43]   Beginning with Mill's *On Liberty* ch. 4. The 1980s saw extensive discussion of the issue, including *Harm to Self* chs 17–19; Dworkin, above n. 27; Kleinig, above n. 28, 67–73; Raz, above n. 11, ch. 15. More recently see, e.g., R. Arneson, 'Joel Feinberg and the Justification of Hard Paternalism' (2005) 11 Legal Theory 259.

a. The Inappropriateness of Penal Censure

One simple, and common, argument against paternalistic criminal prohibitions is that they contravene the aim of paternalism itself, because the deprivations involved in penal sanctions ordinarily would not promote the interests of the defendant.[44] In cases of severe punishment for supposedly self-damaging behaviour such as drug abuse, this argument is manifestly correct: how could a drug user's own interests be fostered through infliction of the lengthy prison terms that drug laws frequently require? This is an *internal* justificatory objection: as paternalism, it fails in its own terms, since the coercion is not in the best interests of those to whom it is addressed.[45]

With reduced criminal sanctions, though, the internal objection would become less compelling. If certain seriously and irreversibly self-damaging conduct were subject only to modest criminal penalties, and if that helped diminish the incidence of such behaviour, it becomes less clear whether criminalisation would necessarily be worse for the person than her own self-destructive conduct.

However, at this point there is a second argument against criminalisation, one that concerns the censuring character of criminal law. As we saw in Part I, both criminalisation and punishment centrally involve censure—that is, the expression of disapprobation for the activity, and of blame directed at the perpetrator for his act. This censuring element plays a crucial normative role: it serves as a moral communication to the perpetrator as well as to others; and it treats the defendant as an agent capable of moral deliberation. The defendant is confronted with disapproval because of the publicly declared wrongfulness of the conduct, and not solely for preventive purposes.

In the context of conduct that is harmful to others, this censuring element can readily be accounted for.[46] When D commits an assault against V, he infringes the legitimate claims that V has to her personal physical integrity; and this infringement, when done intentionally, shows culpable

---

[44] For discussion of this issue, see D. Husak, above n. 41, 76.

[45] Defenders of paternalistic criminal laws might accept this point, but respond that the sanction is to be justified in terms of *general* deterrence: even though D may not deserve or benefit from the quantum of punishment he receives for his act of self-injury, E and F will benefit from it by being deterred from acting similarly. Of course, doubts about the effectiveness of general deterrence may combine with the disvalue for D to undermine such analysis even in its own terms. More importantly, however, this kind of consequentialism—making D suffer for the benefit of others—would be ruled out by the conception of criminalisation we outlined in Chapter 1 and, as we argue in the rest of this section, by the requirement that D's punishment should be deserved. See also A. von Hirsch, *Censure and Sanctions* (Oxford: Oxford UP, 1993) 16–17.

[46] We assume here that the harm is non-consensual. For the alternative case, see Chapter 10 below.

disregard for V's vital interests and constitutes a censurable wrong. In such situations, not only is the conduct wrongful, but the rationale for the state's censuring response lies precisely in that response's public recognition of the conduct's wrongfulness.[47] Even if criminalisation is justified partially in crime-prevention terms,[48] an inescapable feature of the criminal sanction is its retrospective ascription of fault for wrongdoing and its resulting imposition of censure.

When this wrongdoing/censure paradigm is applied to self-injurious conduct, however, it becomes far more problematic. Suppose the 'assault' is committed by D against himself: having just lost his job, he becomes despondent and tries to kill himself. Perhaps he is being most unwise; had he waited, he would have realised that he still has adequate living prospects—hence the argument in § 9.3(a) that limited civil intervention to provide a 'cooling-off' period may be warranted. However, even were we to assume that his conduct violates a moral duty owed by D to himself,[49] a paternalistic rationale would not warrant the deployment of the criminal law to give public recognition to this 'wrong'.

In our discussion of Kleinig's and Dworkin's proposals for a limited paternalism,[50] the basis for intervening related to preserving the person's future life chances. The intervention was not to convey disapproval for her conduct, but to restrain her temporarily in order that she can reconsider, and/or resume, her (apparent) longer-term projects. This ground for intervention is plainly preventive and future-oriented. That same orientation, however, makes the criminal sanction, with its strong retrospective and censuring features, an inappropriate form of response. Moreover, the criminal law's proscription is not temporary—and so cannot be supported by Kleinig's and Dworkin's proposals. It is the wrong *type* of response.

This contention is brought into sharp relief when one considers the quantum of intervention. If attempted suicide were to be censured as a wrong, the criminal law's response would involve a retrospectively-focused, desert-based measure of sanction, determined substantially by the degrees of harmfulness and culpability of the defendant's behaviour.[51] Given the intentional character of the conduct, and the gravity of harm involved, one might expect the deserved sentence to be substantial.[52] But, in paternalistic terms, the concern should be primarily future-orientated:

---

[47] Above, § 1.2.

[48] Above, § 1.3.

[49] cf. above, n. 15. In this and the next chapter, we will leave to one side the possibility of cases in which moral duties are owed to others, e.g. one's young children, the discharge of which is dependent on one's remaining alive. Such duties, if any, would take the case outside the scope of paternalism.

[50] Above, § 9.3(a).

[51] *Proportionate Sentencing* chs 2, 9.

[52] Subject, as always, to circumstances that may excuse or otherwise attenuate blame.

intervention is warranted in order to secure the individual an opportunity to reconsider and reflect on his options. It is hard to see how the criteria of a censure-oriented response can discharge those aims. Especially when considered across the range of offences, the criteria of paternalistic responses do not seem to track those of deserved penal censure.

One might think that these two ambitions need not be in tension; that punishing self-injurious conduct could help safeguard the person's options for the future, by providing a disincentive to self-injurious conduct. With criminalisation, however, the disincentive embodied in the threatened penal response is of a special kind, since it is intimately bound up with censure for the conduct. The 'hard treatment' or deprivation element in punishment serves both as the vehicle through which penal censure is expressed and as a means for discouraging future offending. Hence it is appropriate to invoke punishment as such a disincentive only when and to the extent that the conduct should properly be subjected to penal censure.

b.   The Private and the Public Realms

Conceivably, however, that argument begs a question. Might not self-injurious conduct be, on occasion, worthy of moral censure? In principle, the answer is yes: such conduct can sometimes be wrong, all things considered. In some cases, indeed, it seems that the wrongfulness may be substantial, especially when the consequences of the behaviour are irreversible, and the actor's reasons for attempting self-harm are manifestly short-sighted and unreasonable. Imagine the case of a patriotic pop-music fan, who decides to kill herself should her country do badly (again) in the next Eurovision Song Contest. This seems a ridiculous reason for an attempt at self-annihilation, and the misguided patriot (supposing she survives) might rightly be criticised by friends and acquaintances for seeking to 'throw away' her life and personal prospects for trivial reasons.

As we argued in Chapter 2, however, eligibility for criticism is necessary but insufficient by itself to warrant penal censure. It does not, without more, give reason why morally wrongful but *self-regarding* actions are the business of the state.[53] State coercive intervention, under the limited-paternalism

---

[53] In 'Joel Feinberg and the Justification of Hard Paternalism', above n. 43, 280, Richard Arneson disagrees, asserting that we ought to 'make something worthwhile of our life, something good for ourselves and others', and hence that a person may properly be restrained from attempting suicide for trivial and purely self-directed reasons. Of course, this is not a paternalistic ground for intervention, as it is not concerned with the quality of the person's own life as he would experience it. It is, rather, a species of legal moralism because, as Bill Edmundson has pointed out, it assumes the person 'holds [his own] life in an unconsented trusteeship, subject to the moral community's insistence that it not be wasted or squandered':

scheme discussed in § 9.3, becomes permissible because it accords with a person's own apparent longer-range goals and thus helps to preserve her ability to achieve these goals. In effect, Kleinig and Dworkin borrow the individual's own goals to justify intervention. But a general criminal law prohibition does not. Indeed, it ignores them. Rather than safeguarding his future interests and longer-term preferences, it provides for penal censure of supposedly wrongful past choices.

Wrong as such self-damaging choices might well be, they are essentially private.[54] Any system for social regulation must draw somewhere a divide between public and private, in order that there may be spheres within which the state's co-ordinating and norm-establishing roles can be avoided: wherein individuals can, as it were, 'contract out' of the state's regulatory terms. Those regulatory terms are needed, indeed desirable, to set the terms of interaction *between* individuals; not least in order to maximise the self-determination available to each member of a society. But that justification does not extend to self-regarding conduct. This is part of the point of *self*-determination; to the extent that one's conduct does not impact upon other persons—to the extent that the conduct is not other-determining—then the choice should be up to her. Private or informal expressions of disapproval may well remain appropriate; and friends may be entitled to issue a rebuke. ('What a ridiculous reason for trying to end your life!') But formal, public proscription and condemnation of such behaviour seems incompatible with the commitment to respect human beings as self-determining agents.

9.5 AN EXCEPTION FOR DE MINIMIS INTERVENTIONS?

Our conclusion is that criminal sanctions are not, in principle, an appropriate way of intervening coercively to prevent an actor from injuring herself. Even in cases where limited state intervention of a civil character is justified, recourse to the criminal law should not follow.

This view, which rules out direct paternalism generally in criminal law, raises the question of the appropriateness of criminal prohibitions with restricted penalties, such as seatbelt or motorcycle-helmet laws. Within the Anglo-American legal system, self-injurious conduct in such cases is regulated through criminal laws, but the sanctions are limited—say, to modest fines, which are imposed primarily in order to give some deterrent effect to the rule. The arguments in § 9.4 have rested in large part on the

W. Edmundson, 'Comments on Richard Arneson's "Joel Feinberg and the Justification of Hard Paternalism"' (2005) 11 Legal Theory 285, 290–91.

[54] See also the discussion of privacy in § 11.1.

censuring features of criminalisation and the inappropriateness of penal censure for self-damaging conduct. To the extent that our arguments are dependent on those features, it is arguable that, in virtue of the low levels of the sanctions involved in seat-belt-type laws, no significantly censuring response (of the kind typical of the criminal law) is involved.[55] In German law, such conduct would be deemed violations (*Ordnungswidrigkeiten*) rather than criminal offences. As such, the verdict generally does not convey formal penal censure.[56]

The intervention remains coercive in structure. Unlike taxes or licences, regulatory offences are not permissive. They do not allow the activity provided D pays for it. The conduct is disapproved—prohibited—and should not be engaged in.[57] Even if outside the stigmatic criminal-law archetype, therefore, they too require justification. Here, considerations of degree will be relevant: that the intervention requires only minor precautions and is not unduly onerous or restrictive of meaningful options, while the potential effect on victims' lives and long-term goals is substantial. Moreover, the risks are typically not the subject of considered choices by individuals—they represent the kinds of casual 'miscalculation' that, as we suggested in § 9.2, might legitimately be addressed through intervention.

9.6   OTHER (NON-PATERNALISTIC) GROUNDS FOR INTERVENTION?

What practical difference would such a principle against direct paternalism make in criminal law? It is sometimes suggested that most seemingly paternalistic prohibitions can be rationalised on other grounds—including the Harm Principle.[58] Under scrutiny, however, many such claims are problematic. Let us consider three examples.

---

[55] For discussion, see A.P. Simester, 'Is Strict Liability Always Wrong?' in Simester (ed.), *Appraising Strict Liability* (Oxford: Oxford UP, 2005) ch. 2; compare, however, N. Persak, 'In den Nebengebieten des Strafrechts: Paternalische Interventionen im Recht der Ordnungswiedrigkeiten' in A. von Hirsch, U. Neumann and K. Seelmann (eds), *Paternalismus im Strafrecht; Die Kriminalisierung von selbstchädingendem Verhalten* (Baden-Baden: Nomos, 2010) 173.

[56] See J.R. Spencer and A. Pedain, 'Approaches to Strict and Constructive Liability in Continental Criminal Law' in Simester (ed.), *Appraising Strict Liability* (Oxford: Oxford UP, 2005) ch. 10; Roxin, *Strafrecht AT*, 31–32.

[57] This is part of the reason why 'quasi-criminal' and 'truly criminal' offences are not straightforwardly separated. See Simester, above n. 55, at 40–41.

[58] See B. Harcourt, 'The Collapse of the Harm Principle' (1999) 90 J Crim L & Criminology 105.

a.   Duty of Rescue?

Under much continental European law, individuals have a duty to rescue someone in danger.[59] The public rescue services are also called upon to provide assistance to the person. German writers have sometimes sought by analogy to suggest that, if the state should require its citizens to render emergency assistance to persons in need, it should itself also help to prevent such emergencies, by proscribing suicide or self-harm. Might a prohibition of attempted suicide be derived, or even implied, from the duty to rescue and the rationale behind that duty?

In the normal situation of rescue, the victim is (say) in the river, at risk of drowning, because he accidentally fell in or was pushed. Indeed, if he was pushed, criminalisation under the Harm Principle is already in play, since he has been victimised by the harmful behaviour of an instigator whose act may itself be punishable. The question then becomes whether a bystander (who was not responsible for initially putting the victim at risk) also has an obligation to provide assistance. German criminal law, for example, holds that he has such an obligation, based on duties of 'solidarity' among citizens.[60] Anglo-American law, by contrast, does not impose any comparable obligation of rescue.[61]

With attempted self-harm, the situation is different. The person attempting suicide is in danger because he has decided to put himself in harm's way: he has *jumped* in the river, for example. Rescuing him, in this situation, is plainly a paternalistic intervention—saving him in disregard of his own decision to end his life. Does this mean that no rescue attempt should be permissible? Not necessarily. In the immediate situation, it may be impossible to ascertain his preference for living or dying—so that rescue becomes appropriate because he may in fact wish to survive. And even if he apparently does wish to die, the limited paternalism discussed in § 9.4(a) could allow rescue-type interventions, and possibly a brief period of holding the person to permit reconsideration and reflection. What must be emphasised, however, is that the attempt at *self*-injury alters the rationale for the intervention. The normal basis for the duty of rescue, with its derivation from prevention of harm to others, no longer would suffice to justify the state's intervention. Intervention, to the extent permissible, becomes instead a paternalistic concern with preventing the actor from injuring himself; which should be subject to the limitations discussed in § 9.5.

[59]   e.g. StGB § 323c; *Code Pénal*, Art. 63 (France).
[60]   W. Wohlers, 'Commentary to § 323c' in U. Kindhäuser, U. Neumann and H.-U. Pfaeffgen (eds), *Nomoskommentar zum StGB* (3rd ed., Baden-Baden: Nomos, 2010) 5584; von Hirsch, 'Criminalising Failure to Rescue: A Matter of "Solidarity" or Altruism?' above n. 7.
[61]   *Simester and Sullivan* § 4.1(i).

b. 'Harm' to the State's Health-Protection System?

It has also been argued that attempts at self-injury can generate a form of harm to others, and so fall within the scope of the Harm Principle, because of their indirect financial effects; for example, their effects on the state's rescue and health-funding systems.[62] The person who jumps into the river affects others adversely because he draws upon those costly, tax-supported services. But it must be borne in mind, again, that he does not want to be rescued. He is trying to kill himself. Must he be saved notwithstanding his wishes? In this situation, the expenditure of state money occurs only because the state extends its services to those who have voluntarily sought to do themselves injury. If the attempted suicide is to be punished for supposedly 'abusing' these benefits in virtue of his self-destructive behaviour—without being given the opportunity to withdraw from the state's scheme of assistance—then he is being coerced for his own (supposed) good. Prima facie, the intervention is therefore paternalistic, and should be judged in its own terms. It cannot be justified simply by resort to the Harm Principle.

One limitation of our argument here is the possibility of mistake or ignorance. If the state does not (and, let us imagine, cannot) ascertain the agent's intentions, then it may be morally obliged to seek to intervene and will incur rescue costs in good faith. Intervention in these cases need not, therefore, be paternalistic. Even so, however, this link seems insufficient to warrant criminalisation. It rests on a view of the would-be suicide as selfish or inconsiderate, which seems in this context an inadequate basis of imputing criminal-law responsibility for costs incurred by third parties who voluntarily choose to intervene. In effect, the harm here is too remote for imputation:[63] the choice by third parties (here, the state) to provide rescue services does not suffice to make D's initial action, which is otherwise a matter of D's self-determination, wrong. If attempted self-injury is wrongful at all, it is (as we noted earlier) wrongful for other reasons, i.e. those reasons directly concerning whether one should attempt to harm oneself. In our view, therefore, the distribution and recovery of rescue costs are a matter for the civil law. In any event, the case for invoking criminal proscriptions would demand that an advance opt-out mechanism exist, so that rescues are not compulsory.

---

[62] See Harcourt, above n. 58; *Harm to Self* 134–42.
[63] Above, Chapters 4–5.

c.   Other Remote Harms?

Finally, it is sometimes suggested that many seemingly paternalistic prohibitions, such as those related to drug possession, actually generate long-run harmful effects to others, because they initiate a chain of bad consequences that end with acts of victimisation. Drug prohibitions, it is thus argued, need not rely on paternalist claims in order to be sustainable. Drug use should be proscribed because its prevalent use in neighbourhoods may produce criminogenic conditions that, in turn, generate conduct that is harmful to others, such as increased levels of theft, assault, vandalism, and so forth.[64] This, however, involves *mediating-intervention* liability: the conduct (in this case, drug possession) is proscribed because of its tendency to induce other actors, or the same actor at a later time, to choose to engage in injurious conduct.

The objection to such mediating-intervention liability, as we argued in Chapters 4 and 5, is that the prospect of that eventual harmful outcome is not, without more, the initial actor's responsibility, so that the initial actor's conduct need not be a wrong, and it is therefore unsuitable for the censuring response of the criminal law. This is most obviously the case where the chain of consequences involves other intervening actors. Here, the actor's own behaviour (for example, his drug possession and use) is not in itself injurious to others. It is being proscribed only because subsequent actors, whom the original actor does not control, may decide to engage in further conduct that does or risks harm. To impose criminal liability on the original actor, in such situations, ignores the separability of persons as choosing agents.[65] Liability is appropriate for the original actor only if he does something that generates normative involvement in the subsequent choices, that is, if he, in his original conduct, does something to affirm or underwrite the subsequent actors' harmful choices—which mere drug use does not do. We conclude that paternalistic arguments cannot be replaced readily by claims about remote harm to others.

9.7   IN CLOSING: AUTONOMY AND RESPECT

In general, paternalistic interventions are better done, if at all, outside the criminal law. Civil law measures, or even public information initiatives, may be preferable and more effective. It is also rare for punitive responses

---

[64] An argument criticised by Husak, above, n. 44, at 195–207.

[65] Comparable objections hold in situations in which the same actor but subsequent choices are involved. An example would be where the actor is prohibited from taking drugs because that activity might make him more likely later to commit further harmful (e.g. violent) acts. See generally above, § 5.2(c).

to be in the interests of those to whom they are addressed, and nothing in the discussion here supports the imposition of substantial sanctions for wrongful behaviour that does not harm others.

But it is, we accept, an error to think that consent, or a voluntary choice, to self-harm necessarily prevents an action from being wrong. Choices don't become good ones just because they are freely made. As such, self-harmful acts are capable of satisfying the first condition of criminalisation, i.e. the wrongfulness constraint: that the conduct ought not to be done. Whether we should regulate it involves evaluating the particular nature of the conduct, the restrictions on liberty involved, mediating factors, and the like. It may be that only limited kinds of cases, such as those discussed in §§ 9.3–9.4, where intervention may be compatible with respect for human dignity, are appropriately the subject of paternalistic intervention. Moreover, there are good reasons for thinking that *direct* paternalistic interventions should not normally use the criminal law. At least sometimes, however, criminal law may be the best option, especially in minor regulatory contexts. It is not ruled out entirely.

Autonomy serves our well-being, in as much as we need an adequate range of options with which to pursue a fulfilling life. To the extent that it does so, the good of human welfare is the master value, and not autonomy *per se*. Considerations of human welfare are capable therefore of generating positive reasons for the state to intervene, even at the price of autonomy. At the same time, the right to respect for human dignity generates substantial constraints upon the means of going about that task. It restricts the range of legitimate paternalism, direct and indirect.

10

Some Varieties of Indirect Paternalism

I N THE PREVIOUS chapter, we argued that while limited paternalism might be permissible in civil or administrative law, there should be little room for direct paternalism in the criminal law, especially in regard to serious crimes. In practice, while contemporary criminal law tends to eschew direct paternalistic prohibitions, indirect interventions are more common. As we noted in § 9.2, indirect paternalism operates by pre-emptively removing options, so that individuals are deprived of the potential for being harmed. Those pre-empted risks may be ones of which individuals may or may not be aware. The requirement that manufacturers sell only cars having airbags is an example of removing an option that is typically unconsidered by purchasers. Other options, however, may be genuinely desired, at least by some persons. Perhaps the most extreme case, where the option is consciously sought, is killing upon request, where D kills P at the latter's behest—a crime under most modern penal systems.[1] These kinds of cases present different problems from the case of airbags, and we turn to them in § 10.2.

10.1 REMOVING (UNWANTED?) OPTIONS: AIRBAGS AND THE LIKE

To the extent that coercion involves the negation of free choice, a case could be made that airbag requirements and similar impositions are amongst the most peremptory of all kinds of criminal-law intervention. Unlike directly paternalistic regulation, the beneficiary for whose sake the prohibition exists is not treated even as a rational, choosing actor, let alone as a moral agent.[2] Her choices are not appealed to or influenced by reasons, with prudential incentives attached. The decision is made for her. She has no choice *at all*.

Of course, the immediate target of the prohibition, the manufacturer, *is* treated as a moral agent, and perhaps it oversimplifies the situation merely

---

[1] See n. 7 below.
[2] See above, § 1.1

to describe the beneficiary-driver as 'coerced'. Yet, whatever language one uses to characterise these cases,[3] the central point is that the penal measure is designed to alter the beneficiary's environment so as to remove a self-harming option. Typically, moreover, such health and safety regulations are designed with the cooperation of the manufacturer or its representative body, which is likely to have an interest in having agreed rules about what counts as an appropriately safe product. To that extent, the manufacturer could even be seen as complicit in this kind of paternalism.

Yet should we really object to such measures? Provided the option being removed is genuinely dangerous, and not the sort of self-harming option that consumers are likely to value, is there any serious reservation about health and safety regulation of this sort?

We do think there is ground for concern here. The reason is not, however, that a right to buy cars without airbags is especially important. The main ground for caution is cumulative.[4] Even where no individual regulatory intervention will have a substantial effect on people's lives, schemes of regulation may do so when taken as a whole; hence one should hesitate before adding to the total load. Viewed cumulatively, the problem arises through cost. Airbags must be paid for, and the financial burden falls ultimately on the consumer. Perhaps they are nowadays not so expensive. But if we also take into account the price of seat belt systems, together with other required precautions such as laminated windshields, crumple zones, side-impact protection beams, collapsible steering columns, etc., the overall expense of car ownership rises considerably. Add to that the health and safety costs affecting all our other activities, as well as those incurred by taxpayer-funded public bodies—e.g. local councils, which must comply with safety regulations governing playgrounds and the like—and the result is a significant imposition.

Given that, even in relatively prosperous countries, most people have limited financial means, indirect paternalism of this sort therefore has a real impact on their lives. In a relatively poor nation, that impact is still greater, which is one reason why many developing countries have more limited car safety regulations: people may be better off with less-safe cars than with no car at all. But the point is not restricted to poor nations.

---

[3] Even the label, 'paternalism', may not apply equally to all cases to which we have attached it in Part IV. But we use it for convenience: nothing in the argument is intended to turn on the label itself.

[4] Note that the same worry can apply also to other methods of regulation, such as taxation. This reminds us of the point mentioned in § 9.1, that the objections to various forms of regulation overlap. Yet there remain distinctive features of this kind of intervention, including the coercive removal of the option altogether and the fact that criminalisation speaks in censorious terms about the prohibited activity (above, § 1.2). Each regulatory method calls for justification in its own terms.

Consumers everywhere must either pay more, and forgo alternative uses of their resources; or sacrifice the activity altogether. If a local council is forced to shut its playground, or a retirement home is forced to close, the outcome for the intended 'beneficiaries' is not necessarily beneficial. (Indeed, the cost-effectiveness of airbags themselves has been questioned.[5])

In these instances, the potential objection to paternalism is internal:[6] that is, the case for paternalistic intervention may fail in its own terms. The problem is, first, one of balancing the risk and the seriousness of prospective harms against the value of the activity itself and the burdens imposed by its regulation: to ensure that the intervention really does benefit, overall, those whom it is targeted to protect. The onus of establishing that case should fall, as always, upon proponents of the intervention. Secondly, even if an indirectly paternalistic rule seems sensible in abstract, its justification must also take account of the extent of existing regulation. In practice, it doesn't: indirect paternalism often exhibits 'mission creep'. Cumulatively, it can deprive us of access to options that we might otherwise prefer.

But it should not be concluded that this variety of indirect paternalism is wrong *tout court*: what we counsel is caution, not abstention. Other things being equal, most of us have good reason for preferring safe to unsafe cars. Moreover, as individuals, we are often poorly placed to assess for ourselves how much safety we should choose. Regulation in this area may therefore be justified as an assumption of that risk-assessment and decision-making power; as such, indirect paternalism can be compatible with both our first-order and our second-order preferences. This is a key point of distinction from direct paternalism, which even in justified cases tends to subordinate a person's first-order preferences. While one may rationally prefer to empower the state to make risk assessments, to be implemented via indirect paternalism, this does not carry over to warrant coercion, on a similar basis, of our first-order choices via direct paternalism. (Doubtless, this is why the rule requiring manufacturers to install seat-belts, introduced in the UK in 1967, was so much less controversial than the 1983 rule that required users to wear them.)

10.2   PROHIBITING IMPORTANT CHOICES: KILLING ON REQUEST AND THE LIKE

Some decisions about an activity are not amenable to delegation. Yet even here, a sharp distinction is drawn in the law between direct and indirect paternalistic prohibitions. The former are used sparingly, the latter

---

[5] In the leading survey, Leonard Evans suggests that the mandatory airbag requirement in the US is 'indefensible': L. Evans, *Traffic Safety* (Bloomfield, MI: Science Serving Society, 2004) ch. 12.

[6] See also § 9.4; below, § 10.5.

extensively. Killing another person at her request ('K/R') is prohibited, in different ways, within most modern penal systems,[7] as is (with important exceptions) injuring another with her consent.[8] By contrast, were a person to (attempt to) kill himself directly, his conduct ordinarily would not, and we have argued should not, be criminal;[9] although, in certain jurisdictions, it may be an offence to help him.[10] It remains to be explained why the criminal law should be so much more stringent with harming another on request when it is so permissive of direct self-injury. What difference should it make when the consensual act of termination is carried out by another?

In the K/R situation, P's consent removes the case from the normal scope of the Harm Principle. Admittedly, A's killing P involves a harm. But P has consented to (indeed, requested) that result. Prima facie, therefore, there is no wrong to P. This is not to dismiss the possibility that A's act is still wrongful, in the sense that it ought not to be done, and perhaps P's consent should be disregarded. But if so, this would be on *paternalistic* grounds— that a concern for P's own welfare dictates ignoring his wishes. This returns us to our original question: assuming that paternalistic grounds do not warrant proscribing direct self-harm, should criminalisation be retained on those grounds for indirect self-harm?

a. Framing Some Issues

To help frame the issues, let us begin with a simple hypothetical. Suppose that P wishes to die, but does not wish to face the terrors and uncertainties of attempting suicide himself. So he asks an acquaintance, D, to carry out the deed. After considering the reasons offered by P for wishing to terminate his existence, D decides to act on P's request. He provides P with

---

[7] By way of illustration, D's conduct in killing P at the latter's request is punishable under both German and English law. Under English law, P's consent is simply disregarded in the killing-on-request situation. D is deemed guilty of murder, just as if he had killed P contrary to P's wishes: cf. Homicide Act 1957, s. 4. German criminal law is less Draconian. While D is criminally liable for killing P at the latter's request (StGB § 216), the penalty is much lower than for ordinary criminal homicide, with a maximum of five years' imprisonment.

[8] StGB §§ 223, 228; *Brown* [1994] 1 AC 212.

[9] Above, Chapter 9.

[10] It is a crime in England if D assists P to kill himself, say by supplying P with a lethal drug: not murder, but a separate offence of assisting suicide contrary to s. 2 of the Suicide Act 1961, carrying a maximum sentence of 14 years' imprisonment. (At the time of writing, this provision is under review.) Contrast German law where, if D does not perform the killing directly and merely assists P to commit suicide, she commits no crime at all: see U. Neumann, 'Commentary to § 211' in U. Kindhäuser, U. Neumann and H.-U. Pfäffgen (eds), *Nomoskommentar zum StGB* (3rd ed., Baden-Baden: Nomos 2010) 3556–58.

a swift, painless death by administering a sedative drug to P and, while the latter is unconscious, terminating his life by injecting a quick-acting lethal preparation.

In order to address the normative case for permitting D's response, it is worth first noting some aspects of the transaction that might appear to be morally problematic, and which generate some of the questions of criminalisation that we consider in the following pages.

One difficulty is the risk that the killing might involve a defective consent on P's part. It may be that P is not fully competent: perhaps he thinks that death is his only option because he is under a delusion that the planet is about to be invaded by evil interplanetary beings, Muggly-Umps, and fears the terrible consequences of falling into their clutches. If the consent is defective because of P's lack of competence, then the Harm Principle *does* apply: he is being harmed without his genuine consent, and his entitlement to self-determination would not be undermined by state intervention.

Secondly, even if P is capable of valid consent, D's conduct may still be objectionable because P has been denied sufficient opportunity to reconsider his reasons for wanting to die, and to reflect upon how those reasons comport with his longer-term commitments and aims. As we noted in the previous chapter, a limited paternalism may be appropriate here, in order to help assure that this process of evaluation occurs. If direct paternalism is sometimes warranted on these grounds, the question naturally arises whether indirect paternalism would be too.

A development of this line of thought is found in the German 'inhibition-threshold' theory.[11] Merely requiring a brief period for reconsideration, it is argued, does not give P an adequate opportunity to try to alter his mode of living in a way that makes it less unsatisfactory. Perhaps, therefore, P's options for terminating his existence should themselves be structured to encourage him to make such efforts. Permitting someone to take his own life, while prohibiting another from performing the act for him, might help provide such a structure of incentives. A number of German criminal law scholars have thus contended that the earnestness of the person's will to die is better assured if that person must himself overcome the natural human inhibition against self-destruction. He might then make a greater effort to come to terms with his life, if the apparently easier option of dying by another's hand is closed off. The persuasiveness of this argument remains, however, to be evaluated in § 10.4.

Finally, there is the possibility of identifying a subclass of requested killings for which the case for decriminalisation is especially strong. Even were the K/R prohibition generally sustainable for one or more of the

---

[11]   Below, § 10.4.

reasons just mentioned, might there nevertheless be a broad exemption (say) for situations where the person's health or welfare have deteriorated sufficiently?

With this much in the way of preliminaries, we turn now to normative argument.

10.3   CONSENT AND EVIDENTIAL RISKS

Can we be sure that P genuinely consented? A familiar justification for outright prohibitions of K/R treats the situation as one of *abstract endangerment*,[12] where the risk to be prevented is that of killing under circumstances of defective consent or insufficient opportunity for reconsideration. This kind of analysis argues for prohibiting K/R on an over-inclusive basis,[13] in that even genuine, fully considered requests would be disallowed because of the possibility that other requests will not meet that standard.

The first such risk, were K/R decriminalised, is of imperfect consent. The simple case is where P is demonstrably incompetent: he is delusional, and wants to die because he fears the imminent arrival of sadistic interplanetary creatures. This case seems straightforward enough. D ought not to act at the request of a manifestly mad principal, and should remain subject to criminal liability if he culpably so acts. More difficult to assess would be the risk of D's having an interest in the outcome and hence of having an incentive to pressurise P into asking her to act. Obviously, where D is a commercial operator, profitability may depend on processing a sufficient number of cases. But the same worry exists in other contexts, such as purportedly requested terminations within a family setting.

The second risk concerns situations of potential 'misalignment'.[14] When a person, whose life hitherto suggests a commitment to various continuing projects, attempts suicide or other grievous self-injury after a personal setback (say, the collapse of a marriage or career), temporary intervention may be appropriate in order to secure time for reflection and reconsideration.[15] As with the risk of defective consent, were the current general criminal prohibition of K/R eliminated, how could it be assured that P is afforded an adequate opportunity for reflection, when he requests A to terminate his life?

---

[12]   Above, §§ 4.3(a), 5.2(a).
[13]   See also the discussion of over-inclusion in § 11.4(c).
[14]   Above, § 9.2(a).
[15]   cf. above, § 9.3(a).

a.   A Place for Criminal Law?

In the context of direct suicide attempts, while our conclusion supported certain limited paternalistic interventions by the state, it did not, save at a *de minimis* level, extend to deployment of the *criminal* law.[16] Whereas the quantum of penal censure and punishment should be desert-oriented, direct paternalistic intervention should normally be concerned with safeguarding P's future life opportunities and her second-order preferences. Normally, we therefore argued, only civil or administrative measures should be invoked against the would-be self-harmer.

With respect to killing *another* person at the latter's request, however, the ground for this restriction falls away. Granted, the aim of intervention may be unchanged, i.e. to secure P an opportunity to consider her future options in a more reflected way. But the criminal law's prohibition is not directed at P, whose interests are being protected. Rather, it is directed against D, who acts on P's request to be killed. This creates logical space to argue that D acts wrongfully if he harms P while failing to give sufficient opportunity for reflection and reconsideration.[17] In turn, the criminal law's condemnatory character would no longer be out of place: the criminal prohibition would address D's choice to injure P by acting on his request without providing him with this opportunity.

b.   Over-inclusion

Notice, however, that since the underlying basis of the wrong is unchanged, the rationale for intervention continues to support only a criminal-law norm of limited temporal scope, according to which D may be required to refrain from implementing P's request until she has ensured that P genuinely consents, and has sufficient chance for reflection. The wrong, in effect, lies in acting precipitately. Consequently, unless some further reason can be found why the involvement of a second person is significant, outright prohibitions of K/R generate a serious problem of over-breadth. In § 11.4(c) we argue that avoidable over-inclusion should indeed be eschewed—which militates here in favour of K/R prohibitions of limited scope, designed to proscribe requested killings only where P lacks an adequate opportunity for reconsideration.

But is over-inclusion avoidable? Could safeguards of this nature really be provided in a criminal statute? Presumably, a waiting period could be ensured by requiring a minimum period to elapse between P's initial

---

[16]   Above, § 9.4(a).

[17]   Or indeed, as the German courts have held, if D's homicidal act is not motivated by respect for P's request: see Neumann, above n. 10.

request and its implementation by D. Sufficient opportunity for reflection, however, may be more difficult to ensure. (Has P been spoken to, in a sensitive manner, about his reasons for wishing death? Has he been given adequate opportunity to consider, and perhaps discuss, his longer-term preferences, and what his other options might be?) Often, as in family contexts, there is a concern with the unstructured character of the setting, which makes it difficult for a legal system to evaluate whether adequate precautions have been taken. How can one, for example, identify the kinds of inducements or pressures to which P was exposed before she requested a family member to terminate her life?

At the same time, D needs guidance too. Faced with a request from P, D runs the risk of serious criminal liability if she complies. In so far as possible, the law should clarify D's legal position so that she is not left uncertain about her options. This is a particular problem where the request occurs in an unstructured setting such as the family. Admittedly, D's position is not impossible. She can always refuse P's request. But it is undesirable that she be driven to refusal simply by a lack of clarity about her possible criminal liability.

These are valid concerns. If they cannot be met, they generate prima facie reasons to criminalise on an over-inclusive basis. We cannot resolve all the practical issues here. It may be necessary to increase the formality of such cases, by implementing certain documentation and counselling requirements.[18] With some ingenuity, it should be possible to frame procedurally based exceptions to the K/R prohibition. And if it is possible, the principle against over-inclusion mandates that we should.

c. The Complexity of Consent

While we accept the force of these evidential worries, it is worth cautioning that, even where there *is* some defect about someone's consent, it does not follow that it should always be invalidated, or that legal intervention is warranted. The state's refusal to accept a purported consent as being effective is itself capable of substantially interfering with the freedoms of the person being 'protected'.[19]

By way of illustration, consider the prosecution of David Jenkins in 2000. Jenkins, a care worker at a London housing project for about 100

---

[18]   Or perhaps even to involve court order mechanisms. Cf., in a different context, *In re A (Children) (Conjoined Twins: Surgical Separation)* [2001] Fam 147.

[19]   cf. A. Du Bois-Pedain, 'Die Beteiligung an fremder Selbstchädigung als eigendständiger Typus moralisch relevanten Verhaltens—Ein Beitrag zur Strukturanalyse des indirekten Paternalismus' in A. von Hirsch, U. Neumann and K. Seelmann (eds), *Paternalismus im Strafrecht; Die Kriminalisierung von selbstchädingendem Verhalten* (Baden-Baden: Nomos, 2010) 33, 42–43.

adults with learning disabilities, had a sexual relationship with one of the residents, a woman with severe learning disabilities who was said to have the mental age of a young child. His acquittal of rape, on the ground that she had 'consented', was criticised by the Royal Society for Mentally Handicapped Children & Adults as 'a fundamental miscarriage of justice against a woman who has suffered long term abuse and emotional torment. ... People with learning disabilities are at risk and often seen to be an easy target by abusers. The legal system is there to protect them, not side with their abusers.'[20]

Yet, in crafting forward-looking criminal prohibitions, we need to think carefully about their implications for those we are protecting. On the particular allegations of this case, Jenkins's behaviour was seemingly exploitative and deserving of punishment. But the way forward is not necessarily just to deem all forms of consent by learning-disabled persons as automatically inoperative. That would be to deny such persons the power to have sexual relations, with anyone, *permanently*.[21] Or, indeed, to do anything that requires a valid consent, such as play contact sports. Perhaps, upon reflection, imposing such a stringently paternalistic restriction *is* the best available response. However, that conclusion is not obvious. It needs to be argued for and not assumed.

In the context of sex, consent is rightly seen as bearing upon the difference between acceptable and wrongful conduct by D. But it is not a kind of password that P can simply choose whether to issue. It is not, in short, a thing. Consent is better thought of as a transactional process by which D's and P's (and frequently others') normative relationship—their respective rights, duties, and the like—is altered.[22] While there are other ways in which normative relationships can be altered,[23] consent is a particularly important method in as much as it permits P to control her situation, bringing it partially under the determination of P's own will.[24] The default position, morally and legally, is that D is not free to have sex

---

[20] 'Care worker's release on rape charge prompts CPS to seek review of law' *The Guardian*, 24 January 2000. For a similar case, see J. O'Hara and H. Martin, 'A learning-disabled woman who had been raped: a multi-agency approach' (2001) 94 Journal of the Royal Society of Medicine 245, where P's abilities are described as 'correlating with a mental age of under 7 years'.

[21] A similar burden is imposed in the UK by s. 30 of the Sexual Offences Act 2003 (sexual activity with a person with a mental disorder impeding choice); compare also its more clear-cut predecessor, s. 7 of the Sexual Offences Act 1956 (sexual intercourse with a woman who is defective), under which Jenkins would certainly have been convicted.

[22] Cf. G. Lamond, 'Coercion, Threats, and the Puzzle of Blackmail' in A.P. Simester and A.T.H. Smith (eds.), *Harm and Culpability* (Oxford: Oxford UP, 1996) 215, 233.

[23] e.g., through the legal system, when injunctions are issued or (say) judicial orders are made affecting the parties' respective property rights and duties.

[24] To that extent, consent is rightly seen as having a naturalistic component, in as much as it is contingent upon an expression of P's will.

with P. But P can change that through her choice. The recognition of consent, therefore, fosters P's autonomy.[25] And its negation depowers her.

Yet consent remains a transactional process. And its validity is a normative conclusion, one that should only be reached when there are reasons to give recognition to P's choice. Those reasons will differ in the context of property transactions from that of personal intimacy; hence the criteria of an effective consent are likely to vary according to the setting.[26]

Sometimes, the value of a purported consent-transaction may be negated, as when P's 'agreement' to sex is induced by threats or abuse of authority:[27] in such cases, we have reason not to treat the consent as effective. Here, the wrong by D and the vitiated exercise of will by P go hand in hand. But this will not always occur straightforwardly. In cases of contracts agreed under duress, for example, D is deprived of the power to give a legally-perfect consent, notwithstanding that she retains the capacity to form her own will; indeed, even if she wants the transaction anyway.[28] There, we have some reasons to recognise consent and some to reject it. If we reject it, P's freedom to alter her normative position is restricted, not in virtue of her own choices but because of D's actions. That is the nature of consent. It is a multi-party process, the validity of which is a normative judgement, and a conclusion about the reach of the state, rather than a physical fact.

Consent and Killing on Request

Whether intervention is warranted very much depends, therefore, on the context. Rape differs crucially from K/R in both the character of the wrongdoing and its inherent consequences. Unlike K/R, in the context of rape, the wrong—of sexual intercourse without consent—derives from the

---

[25] Thus we might have reason to treat a consent as valid even when the activity is, as J. Gardner and S. Shute put it, 'depressingly dehumanizing': 'The Wrongness of Rape' in J. Horder (ed.), *Oxford Essays in Jurisprudence* (4th series, Oxford: Oxford UP, 2000) 193, 209.

[26] In the context of property transactions, for instance, the interests of third parties (who may justifiably rely upon apparent transfers of ownership) are likely to be more important than they are in the arena of personal intimacy. Hence property may pass despite some feature that gives rise to an *in personam* claim against the beneficiary. See A.P. Simester, 'Correcting Unjust Enrichments' (2010) 30 OJLS 579, § 3(b).

[27] Indeed, the latter factor seems to have been present in Jenkins's case.

[28] cf. *Barton* v. *Armstrong* [1976] AC 104, where apparently B would have entered into the contract even had A not threatened him: the consent was voidable. Conversely, suppose that an extreme degree of circumstantial (financial or other) pressure induces P Ltd to enter into a transaction with D Ltd on disadvantageous terms that it would otherwise not have contemplated. In the absence of wrongdoing by D, the transaction is not normally voidable.

nature of P's choice,[29] rather than from an independent harm.[30] The criminal law has no basis for prohibiting sexual intercourse *per se*. With K/R, however, matters are different. Prima facie, the consequence is independently and irreversibly harmful: P's death. Where there is a potentially defective consent, so that P's understanding of the nature of that consequence cannot be assured, the case for intervention is therefore stronger. As we argued earlier in this section, killings in such cases are rightly proscribed.

10.4   APPEALING TO P'S INHIBITIONS: THE THEORY OF *HEMMSCHWELLE*

A number of German authors have argued that a prohibition against requested killing, coupled with decriminalisation of direct suicide attempts, may help assure that P terminates his life only if he has given that option careful reflection and fully wills it.[31] Hence the prohibition against K/R is said to provide an 'inhibition threshold' ('*Hemmschwelle*'), safeguarding against a too-easy resort to one mode of terminating life.

The theory certainly has the attraction of simplicity, and avoids the pitfalls of abstract-endangerment arguments. Unlike the risk-based approach in § 10.3, however, it does not call for temporal limits but favours an outright ban of killing on request, even where P has thoroughly considered the matter. With the greater degree of intervention comes reduced scope for self-determination: the person becomes less free to decide such questions of life or death for himself.

Perhaps, though, we should not be unduly preoccupied with self-determination here. The narrowing of an option is not the same as its elimination, and there is no in-principle requirement that every mode of self-demise be permitted by the state—just as there is no requirement that P be allowed to practice law or drive in any manner he likes. What counts is that P has *adequate* access to options. Particularly if assisting suicide is allowed,[32] it may be thought that the available modes are adequate.

---

[29]   cf. above, § 3.2(a).

[30]   This claim leaves open the possibility that, for some learning-disabled persons, sexual intercourse *is* (especially, psychologically) harmful or potentially harmful: hence the impetus to enact specialised offences such as those mentioned in n. 21.

[31]   C. Roxin, 'Die Abgrenzung von strafloser Suizidteilnahme, strafbaren Tötungsdelikt und gerechtfertigter Euthanasie' in J. Wolter (ed.), *140 Jahre Goldtammer's Archiv für Strafrecht: eine Würdigung zum 70. Geburtstag von Paul-Günter Pötz* (Heidelberg: R.v. Decker's Verlag, 1993) 177ff; K. Chatzikostas, *Die Disponibilität des Rechtsguts Leben in ihrer Bedeutung für die Probleme von Suizid und Euthanasie* (Frankfurt a.M.: Peter Lang, 2003).

[32]   See n. 10 above.

Two lines of argument are advanced in support of the 'inhibition-threshold' argument for proscribing K/R. The first is, in effect, evidential. The earnestness of P's wish to die is, assertedly, better demonstrated if P must undertake the final step of exiting life himself, and thus must overcome natural human inhibitions against self-destruction. The second is incentive-based. A spur to further reflection is built into the permitted options, in as much as, by being denied the supposedly easier option (of having someone else terminate his life), P may be induced to reflect more carefully before resorting to the remaining but more intimidating option of killing himself directly.[33]

Both lines of argument are problematic. As we saw in § 10.3, the evidential argument tends to promote over-inclusion. One should not underestimate the very real terror that some individuals have of personally hurting themselves; a person may truly wish to die, yet still recoil from leaping off a building or ingesting a lethal potion. For such people, a K/R prohibition may effectively preclude their choice to die altogether. Additionally, by conflating failure to commit suicide with unwillingness to die, the argument ignores the problem of severely disabled persons, for whom suicide may be impossible.[34]

a. Barriers *in Terrorem*

But there is also, we think, a more fundamental objection to the 'inhibition-threshold' arguments than over-inclusion. In § 9.2(a), we noted the importance of treating individuals with respect, something grounded in the right of human dignity and from which coercive measures tend to detract. Sometimes, as we have seen, such coercive measures are susceptible of justification, provided the justifying aim is compatible with the aspiration to fully responsible agency. But the *Hemmschwelle* analysis departs from that perspective. It operates with incentives and disincentives that do *not* address the actor as a moral agent, a person capable of acting for considered reasons related to the quality of his own existence. Instead, it uses a crude deterrence mechanism. The strategy is to preclude more palatable methods of exit (namely, through the instrumentality of another), in the hope that with only the more unpleasant and frightening form of exit available, the person will not himself attempt an end to his life. In short, the theory relies on *intimidating* the would-be suicide into continuing his life.

---

[33] In Germany, with or without assistance. See, e.g., Chatzikostas, above n. 31.
[34] Perhaps *Hemmschwelle* advocates might negotiate this case by means of a special provision.

In our view, even coercive interventions should operate *through* giving reasons, thus being respectful of individuals' capacities for moral agency.[35] Notwithstanding that the intervention limits the person's self-regarding choices, as paternalistic measures necessarily do, it should treat the addressee as one capable of considering how he should deal with his life. Imposing a procedure fashioned to encourage reflection upon one's reasons for wishing to die (as contemplated in the previous chapter), and perhaps to consider alternative ways of living, can meet that standard. But seeking similar outcomes simply by playing upon a person's inhibitions, aversions, and fears does not. As such, it is an illegitimate form of paternalism.

b.   Ambitions for State Intervention

Other concerns too are raised by the incentive-based approach of the *Hemmschwelle* theory. Consider the case of a pop musician, who has enjoyed the fame, wealth, and popular acclaim of such a life, but whose music and persona have now gone out of fashion. He thinks that death is preferable to a life of obscurity and frustration. However, direct suicide frightens him: he wants someone else to perform the deed. Our pop singer case is an example where a change in circumstances leaves the person with frustrated life goals. He retains his ordinary capacities to function, but wants to terminate his existence because his central aims now have little chance of being fulfilled. The example may be esoteric, but there are many more ordinary cases of this character: the painter disabled by bad eyesight from pursuing his work; the elderly person who wishes to continue living independently but must now move to a nursing home. Such persons have more conventional lives and focal aims than our musician—which, because of a major setback, they can no longer fulfil.

Despair is not inevitable. The pop singer may undergo a life transition: for a satisfactory existence, he needs to find new priorities for his life. If he has no easy way of ending his life, he may have an incentive to try out another, perhaps more modest, way of living. While he may feel alienated and disoriented for a while, he may eventually find new interests and activities to replace his old. Have not many ex-celebrities found alternative, tolerable and often successful, ways of living? And have not many ordinary people also found alternatives, once their former way of life became no longer viable?

This is deep variety of paternalism. Intervening with the purpose of securing changes in someone's life goals would, by definition, not comport with that person's existing longer-term preferences. (Our hypothetical pop

---

[35] cf. the discussion in Chapter 1; also § 10.1 above.

musician, for example, never had any stable preference to go on living once his fame ended.) In turn, this generates a worry concerning the proper ambitions for state power. Is it an appropriate aim of coercive state intervention to encourage citizens to reorder their life's priorities, even if the ultimate aim is thereby to make possible a mode of existence they would come to think satisfactory?

There is a fine distinction to be drawn here, between (coercive) interventions with the purpose of changing someone's goals, and interventions with the purpose of encouraging him to reflect upon what his own goals should be. Fine, but crucial. The latter is compatible with respect for the individual as an autonomous moral agent; the former is not. As we argued in the previous chapter, the state may foster and support valuable options and forms of life but, save in respect of incompetent actors, it should not impose them. It is for this reason that temporary interventions may be permissible; but, to the extent that the rationale of the *Hemmschwelle* approach is to utilise compulsion-based measures to bring about changes in P's life goals, it is unjustified.

10.5   EXISTENCE WITHOUT LIFE-CHANGES, AND THE BURDEN OF SELF-REFORM

A person barred from exiting his life may come to find new goals, a new career, and renewed fulfilment. But this is a contingent matter: some will prosper, others will not. Not everyone will benefit from the prohibition. Sometimes, P will limp on with unchanged life goals, in an unfulfilled and tiresome existence. In such cases, merely inducing a prolongation of P's life is not necessarily in his interest, in as much as he is compelled to continue an unfulfilled existence. The result may be not even a neutral outcome, but a negative one, where the prohibition achieves no paternalistic success.

This concern is internal to the paternalistic argument. The case for temporary intervention is that P might be deprived of a degree of freedom now for his own subsequent good. But that good must involve a mode of living from which P can eventually derive satisfaction. Where P continues to be alienated from his life, the intervention cannot be described, from P's point of view, as a success.[36] Well-being depends not only upon the successful pursuit of the goals that make one's life worthwhile; it depends also upon those goals' being one's own. When a person is forced indefinitely to live an unchosen life, from which he continues to derive no satisfaction, ultimately the intervention should not be characterised as beneficial. Thus, according to the internal objection, compelling P to live a

---

[36] cf. § 9.4.

mode of life which he has not chosen and continues to regard as unacceptable does not qualify as a successful form of paternalism at all.[37]

Admittedly, the internal objection does not deny that such a mode of life could be valuable. Perhaps P is a generous and kind person, and the lives of others are enriched by his conduct and ongoing existence. It is not a misuse of language to describe such a life as 'good', or in a sense as 'successful'. But it is not, *for P*, a good life. Even accepting that part of the state's role is to safeguard the means by which citizens can live good lives, what counts as a good life must depend, ultimately, upon the preferences of the person himself. The goals, aims, and affiliations with which a person identifies ultimately should be up to him, not the state. Perhaps P's identifications are misguided. His goals and affiliations may be worthy of criticism. We don't have to endorse them. But we still have to respect P. And this constraint is particularly important in the context of coercive, long-term state intervention. Provided P does no harm to others, we should not use the criminal law in particular to impose a 'good' life, on the basis of which citizens might be compelled indefinitely to pursue modes of living that they themselves find repugnant.

a.   Risks and Standard Cases

Note, too, that it is not just the long-term outcome that is problematic: in some cases, even temporary interventions may impose significant burdens. Suppose, for example, that P has come to suffer from major disabilities that greatly impede his activities, even quite ordinary ones. Let us say, for example, that he experiences a grave loss of physical mobility. He is precluded by his condition from many everyday pursuits, and can undertake others only with much additional effort and to a substantially reduced extent. With necessary commitment and determination, he nevertheless may succeed in achieving a satisfactory existence, and many persons so situated do just that. Yet, if he does not wish to undertake such efforts, even the temporary restraint upon K/R contemplated in § 10.3 can impose enormous burdens; making P live what is, in his own eyes, an unwelcome existence.

This is, of course, part of the calculus of temporary interventions. The long-term prognosis of such cases is inherently uncertain. One who has had an accident leaving him seriously disabled, for example, may over time adjust to his situation and find a new, or renewed, purpose in life. So the potential long-term gains may be worth the considerable, short- or

---

[37] Some writers would none the less describe such an intervention as being 'paternalistic' in character, meaning that it is *motivated* by concern for P's supposed interests. In that case it would be misguided paternalism.

medium-term, burdens along the way. A permanent proscription, however, risks imposing a protracted joyless existence; a result that cannot be justified on paternalistic grounds.

But perhaps there is also a calculus of permanent interventions? Suppose we knew that 80 per cent of would-be suicides would, if prevented from terminating their lives, find new fulfilment. Would this matter?

Were we speaking of the Harm or Offence Principles, it would. Other-affecting criminalisation decisions necessarily proceed in terms of standard effects and risks, accommodating the likely extent and severity of the effects that an act is likely to generate. But in those contexts, the involvement of potential victims is not voluntary and, consequently, the state's involvement is not entirely voluntary either.[38] In respect of other-affecting behaviour, the prospect for conflict between individuals tends to place the state in the position of referee, negotiating the boundaries of permissible social inter-action. It cannot simply decline to intervene, since—in a situation of conflicting actions and interests—that establishes a rule too.

The same line of reasoning seems weaker in the context of paternalism, which involves no such impact on other persons. Here, the state's interven-tion is not that of a referee. The responsibility for unsuccessful interven-tions therefore falls directly, and solely, on the state. It cannot be justified as a matter of trade-off between the competing interests of other persons, through which a middle path must be negotiated.

10.6   PARTIAL DECRIMINALISATION AND THE CONCEPT OF THE LIVING STANDARD

So far, we have argued for the importance of self-determination in paternalism cases. We have also argued that permanent prohibitions of killing on request may under some circumstances fail to serve the person's interest—wherefore they cannot be justified in paternalist terms. However, the chances of a full repeal of the K/R prohibition seem remote, at least for the foreseeable future. Consequently, it is worth considering the case for partial decriminalisation. Are there specific contexts where legalising K/R is a matter of especial importance?

In Germany, there has been continuing scholarly interest in a 1986 proposal to permit K/R in restricted form. The 'Alternative Draft on Assisted Suicide' would allow killing-on-request in certain cases involving

---

[38] This point is at the heart of the distinction between indirect paternalism and ordinary situations of harm to others, which fall to be dealt with under the Harm Principle. Cf. § 10.3(c) above.

'the termination of unbearable suffering'.[39] This proposal addresses the situation of deteriorating terminal patients who are experiencing intense physical pain. In such situations, it is suggested that an exception be made to § 216 of the German Penal Code, such that the lives of those suffering individuals may be terminated at their request. This approach is narrow in scope, but has the merit of illustrating dramatically what is problematical about invoking paternalistic justifications in such cases. The proposed amendment to § 216 implicitly acknowledges that, under certain circumstances, constraints on terminating a person's existence through the instrumentality of another would condemn that person to further grievous suffering. The concern is not just that criminalisation intrudes upon P's autonomy, but that making P live under such adverse circumstances may not actually be in his interest.

A case can be made, in our view, for extending the logic of partial decriminalisation beyond the narrow scope of the Alternative Draft—beyond the Draft's scenario of intense pain and imminent death—to further situations where prohibiting K/R may condemn someone, against his will, to continuing a burdensome and unwanted existence. On a partial decriminalisation approach, however, what conceptual tools can be offered for determining the law's reach? If one allows an exception to § 216, on what basis could its scope be delimited?

One possible approach to these questions draws upon Amartya Sen's concept of the 'living standard'.[40] The living standard, in Sen's account, is not concerned with a person's individual, actually-experienced sense of well-being. It addresses, instead, the *means* and *capabilities* that a person has for achieving quality of life. Someone has, for example, an adequate standard of living when she has the resources, material and immaterial, that would ordinarily provide for a satisfactory level of well-being. Severe deprivation, on this perspective, can be defined as a person's suffering a serious deficiency of such standardised means and resources.[41]

While a living-standard analysis does not offer a litmus test for deciding the scope of decriminalisation, it may help to furnish a generalised approach to the question when a person's quality of life has deteriorated sufficiently to represent profound deprivation. In the present context, it permits a focus on those deprivations and disabilities that make ordinary living tasks unusually difficult or burdensome, and which therefore tend to make prohibition of K/R and assisted suicide so onerous for one who has a

---

[39] J. Baurmann et al., *Alternativentwurf eines Gesetzes über Sterbehilfe* (Stuttgart: Georg Thieme, 1986).

[40] A. Sen, *The Standard of Living* (ed. G. Hawthorn, Tanner Lectures in Human Values; Cambridge: Cambridge UP, 1987) 20.

[41] Note that, although the concept is the same, it is used here in a context which differs from that of gauging and ranking crime seriousness, as discussed in A. von Hirsch and N. Jareborg, 'Gauging Criminal Harm: A Living-Standard Analysis' (1991) 11 OJLS 1.

settled preference not to live such a life. The governing idea is that the exception would cover those cases where P suffers such a severe deficit in the resources ordinarily needed to manage his life that dealing with everyday tasks becomes extremely difficult; and where P explicitly and unequivocally expresses the wish for an end to his life.

By its nature, the living standard involves a durational element: that P's disability can be expected to be protracted. Suppose that P is in a full body cast in hospital for a few months. This interferes *for the time being* with most activities P might wish to undertake. But the prospect remains of a full life thereafter. Like harm itself, the living standard is a prospective matter. It is only long-term deprivations and disabilities that count as undermining a person's prospects for well-being.

Admittedly, creating such an exception to the K/R prohibition has limitations. It excludes the other class of cases that we addressed earlier in the chapter, of persons who are not disabled but who have focal aims for their lives that they can no longer fulfil.[42] Moreover, it generates complexity. Cases of serious deprivation would need to be distinguished from lesser ones. Legal standards concerning the scope of the K/R exception would need to be developed, and these may not be easy to formulate even with the assistance of the living-standard conception. The source of the latter problem, however, lies in the case for criminalisation, such as is made by supporters of the *Hemmschwelle* theory. To the extent that K/R and assisted suicide prohibitions are justified on paternalistic grounds, it is those justifications themselves that generate the need to distinguish exceptions where no such paternalistic aim is realistically achievable. Were the general prohibition eliminated (or subjected to the temporal limits discussed in § 10.3), the pressure would ease to define an exception, with its attendant problems of conceptualisation and formulation.

Two important provisos must be re-emphasised here. First, as we said in § 10.5 and § 10.5(a), persons with major physical disabilities may and often do achieve fulfilling lives. Our concern here is with a person who demonstrates a settled preference *not* to live such a life. Moreover, as we said in §§ 10.2–10.3, that wish must be demonstrated by an explicit and considered request, made by one with the capacity for reflective choice. This discussion is not intended to offer support for any kind of involuntary euthanasia.

---

[42] Above, § 10.4(b).

10.7   KILLING VERSUS OTHER FORMS OF SELF-INJURY

The living-standard approach is also useful in the context of a second set of issues for indirect paternalism, arising where P requests D to inflict serious physical injury upon him falling short of death.

Both killing and maiming adversely affect a person's capacities for well-being. However, they do so in different ways, and the distinction is not merely one of degree. Life is *a prerequisite*, rather than constitutive, of well-being. This helps to explain why people sometimes claim that there are modes of life worse than death. Strictly speaking, the claim is not quite right: death is not a mode of life at all, so that qualitative comparisons do not lie. But one element of truth in the claim is that, on a qualitative scale, being dead is not at the bottom (or anywhere else). Unlike the slave, for example, someone who is dead does not have to live an unfree or unwanted life.

This distinction between killing and other forms of self-harm introduces a point of divergence into the arguments concerning indirect paternalism. Serious injury (e.g. amputation) is a form of harm that is likely constituently to set back one's well-being.[43] While death is certainly also a harm—a profound one, in that it deprives the individual of all opportunities for well-being—P does not have to live with the consequences. Hence there may be reasons to prohibit maiming on request which go beyond those that militate against K/R.

One might seek to express this distinction purely in terms of autonomy: the consequence of serious self-injury is that P must now live a life that lacks an adequate range of opportunities. Yet cutting down one's own options need not be, in itself, problematic. Indeed, it is part of the point of autonomy that a person can mortgage her own future—that she can make present choices which limit her future options. Many successful forms of life require a commitment, made in advance and often with no guarantee of success, that forecloses other potentially fulfilling paths. The budding tennis player may have to choose between professional sport and law, the would-be actor between drama school and university. And so on. There is nothing wrong with this. We cannot keep open all our options. A successful life frequently, even typically, requires that we do not.

So describing the difference in terms of autonomy is not entirely illuminating. More helpfully, it concerns the prospects of a successful life. Ordinarily, serious self-injury is likely simply to worsen P's ongoing quality of life, without being a constructive step toward P's opportunities for future well-being. It is intelligible that sacrificing future options can be justified by the welfare goals that autonomy itself serves. But not, ordinarily, in this case.

---

[43]   Absent, we assume, medical justification.

As such, there do seem to be additional reasons for intervention to save P from arranging with another to inflict serious injury on him, reasons that are in the long term compatible with P's well-being and dignity. Moreover, a case can even be made for intervention on the basis of 'misalignment',[44] in as much as the probability is substantial that, having to live with the consequences, P will come to regret them.

A living standard test can help to capture these rather extreme cases, without extending the realm of intervention to anything that might happen to be bad for P—for instance, prohibiting sale and supply of pizzas and other fatty foods. It does so by helping to distinguish serious and long-term injury from lesser forms of self-harm. Having one's arms or legs amputated will have a drastic and permanent effect on a person's standardised means and capabilities for having a good life. Arranging the infliction of lesser forms of injury need not.

This last point reinforces the conclusion that inflicting petty injury on another in the context of sexual play, as in *Brown*,[45] ought not to be criminalised. The objection is not just an issue of privacy concerning people's sexual preferences and conduct. It is also that, where no serious injury is involved, the interest-based claim that is necessary to a paternalist argument is not made out; hence, the paternalist argument should have no traction.

10.8 IN CLOSING

Paternalism, direct and indirect, involves a trade-off between autonomy, understood as self-determination, and well-being. Autonomy need not require us to respect a person's bad choices. Still less does autonomy require us to respect bad choices that set back that person's well being. We don't have to facilitate or encourage those choices. But considerations of human dignity require us to respect that person's *right* to make bad choices. We should not coerce them not to do so. Their free choices do not acquire value just by being free: the value lies in their being free to make them.

This injunction is most compelling in respect of persons' second-order choices, about what kind of life they want for themselves. As Joseph Raz has put it, 'we cannot deny them sovereignty over defining for themselves what their way of life is, and what is integral to it.'[46] Living with goals one

---

[44] Above, § 9.2(a).

[45] [1994] 1 AC 212; above, §§ 3, 4.3(b).

[46] J. Raz, 'Free Expression and Personal Identification' in *Ethics in the Public Domain* (revised ed., Oxford: Oxford UP, 1995) 146, 162. Neither does Mikhail Valdman argue that we can 'outsource' decisions about our deep commitments: M. Valdman, 'Outsourcing Self-Government' (2010) 120 *Ethics* 761.

rejects is a recipe for a failed life. We rightly hope that those who do not value their lives will, in time, come to embrace an altered way of living. But, in the end, it should be up to them. The criterion for paternalistic intervention should, therefore, reside ultimately in P's own preferences. This is the basis of legitimate paternalistic interventions in cases of miscalculation or misalignment. And it applies even to profound choices, such as seeking death. If, having been constrained to continue his existence for a period in order to give him the opportunity for reflection, P still finds his life not worth living, he ought to be entitled to find an exit without hindrance.

We have not sought in this chapter to give a comprehensive account of indirect paternalism. Indeed, perhaps the main lesson of Part IV is that there are no universal answers. More generally, nothing in our analysis rules out the possibility of complementary reasoning. Paternalistic rationales can supplement, and be supplemented by, other penal rationales. Those rationales can augment each other in building a case for criminalisation. But different rationales come with different internal structures and constraints. In this book, we have sought to bring out some of those differences, and to investigate more closely what kinds of cases have to be built by those who favour using the criminal law to regulate the lives and choices of their fellow citizens.

Part V

Drawing Back from Criminal Law

11

Mediating Considerations and Constraints

BROADLY SPEAKING, WE can classify into three types the criteria that must be met if the creation of an offence is to be morally legitimate. There must, first, be a prima facie *positive* case for state prohibition, in that the activity at issue must be sufficiently problematic to warrant intervention. In general, as we have seen in Parts II–IV, this requires that the conduct leads to significant levels of harm and/or offence suffered by others, although there may also be limited occasions for paternalistic intervention.

Secondly, certain mediating constraints should be taken into account. While we have considered mediating factors already in the context of the more particular positive grounds of criminalisation such as harm and offence, some of these constraints cut across those more particular grounds, to limit the criminalisation of conduct more generally. These mediating constraints lack the priority of the wrongfulness requirement discussed in Chapter 2. Neither do they operate as complete bars to prohibition of the relevant conduct. None the less, their importance is not contingent on such factors as the degree of riskiness of the conduct, or the extent of the harm that may result.[1]

Finally, at the level of implementation, further *negative* constraints must also be met. In particular, it must be shown that the *criminal* law offers the most appropriate method of regulation, being preferable to alternative methods of legal control that are available to the state; and the practicalities must be considered of drawing up offence definitions in terms that are effective, enforceable, and meet rule of law and other concerns. It may be, if these negative constraints cannot be met, that the state ought not to criminalise certain types of conduct, notwithstanding that initially there is a positive case for doing so.

Over-criminalisation, thus, can result from more than one source. Most obviously, it may arise from the proscription of conduct that is, morally

---

[1] Feinberg uses the term 'mediating principles' to refer to a wider variety of factors, including the likelihood and magnitude of the eventual harm. We have separated these different kinds out for the sake of clarity.

speaking, ineligible—of conduct that should not be considered for criminalisation at all, because it fails to cross the kinds of thresholds discussed in Parts II through IV above. Very often, however, the case against criminalisation is less straightforward: that while the conduct is in principle eligible for prohibition, the criminal law is not in this case the right response. In this chapter, we offer thoughts concerning this second type of case, outlining some of the general limiting factors that should also be considered before the decision to criminalise is taken.

11.1 PRIVACY

Most European penal systems prohibit an adult from engaging in sexual intercourse with young adolescents. In Germany, for example, sexual conduct with a person aged under 16 years is a crime when committed under circumstances of exploitation of the affected person's insufficient capacity for sexual self-determination.[2] The aim of the prohibition is to prevent the harm of sexual abuse of young adolescents not sufficiently mature to give proper consent. However, there are categorical exemptions from criminal liability for cases in which the alleged perpetrator is himself a young person: the German prohibition becomes inapplicable if the actor is aged 21 years or younger (unless his sexual partner is *very* young—under 14 years).[3] In France, the crime of consensual sex with minors excludes defendants who are themselves under the age of 18.[4] In Italy, the equivalent offence also exempts young persons, unless the partner is aged under 14 or there is more than three years' difference in age between them.[5]

Why these exemptions? Why not, instead, follow the approach of recent English legislation,[6] which prohibits virtually all sexual activity with or among young adolescents, even where the activity occurs among persons of similar ages?

One conceivable ground for restricting the scope of this prohibition could be that less criminal harm or risk is involved: the greater danger of sexual exploitation of young adolescents comes from adults, with their greater seeming power and authority. Another possible ground might be pragmatic concerns about enforceability: given the prevalence of sexual

---

[2] StGB § 182(3).
[3] StGB § 176(1).
[4] *Code pénal* art. 227–25.
[5] *Codice penale* art. 609 *quarter*, para. 5.
[6] Sexual Offences Act 2003; confirmed in G [2008] UKHL 37. For analysis of this legislation, which criminalises sexual activity with someone under 16 even when the defendant is of the same (or lower) age, see Spencer, 'Child and Family Offences' [2004] Crim LR 347.

activity among young teenagers, an English-style blanket prohibition of sex among them would be largely unenforceable, except on a discriminatory basis.[7]

These are valid points. However, they do not fully reflect what would be most problematic about such a general criminal prohibition: namely, a concern about personal privacy. In a free society, a person's intimate life should be a matter for disposition by the person herself, in large part free from coercive intervention from state authorities. This claim of privacy holds not only for adults but for teenagers also: their intimate lives should likewise be substantially free of state intrusion. Even if wrongs might result—and some sexual contacts among teenagers may indeed involve undue pressure or influence by one of the parties—it remains important to assure young persons of a significant degree of autonomy in their intimate choices. To ensure this broad autonomy, the intimate lives of teenagers, as well as adults, should prima facie be exempt from state scrutiny and the intervention of the criminal law. Here, then, is a mediating ground for withholding criminalisation that is based on notions of privacy.

Of course, such privacy constraints are not absolute bars to criminalisation. Sexual intercourse with a *very* young person may properly be criminalised, notwithstanding that the alleged perpetrator is also relatively young. German law recognises this, by proscribing sexual intercourse with someone aged 13 years or younger, even where the sexual partner is under 21. The force of privacy claims can be overcome when the harm or risk of harm is sufficiently great; and very young adolescents are particularly vulnerable to exploitation and abuse. The claim to an intimate sphere protected from state scrutiny and intervention becomes less plausible, moreover, the younger is the person involved.

Consider another illustration. In most modern penal systems, it is a criminal offence for a person to obtain money or property of another through false pretences.[8] However, there generally exists no comparable prohibition concerning the sexual or intimate sphere, or indeed for other day-to-day social and personal interactions. The person who initiates a romantic or sexual relationship with another by misrepresenting his motivations, feelings, skills, achievements, resources, or marital status behaves reprehensibly, but he commits no crime under existing law. Should prohibitions concerning criminal misrepresentations be extended to such contexts? We think not.[9]

---

[7] As Spencer notes (*ibid.*), 'So far are these provisions … out of line with the sexual behaviour of the young that, unless they provoke a sexual counter-revolution, they will eventually make indictable offenders of the whole population.' See also below, § 11.4(c).

[8] cf. Germany's Penal Code, § 236; Fraud Act 2006 (UK).

[9] Although one British commentator has proposed such an extension: J. Herring, 'Mistaken Sex' (2005) Crim LR 511. This is not to assert that misrepresentations should

One basis for withholding criminal liability might be practical and instrumental, of avoiding specious claims: the criminal courts should not become a battleground for numerous estranged couples, charging each other with criminal misrepresentation. Such instrumental reasons, however, do not fully express what appears to be the most persuasive reason not to intervene—namely, the protection of personal privacy. To ensure broad autonomy within the intimate and other personal spheres, even various forms of misrepresentation should be exempt from state scrutiny and intervention. When A and B commence an acquaintanceship potentially involving sexual intimacy of some kind, it is important to its naturalness and spontaneity, and to their sense of control over their own intimate lives, that they feel free to address each other in terms that they choose, without fear that claims they have made about themselves might be subject to inquiry by the state's penal authorities. Here, again, the mediating ground for withholding criminalisation is based on notions of privacy.

a.   A Constitutional Matter?

Nowadays, privacy claims sometimes have a constitutional character, and may operate to invalidate some acts of criminalisation. While that development is welcome, it does not exhaust the role of privacy (and similar mediating) considerations. Privacy is applicable as a mediating value whether or not it is a constitutional trump. The extent to which constitutional privacy limitations apply to a given piece of legislation depends on the character and scope of the privacy guarantee within the constitution of a particular jurisdiction.[10] Constitutional constraints, moreover, concern themselves to a large degree with the restriction of legislative authority. There may well exist privacy concerns that are important enough to warrant legislative abstinence—the legislature's opting in principle against criminalising the conduct—without necessarily possessing such especial importance as to warrant the constitution's barring the possibility of such legislation categorically. Thus, even if an applicable constitutional privacy guarantee is not so sweeping as to invalidate criminal prohibitions of sexual contacts among teenagers (or misrepresentations among adults in the sexual sphere), the concern for privacy generally could provide the legislature with a principled (mediating) reason for not enacting such prohibitions.

---

never vitiate a partner's consent, especially when they relate to D's identity; but the matter is more nuanced than Herring allows. For discussion, see *Simester and Sullivan* § 21.1(iii)(d)–(e).

[10]   It seems that in the UK, the constitutional role of privacy in the criminal law is a limited one, at least according to the majority of the House of Lords: G [2008] UKHL 37.

11.2   REGULATORY ALTERNATIVES

Suppose that we can establish a positive case for prohibiting some activity through the criminal law. We need then to ask whether, nonetheless, there are reasons *not* to criminalise.[11] One important element of the enquiry involves considering whether the criminal law is the most appropriate tool for regulating the activity. In particular, the advantages and disadvantages of using the criminal law should be measured against those accruing to alternative regulatory mechanisms. As a general rule, if some other form of state intervention falling short of criminalisation would be effective to regulate the conduct at issue, that alternative should be preferred.

a.   Tax

On occasions in the past, various Western governments have attempted to restrict alcohol consumption through criminal prohibition. The results were disastrous; sales and consumption went underground, creating a black market ripe for extortion and racketeering. Nowadays, control is exercised via licensing arrangements and tax. One of the standard functions of a tax on liquor sales is to reduce consumption by raising the price of alcohol.[12] The mechanism is thus one means by which the state can influence the behaviour of citizens, without resort to outright prohibition. An explicit rationale for tobacco and alcohol duties is to provide a disincentive against smoking and drinking and, at least in part, to ensure that the price of cigarettes and alcohol reflects the true social cost (including healthcare costs) of these products.

Consumption taxes of this sort do, of course, affect options. If the price of cigarettes is increased, smokers will have less money left for other activities. In the absence of offsetting income tax rebates, such measures also tend to have a regressive effect on the poor. As such, tax measures are both an improvement on criminalisation in so far as they are less coercive and preserve more options for citizens and, at the same time, less equitable than criminalisation in so far as they are likely to affect different socio-economic classes differently.

---

[11]   Thanks are due here to Bob Sullivan, co-author of *Simester and Sullivan*, from which parts of the following discussion are drawn.

[12]   Usually to inhibit choices, as in the case of tobacco; but sometimes to support them. One reason for providing benefits (which can be thought of as negative taxes) and/or tax credits to parents, for example, is that children are, *inter alia*, public goods; hence the state has reason to subsidise part of the cost of their upbringing.

b.   Tort Law

A second option is for the state to regulate an activity by means of a statutory or common law tort. Intervention through the civil law involves a substantial intrusion into people's lives, but remains less coercive than the criminal law: there is no arrest, no imprisonment, and no record of a criminal conviction. In some situations, therefore, the creation of a statutory tort may be a useful alternative to criminal sanctions. This is especially so when considering compliance incentives for large corporations. An industrial accident costing many lives might lead to a company being fined some tens of thousands of pounds: that same company might be far more concerned by the millions of pounds it may incur in tort damages.

It is not a complete alternative. Tort law effectively prices rather than prohibits; it lacks the mandatory and condemnatory character of the criminal law, and requires a claimant with adequate resources to bring a legal action. Moreover, in many instances tortfeasors may be able to defray the costs of liability by means of insurance.

c.   Other Mechanisms

There is a variety of other methods for addressing harmful or offensive behaviour, including advertising and licensing. A classic example of the former is the publicity campaign against drink-driving, which has been instrumental, alongside the criminal law, in bringing about a change in public attitudes toward the wrongfulness of driving while under the influence of alcohol. Although not appropriate to all varieties of wrong (for example, there is normally no need to polemicise against performing acts that are already widely perceived as *mala in se*), education and advertising can in some instances raise awareness of the potential harmfulness of an activity, in circumstances where that harmfulness was previously not well understood.

Licensing is also a familiar form of modern regulation. The performance of many activities—e.g. running a public house, possessing a firearm, and even driving—requires a licence. All of these activities involve risks of harm, either direct or remote. But each is valuable, and it may be inappropriate, because of the social costs, to forbid the activity outright. So the activities are permitted, but only under conditions prescribed by licensing systems. The criminal law, in turn, remains in the background to prohibit persons from carrying out the activity without, or in breach of, the licence. Licensing systems represent a significant limitation of individual liberty, but fall well short of outright prohibition. Moreover, they offer a more flexible tool than do generalised criminal statutes, since the terms of each licence can be adapted to specific cases by the authorities responsible for administering that licence.

An increasingly common device for the monitoring of specialist commercial activities is the establishment of activity-specific regulatory agencies equipped with powers to impose sanctions, including disqualifications and financial penalties, for norm-violating behaviour. These kinds of agencies are now particularly familiar in the financial services industry and the delivery of public utilities. There are certainly dangers in these kinds of regulation,[13] not least of which is the risk of having a punitive system without the protections embedded in the criminal law. As a means of administering standards of conduct for commercial actors, however, they can offer a useful alternative to the use of strict-liability criminal offences, while not displacing the role of the criminal law in more serious forms of wrongdoing.[14]

On occasion, it may even be appropriate for the state to allow remedies of self-help by private citizens. The common law, for example, permits abatement of a public nuisance. If a barrier is erected across a public footpath, any person lawfully using the path is permitted to remove the barrier, provided that she can do so without causing a breach of the peace. Similarly, if an inanimate item belonging to P is on D's land without permission, and there causes damage or disruption, D may freely move the item and indeed retain it until P compensates her for the loss suffered.[15] These kinds of measures which bypass the legal process altogether can be simpler and more efficient.

d. Specialised Prohibitions

A familiar distinction exists between criminal prohibitions applicable to the general public and those which deal with more specialised activities. This distinction, too, supplies an important way of narrowing the range of criminalisation. Restricting the number and scope of proscriptions of

---

[13] See, e.g., J. Braithwaite, *Regulatory Capitalism: How it Works, Ideas for Making it Work Better* (Cheltenham: Edward Elgar, 2008) 4: 'the reciprocal relationship between corporatization and regulation creates a world in which there is more governance of all kinds. *1984* did arrive.'

[14] cf. R. Macrory, *Regulatory Justice: Sanctioning in a Post-Hampton World* (London: Cabinet Office, 2006). The Macrory Review recommends introducing into English law a civil-law regime of non-fault monetary administrative penalties. The difficulty any regulatory system of this kind faces, of course, is to avoid issuing judgments involving censorious hard treatment—in which case, the process becomes in-substance criminal: cf. *Öztürk* v. *Germany* (1984) 6 EHRR 409.

[15] The remedy of distress damage feasant. Another example is recaption, whereby D may seize from V's possession goods that rightfully belong to D.

general applicability helps to ensure fair warning,[16] safeguarding the ordinary citizen against liability that she cannot readily anticipate. Suppose that aerosol sprays can be manufactured using different forms of chemical reagent, but that certain kinds of spray are likely to damage the ozone layer and create long-term health hazards. Criminalising the purchase or possession of those particular sprays would remain problematic: it may be asking too much of the ordinary citizen to understand the different effects of each kind of aerosol.[17] A company that specialises in manufacturing aerosols, by contrast, is in a better position to familiarise itself with the applicable rules. Restrictions on manufacture will, of course, affect the options of citizens indirectly, making it more difficult to purchase certain kinds of aerosol sprays (perhaps the most effective ones). But the means of prevention are considerably less coercive of ordinary people than is threatening them directly with punishment.

Distinguishing between general and special penal measures also alleviates the problem of cumulative prohibitions. Generally applicable prohibitions, when too frequently adopted, impinge together to restrict the life and freedom of the ordinary citizen. If, for example, the use of each hazardous product is generally proscribed, an ordinary person would have to inform herself of and observe a broad band of constraints. Special prohibitions are different, in that persons are not likely to engage in more than one or a few specialties. The aerosol manufacturer would have to concern itself with the restriction on sprays, and the lobsterman about the restrictions on undersize catches, but few are likely to need worry about both kinds of prohibition.

The difference seems especially pertinent in the context of remote harms. There are, we suggested in § 5.2(d), certain basic duties of cooperation which each person owes in his capacity as citizen. These concern such matters as the payment of taxes, administration of justice, etc., and would support generally applicable prohibitions. Beyond these, however, responsibility for cooperating to prevent remote harms should typically be role-related. On a role-based conception of imputation, the duty of cooperating to forestall a given eventual risk falls naturally on those most closely associated with the activity involved—on the specialists in that activity. A firm which manufactures aerosol sprays makes the consequences of that activity its business, in a way that a mere occasional user does not.

The general-special distinction exists in the law already, in the sense that there are a great many more specialised regulations and prohibitions than

---

[16]   Below, § 11.3.

[17]   This concern about fair warning might be met by giving adequate publicity to the prohibition. However, that remedy could only be achieved selectively: a few measures aimed at remote harms might be publicised, but the more numerous the proscriptions are, the less feasible it would be to provide the public with any real notice.

there are prohibitions of general applicability. What we are suggesting, however, is that the distinction be reinforced in the following respects. First, the scope of general prohibitions should be kept reasonably narrow. Not only should the potential for harm be imputable to the actor, as discussed in Part II, but the conduct should be sufficiently obviously reprehensible for its wrongness to be apparent to ordinary persons. Included would be *mala in se* crimes of ordinary victimisation,[18] plus infringement of certain basic and well-understood public duties, such as paying one's taxes. By contrast, the scope of prohibitions affecting special-ised activities need not be so greatly restricted. No requirement of *obvious* reprehensibleness need be imposed. Accumulative harms (for example, those affecting the environment) could be addressed, and abstract endan-germents could be proscribed. However, basic imputation constraints should continue to apply: if good reasons (including reasons relating to public obligation or duties of cooperation) cannot be supplied for holding the actor accountable for the prospective eventual injury, then the prohibi-tion should fall. Intervening-choice risks, for example, should ordinarily be considered suspect as grounds for criminalisation.

e. On the other Hand: No *Ultima Ratio*

The criminal sanction is the most drastic of the state's standard tools for regulating the conduct of individuals. It represents the most severe infringe-ment of a person's liberty, and should be deployed only where there is clear social justification for doing so. However, while alternative methods of regulation, if practical, should *normally* be preferred to the criminal law, there are certain advantages in resorting to criminalisation. Unlike any other area of law, the criminal law systematically condemns activities (through prohibition) and persons (though conviction and punishment). And sometimes such condemnation is appropriate. The public significance of enacting that some activity is a criminal offence can, on occasion, militate in favour of criminalisation. If used selectively, criminal prohibi-tion can be a tool for communicating to the public that the prohibited activity is wrongful and must not be done.

As we noted in our discussion of the Harm Principle, and as Feinberg's account allows,[19] the potential for harm can supply a positive reason to criminalise. It is not just a licensing condition. For this reason, we doubt

---

[18] Most of these would, in any event, involve actual harm or concrete endangerment. Note that the argument for the restriction proposed in the text is grounded in considerations of onerousness and fair warning; it is not that the conduct must be extra-legally wrong (cf. the discussion of *mala prohibita* offences, in § 2.3(b) above).

[19] Above, Chapter 3.

the Continental principle of *ultima ratio*,[20] that criminal law should only be used as a last resort, when other mechanisms are ineffective. In any civilised society, murder *ought* to be condemned through the criminal law. A swingeing tax will not do, however effective it might be as deterrent; because it does not articulate the normative status of murder. This preference for criminal law holds, we think, for all serious *mala in se* wrongs.

There are also some practical benefits, especially when contrasted with tort law. For one thing, tort law requires a victim. But certain activities, e.g. forms of environmental pollution, may wrong no identifiable victim with standing to sue. Alternatively, even where there are particular victims, the aggregate harm to individually wronged plaintiffs may be less than the overall social cost that the activity imposes. Relying exclusively on tort law is likely, in these cases, to result in under-enforcement.

Additionally, given that the state pays the costs of investigating, prosecuting, and punishing offences, it may be better placed to address wrongs than are private individuals through tort. Suppose that my next-door neighbour throws a stone through one of the panes in my greenhouse, which it will cost £100 to replace. It is likely to be impractical for me to pursue her through the law of tort. But a criminal prosecution requires only my time. In this respect, criminal regulation by the state may augment the rule of law, through increasing the consistency with which legal rights are enforced in like cases, rather than leaving the matter to irregular enforcement by individual claimants.

11.3   FAIR WARNING

Even where the creation of offences to regulate an activity is justified in principle, the enactment itself may not be. It is beguilingly easy for a government to misuse criminal law as a convenient means of social ordering. The criminal legal system, in seeking to secure benefits to society at large, can be a major threat of *in*security for individuals charged with the commission of a crime. Accordingly the state, while endeavouring to control and reduce criminal conduct, must be sensitive to the rights and legitimate expectations of those charged with crime.

Central to the protection of those rights and expectations is the rule of law, which demands that those under the state's control should be dealt with by explicit and knowable law, and not according to the discretion of

---

[20]   On which see N. Jareborg, 'Criminalisation as Last Resort (*Ultima Ratio*)' (2005) 2 Ohio State LJ 521; W. Wohlers, 'Strafrecht als Ultima Ratio: Tragender Grundsatz eines rechtstatlichen Strafrechts oder Prinzip ohne eigenen Aussagegehalt?' in A. von Hirsch, K. Seelmann and W. Wohlers (eds), *Mediating Principles: Begrenzungsprinzipien bei der Strafbegründung* (Baden-Baden: Nomos, 2006) 54.

state (including judicial) officials. As such, the rule of law embodies a cluster of legal values, including certainty, clarity, and prospectivity, which have at their heart not merely the constitutional premise that government should operate under the law, but also the ideal that citizens should be able successfully to live within the law, by deriving guidance from the law itself.[21] The criminal law is not there solely to tell police and judges what to do after someone offends, but also to tell *citizens* what not to do in advance. Criminal convictions are not like birthday presents. (Surprise!) People need reasonable opportunities to avoid them. This, in turn, requires that the criminal law must be a well-structured, ascertainable, system of legal rules. The law should give fair warning, by defining the prohibited activity with sufficient certainty. It needs to be understandable, predictable, and not vague.[22] The more clearly defined the offence, the less potential there is for injustice with respect to those whose conduct falls close to its limits. If individuals understand the law, they will be able properly to decide what to do in light of the guidance that the law is meant to provide. Only then do citizens have a fair opportunity to steer themselves clear of criminal liability. If a law cannot be drafted to meet this challenge, it should not exist.

a. Non-material Elements

A legal system, then, should seek to provide as much guidance and predictability as it can. But absolute certainty is not required. This holds particularly for details of the offence specification that are not germane to the defendant's wrong. Normally, these will be non-material elements,[23] such as a jurisdictional requirements or time-limitations. Under English law, if death occurs more than three years after D's homicidal act, her prosecution requires the consent of the Attorney General.[24] Yet this uncertainty generates no objection: it is a condition that does not affect D's substantive guilt with regard to the homicide.

---

[21] J. Raz, *The Authority of Law* (Oxford: Clarendon Press, 1979) ch. 11; E. Colvin, 'Criminal Law and the Rule of Law' in P. Fitzgerald (ed.), *Crime, Justice and Codification: Essays in Commemoration of Jacques Fortin* (Toronto: Carswell, 1986) 125.

[22] cf. *Misra and Srivastava* [2004] EWCA Crim 2375, paras 29–34; *Papachristou v. City of Jacksonville* 405 US 156 (1972) (vagrancy ordinance void for vagueness); *Skilling v. United States*, 130 SCt 2896 (2010) (restrictively interpreting 18 USC § 1346, which makes it a fraud 'to deprive another of the intangible right of honest services').

[23] Compare § 1.13(10) of the Model Penal Code (1985): an element is material where it 'does not relate exclusively to the statute of limitations, jurisdiction, venue, or to any other matter similarly unconnected with (i) the harm or evil, incident to conduct, sought to be prevented by the law defining the offense, or (ii) the existence of a justification or excuse for such conduct.'

[24] Law Reform (Year and a Day Rule) Act 1996 (UK).

b.   Use of Evaluative Components

Explicitness is also, necessarily, compromised in offences that involve open-ended concepts such as 'unreasonable', 'rash',[25] and 'fraudulent'. Similarly, if we drive a car we know, or should know, that we must drive with 'due care and attention'. The phrase sets a standard for a myriad of driving contexts and inevitably must leave an evaluation to the court. If the criminal law is to involve itself with standards of safety, which surely it must, it cannot give a rigid specification of the circumstances under which criminal liability will follow.

Difficulty always accompanies the use of evaluative components within offence definitions. Consider, for example, the imposition of negligence-based criminal liability, through offences which are typically couched in terms of the 'unreasonableness' of the defendant's behaviour. The touch-stone, be it 'unreasonable' or 'negligent', is not susceptible of accurate or formal definition. What is 'reasonable'? Nowhere does the law say, and to some extent the individual must judge the law's standard for himself, and risk the court's disagreeing with him. Such gambles ought to be minimised,[26] and where possible these discretionary terms should be replaced by more concrete definitions of what counts as illegal, and what as legitimate.

This reservation should not be overstated, and it cannot be claimed that such terms deprive individuals of advance warning altogether. The defendant's judgement is not purely a guess: words such as 'reasonable' are not meaningless.[27] We understand them, and know how to apply the implicit judgements they import. The use of broad evaluative terms such as 'negligent' and 'fraudulent' may well provide an acceptable level of guidance where there is a high degree of social consensus about appropriate behaviour in the area of activity under regulation. One may assume that degree of necessary consensus, for instance, in matters of road safety; accordingly a requirement to drive with due care and attention may tell us all we really need to know.

Moreover, evaluative standards are useful. Terms like 'reasonable' and 'dangerous' give the law flexibility to deal with cases that a legislator might not foresee. It is too much to expect a statute to list every single mode of negligent homicide, and meaningful terms like 'unreasonable' save us from being straitjacketed by a rigid specification of the circumstances under which criminal liability will or will not follow.[28] Without such flexibility,

---

[25]   Insolvency Act 1986 (UK), s. 362.
[26]   cf. J. Rawls, *A Theory of Justice* (Cambridge, MA: Belknap Press of Harvard UP, 1971) 239; *Conally v. General Construction Company* 269 US 385 (1926).
[27]   Lucas, 'The Philosophy of the Reasonable Man' (1963) 13 Phil Qtrly 97.
[28]   cf. *Kokkinakis v. Greece* (1993) 17 EHRR 397, para. 40; T. Endicott, 'The Impossibility of the Rule of Law' (1999) 19 OJLS 1.

the law would be impracticable. There will always be matters which require regulation, but where a degree of imprecision is inevitable.

Nonetheless, evaluative terms *are* imprecise, and for that reason, at least in serious crimes, they should normally be used only sparingly and for clear cases of wrongdoing. Sometimes, the imprecision is such that these terms ought not to be used at all. For example, it is doubtful whether there is a sufficient degree of consensus about the acceptable contents of literature, plays, and film to render the standard 'tendency to deprave and corrupt', employed in English obscenity law,[29] a sufficient guide to producers and publishers operating in those fields. If a government wishes to maintain a regulatory presence there, it is better that it regulates by description, expressly identifying those things which are not to be written, photo-graphed, or filmed; preferably through the use of a formal classification system.[30]

c. Crimes of Negligence

The requirement of fair warning is especially relevant to certain kinds of crimes, such as those involving negligence. It is one reason why criminal liability for serious crimes should normally be confined to reckless or intentional wrongdoing. If there were widespread exposure to state inter-ference for inadvertent wrongdoing, it would become much harder for citizens to plan and get on with their lives, without fearing the unforeseen disruption that criminal charges entail.[31] This argument is not insuperable. To the extent that the rule of law enjoins unpredictable interference by the state, liability for negligence is reasonably predictable. None the less, it is a concern militating against criminalisation.

The concern is strongest in the context of offences that are not conduct-specific: typically, in crimes of omission, where the complaint is that the defendant failed to conduct himself in a particular manner; or in result-crimes, where the actus reus involves any act that causes a desig-nated outcome (such as property damage or injury to another). In these contexts, there may be little or nothing about the defendant's conduct to put him on notice that harm is in the offing. Criminal liability in such cases ought to require advertence or, at the very least, gross negligence. Contrast activity-specific injunctions, where the context itself is associated with

---

[29] Obscene Publications Act 1959 (UK), s. 1; *Hicklin* (1868) LR 3 QB 360. While the *Hicklin* test is no longer good law in the USA, it has been explicitly accepted by the Supreme Court that what counts as obscene may vary across states: *Miller* v. *California* 413 US 15 (1973).
[30] As under the Video Recordings Act 1984 (UK).
[31] A point made by Hart: 'Punishment and the Elimination of Responsibility' in *Punishment and Responsibility* (Oxford: Clarendon Press, 1968) 158, 181–82.

specific duties and risks. An aeroplane steward can be expected to remember to lock the door; indeed, this is a standard advantage of framing specialist prohibitions.[32] The same distinction underpins the familiar argument for criminalising negligence regarding a lack of consent in sexual intercourse, since issues of consent are so intimately bound up with the activity that actors are implicitly on notice that such matters are in play.[33]

Much the same analysis applies to constructive liability offences, such as dangerous driving causing death. In offences of this type, some initial or 'gateway' wrong, e.g. dangerous driving, is 'constructed' up into a more serious offence once some further event then occurs (in this case, death).[34] Constructive liability may be legitimate even where there is no requirement that the death be foreseen. Provided the risk of that outcome was intrinsic to the wrongness of the initial conduct, requirements of fair warning have less force in demanding that D be aware of the potential consequences. This is not to suggest that the legal significance of those consequences need not be spelled out clearly and predictably, wherever they affect D's potential conviction or sentence; merely that a mens rea requirement of foresight with respect to such elements need not be specified. D already has a fair opportunity to steer clear of criminal liability.

11.4   FAIR LABELLING AND THE MULTIPLICITY OF CRIMES

Besides *ex ante* guidance, clarity about offence definitions fosters other rule of law goals too. When a crime occurs, justice must not only be done, it must be seen to be done. The law needs precision in order to identify exactly what kind of misconduct has been perpetrated. If he is publicly convicted of 'murder', D should *be* a murderer and not (say) a robber.

At the same time, it would be unsatisfactory for the law simply to label all convicted offenders non-specifically as 'criminals', for that would equate the convictions of rapists with those of pickpockets. The criminal law speaks to the public as well as wrongdoers when it convicts them, and it should communicate its judgment with precision, by accurately naming the crime of which they are convicted. This requirement is known as the principle of fair labelling.[35] The law must make clear what sort of criminal each offender is—what the conviction is *for*. It should communicate this to

---

[32]   Above, § 11.2(d).

[33]   For a fuller discussion of these issues, see W. Chan and A.P. Simester, 'Four Functions of Mens Rea' (2011) 70 CLJ 000.

[34]   See *Simester and Sullivan* § 6.5.

[35]   A. Ashworth, 'The Elasticity of *Mens Rea*' in C. Tapper (ed.), *Crime, Proof and Punishment* (London: Butterworth, 1981) 45, 53–56; G. Williams, 'Convictions and Fair Labelling' [1983] CLJ 85; B. Mitchell, 'Multiple Wrongdoing and Offence Structure: A Plea for Consistency and Fair Labelling' (2001) 64 MLR 395, 398–400; J. Chalmers and F. Leverick, 'Fair Labelling in Criminal Law' (2008) 71 MLR 217.

the defendant, so that he may know exactly what he has done wrong and why he is being punished, in order that his punishment appears meaningful to him, not just an arbitrary harsh treatment.

Not only to the defendant. The law must also communicate the crime with precision to the public, so that it too may understand the nature of D's transgression. Criminal law is not a private colloquy. When labelling D guilty of a stigmatic crime, the state is bound by the public meaning of the words it uses. Thus, for example, Parliament cannot legitimately enact an offence of 'paedophilia', defined as 'parking for more than one hour on a central London street.' It cannot do so because that is not what paedophilia means. Even if all participants in the trial, including D himself, understand that the label is a technical usage, the state may not disregard the rest of its audience, and the effect that such a label will have on D's life. The public record matters. While an employer may have few qualms about hiring a convicted insider-trader as an orderly in a children's hospital, it would be an entirely different matter to contemplate employing someone found guilty of a child sex offence.

a.   Individuating Offences

This demand for precision in labelling presents an important challenge to the possibility of rationalising our mushrooming canon of offences. The more precise the label, the more offences are required. But how many offences do we need? Do we really need to distinguish theft from deception, rape from sexual assault, or between various degrees of injurious assault? Or would it be enough to have just a few generic crimes including, say, violation of another's property right; violation of another's person; damaging the environment; and so on? The answer to the last question is no. While the law may sometimes draw unnecessary distinctions, broad category offences would be inappropriate. Enacting only generic crimes would disregard the fact that, within each field of harmful wrongdoing, each of our existing offences may involve a different wrong, a different harm, or both. It is for this reason that they are rightly separate offences.

In looking to explain and justify the existence of any offence, it is necessary to identify what harm, and what wrong, is addressed by that crime. Obtaining property by deception may, for example, lead to much the same immediate harm as does theft—a diminution of V's resources—but the wrong is different. The thief bypasses ordinary mechanisms for allocating and transferring property. The deceiver exploits them, and induces V to make the transfer herself. Thus deception is not inconsistent with V's proprietary rights in the same way that is theft; as such, the two are rightly distinguished by criminal law.[36]

The need to make these distinctions follows from the principles of fair warning and fair labelling. Both principles require that each offence is labelled and defined in such a way that it conveys to citizens an accurate moral picture of the prohibited conduct, one that is not misleading, vague, or over-generalised. Offences should, so far as is practical, reflect meaningful distinctions in the public mind between different types of culpable wrongdoing. This mandates that they are drawn up in such a way that they capture, and differentiate, significant differences in the harmfulness, wrongfulness, and/or culpability of various types of action.

By way of illustration, the distinctions between murder, maiming, and criminal damage are significant because the harms (and indeed the wrongs) at stake are quite different; and the moral resonances of those differences are sufficient to warrant enacting separate offences. Attempted murder, too, is rightly distinguished from murder because of the difference in resulting harm. Likewise, although the harms of theft and of criminal damage are similar, the manners in which they are inflicted involve two different forms of wrongdoing; forms that are sufficiently distinct in the public mind to warrant independent recognition by the criminal law.

The same need to individuate wrongs also explains why we should not combine arson and vandalism into a single crime of criminal damage, as once was proposed by the Law Commission for England and Wales.[37] These offences, again, involve two different types of wrongdoing, and the communicative function of the law would be impaired were the law to blur the difference.[38] Occasionally, too, there may be a case for distinguishing between two harmful activities on the grounds of culpability. An assault that is negligent with regard to its consequential risks to life typically lacks the culpability of an assault that is reckless about those same risks—and, if ever worthy of being criminalised as a form of a homicide (which we doubt), ought surely to be a separate offence and not lumped in with murder or reckless manslaughter.

At the same time, not every difference is worthy of capture. Structurally, individual offences can only be justified as a distinct form of criminality if they capture a distinctive harm or wrong. Moreover, distinctions between different harms and wrongs will only acquire salience for a criminal justice system if to override the distinctions will send misleading or incomplete

---

[36] For elaboration, see A.P. Simester and G.R. Sullivan, 'On the Nature and Rationale of Property Offences' in R.A. Duff and S. Green (eds), *Defining Crimes: Essays on the Special Part of the Criminal Law* (Oxford: Oxford UP, 2005) 168, 188–90.

[37] Law Commission Working Paper No. 23, 'Malicious Damage' (London: HMSO, 1969) para. 22.

[38] J. Gardner, 'Rationality and the Rule of Law in Offences Against the Person' [1994] CLJ 502, 504–06, 512–20.

communication, either (*ex ante*) as guidance to potential offenders or (*ex post*) from the fact of conviction, or will suppress considerations that should inform the kind and range of sentence. Thus, even though many US states follow the old common law in drawing a rudimentary distinction between petty and grand larceny, nobody would suggest that there should be a much more refined scale of theft offences, graded in minute detail (say, theft of less than £50 value; theft of less than £100 value; theft of less than £200 value; and so on). Excessively specific offences risk clogging the trial process with unmeritorious technical argument, and obfuscating the moral clarity of the law's communications.

At least in the context of non-specialist activities such as property offences, people (both *ex ante* and *ex post*) need to know the law's requirements in gist and not precisely. As such, meaning is better conveyed through publicly shared moral distinctions that are broadly rather than narrowly significant, provided those broader distinctions communicate an adequately nuanced statement of the prohibited wrongdoing. The degree of specificity that the law should adopt when distinguishing various harms and wrongs is, therefore, a trade-off that depends in part on the range of moral differentiations informing the public imagination. The fragmentation of the particular must be balanced against the vagueness of the general.

b.   Offence Classification and Scope

Focusing on the rationale of each offence also has significant implications for their scope and classification. For example, many wrongs that arise in property-related contexts, such as exploitation or unfair competition, are not themselves proprietary wrongs and should not be categorised as such. Insider trading is not theft. It is not really a property offence at all. Rather, it is a covert transactional wrong of exploiting market conditions through unequal access to information. D does not violate V's property rights in the shares. He buys them. But he cheated.

So too for blackmail, which under English law is a (substantive-inchoate) property offence, in that D's benefit, or the loss he seeks to impose on V, when he makes an unwarranted demand on V fortified by menaces, must be a gain of money or property.[39] But a closer examination of the harm and wrong of blackmail shows that this scope is unconnected to its rationale. The restriction to money or property is, normatively speaking, arbitrary. The wrong of blackmail has no connection to the sorts of wrongs addressed by an offence such as theft. Consider a case where D and V are employed by the same company. D threatens to expose V's

---

[39] Theft Act 1968 (UK), s. 21.

criminal past to the company's management unless V makes regular payments to him from her salary. This might be described as the dishonest appropriation of property belonging to another and, therefore, under that description, a case of theft. But to describe the conduct in those terms is to miss the mark. From the perspective of the victim, this is something very different from finding a purse missing from her desk, however much money was in the purse. The pressures inducing surrender to these threats may well be, according to the circumstances, enormous, and succumbing may well entail a form of life that comes close to servitude. It is D's preparedness to put his victim through that experience—to subjugate V to his will—which is the essence of his wrongdoing. Blackmail, therefore, is in truth a serious offence against the person even where the threat is one of exposure rather than violence. The wrong of blackmail is committed by making the (conditional) threat, *whether or not* any property ultimately is transferred. Moreover, the same wrong is perpetrated even if the condition has nothing to do with payment; if, say, D threatens exposure unless V fires a colleague or herself resigns. It is this wrong, together with the need to protect citizens from unjustified coercion by others, which brings black-mail within the scope of the Harm Principle independent of any propri-etary character that, at least under English law,[40] it may happen to possess. Perhaps the English limitation is designed to narrow the practical scope of the offence: but the *concept* of blackmail is free of property.

c. Over-inclusion and Discretionary Enforcement

Specificity of drafting has an additional dimension, in that more narrowly defined crimes are less likely to lead to discretionary enforcement. Wherever an offence is over-inclusive, so that it requires selective prosecution, the liability of defendants is, in effect, remaindered to the decisions of officials—creating the risk of unfair, inappropriate, or potentially even discriminatory prosecutions. Thus Anti-Social Behaviour Orders have become a technique—not intended by Parliament—for use against prostitutes and beggars.[41] And, in the absence of any statutory provision creating an exception for young persons in the Sexual Offences Act 2003,[42] prosecutions may be launched against children for consen-sual sexual activity with other children,[43] notwithstanding an assurance

---

[40] Contrast the Crimes Act 1961 (NZ), s. 237 (as amended).
[41] E. Burney, '"No Spitting": Regulation of Offensive Behaviour in England and Wales' in *Incivilities* 195, 206. See further Chapter 12.
[42] See also above, § 11.1.
[43] e.g. *R(S)* v. *DPP* [2006] EWHC 2231 (Admin); *D* [2006] Cr App R (S) 330; *C* [2006] All ER (D) 293.

by the Government, when bringing the legislation forward, that this would not occur.[44] It is the boy who is typically prosecuted even though his partner is equally liable.[45]

In practice, the use of over-inclusive legislation, reliant on filtering through discretionary prosecution, is common. This is especially true of the public-welfare regulatory sphere, where regimes of strict liability offences are administered by enforcement agencies which, in practice, tend to use the prospect of strict liability as a discretionary bargaining tool in securing compliance by potential defendants.[46] Typically, prosecutions are brought only in cases where the accused was actually at fault.[47] Indeed, as a matter of legal doctrine, they should be brought only where doing so is in the public interest;[48] as Parker J observed in *James & Son* v. *Smee*, 'Where legislation, as here, throws a wide net it is important that only those should be charged who either deserve punishment or in whose case it can be said that punishment would tend to induce them to keep themselves and their organization up to the mark....[49]

Unfortunately, the lack of public interest in a prosecution is not, as such, a defence. Consequently, defendants are on occasion found guilty of offences even though, in the view of the court, a prosecution should not have been brought.[50] This dependence on dispensations by the enforcement agency puts at risk the rule of law, in so far as it leaves the prospect of criminal conviction to the discretion of enforcement officers. Wherever it is possible to frame prohibitions in a manner that is not over-inclusive, that

---

[44] 'The Government considers the discretion of the prosecutor is key to ensuring that clause 6 is used proportionately and the Government intends to make this clear during the passage of the Bill in Parliament. In exercising his discretion as to whether or not to prosecute under clause 6, the prosecutor must always consider whether there is a public interest in prosecuting and must also, by virtue of the Human Rights Act 1998, consider whether a prosecution would be compatible with Article 8. ... Where the sexual activity is genuinely consensual, is low level sexual activity and involves two children close to the age of 13 and of a similar age to each other, the Government expects that, even where this comes to the attention of the authorities, it is almost inconceivable that it will be in the public interest to bring a prosecution.' Home Office Memorandum (reprinted), Joint Committee on Human Rights, *Twelfth Report* 9 June 2003, Appendix 2.

[45] e.g. C (2009) 173 CL & JW 303.

[46] See, e.g., K. Hawkins, *Environment and Enforcement: Regulation and the Social Definition of Pollution* (Oxford: Oxford UP, 1984); B. Hutter, *The Reasonable Arm of the Law: Law Enforcement Procedures of Environmental Health Officers* (Oxford: Oxford UP, 1988). Prosecution is, it seems, a last resort: K. Hawkins, *Law as Last Resort: Prosecution Decision-Making in a Regulatory Agency* (Oxford: Oxford UP, 2002).

[47] G. Richardson, A. Ogus, and P. Burrows, *Policing Pollution: A Study of Regulation and Enforcement* (Oxford: Clarendon Press, 1982).

[48] Code for Crown Prosecutors (www.cps.gov.uk) § 6; *Smedleys Ltd* v. *Breed* [1974] AC 839, 856 (Viscount Dilhorne).

[49] *James & Son* v. *Smee* [1955] 1 QB 78, 93. In our view, even this passage is too permissive (in the second limb).

[50] e.g. *Smedleys Ltd* v. *Breed* [1974] AC 839; *Hart* v. *Bex* [1957] Crim LR 622; cf. *James & Son* v. *Smee* [1955] 1 QB 78.

should be done. Convenience is not a good enough reason to expose citizens to unjustified, discretionary, and unpredictable criminal liability for doing something that is not wrong. And we should not delegate to prosecutors the job that belongs to Parliament.

No Absolute Bar

That said, we should emphasise our belief that over-inclusive criminal proscriptions are not always ruled out. As we noted in §§ 2.3(b) and 5.2(a), frequently it will be impracticable to draft an offence that encompasses all, and only, instances of the conduct at which the prohibition should ideally be aimed. Thus setting a maximum road-speed limit criminalises some cases of driving at higher speeds even where there is no significant risk of an accident. In principle, such over-inclusion is capable of being justified; *provided* the offence is no more extensive than is required to achieve its (otherwise legitimate) objectives.[51]

Even if necessary,[52] however, the extent and significance of the over-inclusion should be taken into account when assessing whether the prohibition is justified overall—or whether, instead, an *under*-inclusive version should be preferred. Within the Standard Harms Analysis,[53] the sacrifice of additional, harmless options counts in the normal way as a factor militating against enactment of any proposed offence.

An over-inclusive prohibition may therefore fail to be justified for two types of reasons. First, the over-inclusion may not be necessary—it may be practically possible to draft a more focused version of the offence, one more tightly confined to proscriptions of the conduct at which it is ultimately targeted. Secondly, taken as a whole, countervailing factors such as the social value of the conduct prohibited by the proposed offence, and the degree of intrusion upon citizens' lives that it would involve, may defeat the positive case for the prohibition, which under the Standard Analysis is grounded in the gravity and likelihood of the potential harm. In either case, a less inclusive offence may (or may not) be justified.

11.5 PRACTICAL CONSTRAINTS

Finally, in addition to rule of law constraints, a variety of other considerations should be taken into account before concluding that criminalisation

---

[51] To this extent, we agree with Douglas Husak's presumption against over-inclusion: *Overcriminalization* 154ff. However, we do not adopt Husak's preferred solution for risk-prevention offences (*ibid.*, 174): see above, § 5.1(a), especially at n. 9.

[52] For a nuanced take on what can make over-inclusion necessary, together with a helpful note of the literature, see S. Buell, 'The Upside of Overbreadth' (2008) 83 NYULR 1491.

[53] Above, §§ 3.2(a), 4.2.

through the proposed offence is the right response. Without aiming to be comprehensive, we sketch some of those factors here.

a. Side-effects of Criminalisation

Suppose a clearly drafted law is proposed that criminalises the knowing failure to disclose one's HIV-positive status to a sexual partner. One thing to consider before enacting such a law is whether it will have the effect of deterring those persons who are most at risk of contracting HIV from being tested. By not knowing their status, they keep themselves outside the scope of the offence—but without advancing the underlying aim of the offence, which is to protect their partners. In these sorts of cases, the legislator should consider whether, in effect, enacting the proposed law will do more harm than good.

It has not escaped judicial notice that one of the concerns about the use of drugs is consequential criminality: the prospect that drug users will steal, deal in drugs, or commit other crimes in order to finance their habit.[54] But a responsible legislator might also think that these considerations argue for *decriminalisation*.[55] The price of illegal drugs is high *because* the drugs are illegal—which artificially constricts supply. If not illegal, no doubt users would need less money to pay for their habits, leading (it may be thought) to a significant reduction in consequential crime. Compare, too, the era of alcohol prohibition in the USA, which led to an upsurge in violent conflict between gangs involved in the black market that arose to replace the licit trade. If criminalisation of an activity is likely to produce such undesirable consequences as these, that is a powerful reason not to prohibit.

b. Pragmatics of the Criminal Justice System

A proposed enactment might also be rejected for reasons of implementation.[56] In particular, the offence needs to be capable of being administered, by enforcement authorities and prosecutors. Ideally, it will be specified in clear and unambiguous terms, so that (as well as giving fair warning to citizens) those responsible for its administration will be able to use the new

---

[54] *Aramah* (1982) 4 Crim App R (S) 407, 408–09 (Lord Lane CJ). See more generally P. Alldridge, 'Dealing with Drug Dealing' in A.P. Simester and A.T.H. Smith (eds), *Harm and Culpability* (Oxford: Oxford UP, 1996) 239.

[55] D. Husak, *Legalize This! The Case for Decriminalizing Drugs* (London: Verso, 2002).

[56] For general discussion, see H. Packer, *The Limits of the Criminal Sanction* (Stanford, CT: Stanford UP, 1968); N. Morris and G. Hawkings, *The Honest Politician's Guide to Crime Control* (Chicago, IL: University of Chicago Press, 1970).

law with predictable outcomes. Further, the terms it uses will cohere with and not reinvent existing legal concepts, facilitating understanding by professionals within the criminal justice system.

Another consideration is policing. The detection of some proposed crimes may be too difficult: this is one reason not to criminalise, say, smoking in bed as a fire hazard. Alternatively, crimes may be detectable only by invasive methods of surveillance; it needs to be considered to what extent the power to use such methods is desirable. There is also the question of cost: how expensive are the means of investigation? Will enforcement agencies be able to afford to monitor the new offence? Will effective policing of the offence require additional resources and legal powers? Criminal justice is very expensive. It is surely the case that, if every instance of harmful or potentially harmful activity were criminalised, administration of the criminal law would be not merely cumbersome but unaffordable. This being the case, even conduct that is prima facie eligible for proscription should be subject to a 'priority' test. Is it important enough to warrant the cost, or are there other offences that are more important? The same test should, incidentally, be applied to existing as well as proposed offences, especially as the modern world evolves: perhaps some older criminal laws no longer justify their continued existence, and the resources they soak up should be redirected toward regulating new forms of wrongdoing.

A third issue is efficacy. Save perhaps in the context of very serious wrongs,[57] there is little value in creating offences that are unlikely to reduce the incidence of harms or wrongs that they are designed to address; as Bentham put it, 'where it cannot act so as to prevent the mischief.'[58] This constraint follows from the instrumental aspect of the criminal law, as a regulatory system directed at *preventing* harm or offence. To the extent that it cannot be expected to do so, the justification for its enactments largely falls away.[59] Moreover, such offences risk diminishing public respect for the criminal law as a distinctive form of regulation.[60]

There are many other issues that must be resolved when a new offence is created (mode of trial, evidential requirements, sentencing options, etc.). We cannot do justice to them all here. The key point is that, even though a prima facie case can be made in favour of criminalising an activity, e.g. because it is harmful to others, it does not follow that criminal legislation is the best response. Other forms of intervention need

---

[57]   cf. § 11.2(e) above.

[58]   *Introduction to the Principles of Morals and Legislation* (1789) ch. 13, esp. § 13.3.

[59]   The importance of this point is rightly emphasised in Husak, *Overcriminalization* 145–53.

[60]   cf. Kadish, *Blame and Punishment: Essays in the Criminal Law* (New York: Macmillan, 1987) 23, 57.

to be considered; sometimes, it may be best not to legislate at all. The criminal law is a powerful, expensive, and invasive tool. It should not be deployed lightly.

12

Two-step Criminalisation

12.1 CONSTRAINING THE CRIMINAL LAW

WE HAVE OBSERVED that, by contrast with much of the rest of the legal system, the criminal law has a distinctively moral voice. Criminal prohibitions and sanctions convey censure: both *ex ante* of the proscribed activity, which is marked out as something that ought (as well as must) not be done, and *ex post*, through conviction and punishment of any individual who is found nonetheless to have perpetrated that activity. As such, the criminal law should, and generally does,[1] couch its prohibitions in a manner designed to engage with agents capable of moral deliberation.[2] It does not merely coerce; it also makes a moral appeal to citizens to desist. Its sanctions are not merely instrumental; they also express disapproval of the offender's wrongful conduct.

Given the criminal law's censuring character, and the potential severity of its sanctions, it is appropriate for the creation and implementation of criminal prohibitions to be subject to important safeguards. Some of these safeguards have constitutional status, and constrain the legislatures of particular jurisdictions. But all of them are, at the very least, norms to which any decent state should aspire. In this book, we have argued that the scope of prohibitions should be limited to certain kinds of wrongful conduct, in particular those activities satisfying a properly defined Harm Principle or Offence Principle. In the previous chapter, we also claimed that prohibitions should give fair warning. They should be specified and labelled in terms that are sufficiently clear and unambiguous—so that citizens have suitable advance guidance about the law's requirements, and so that a conviction accurately names what it is that the defendant has done wrong.

In addition to those constraints, others may be mentioned. First, the specification of prohibitions should include appropriate culpability elements; usually, by requiring mens rea and making the offence subject to

---

[1] But not always, for example in some cases of strict liability: A.P. Simester (ed.), *Appraising Strict Liability* (Oxford: Oxford UP, 2005).
[2] cf. the discussion in Chapter 1.

exculpatory defences.[3] Secondly, it is necessary to ensure a fair trial: when a person is accused of violating criminal prohibitions, stringent procedural and evidential limitations must be observed, including high standards of proof, in order to ensure the integrity and fairness of the criminal justice process.[4] Thirdly, an appropriate range of penalties should be specified. Upon a finding of guilt, the determination of the resulting sanction should observe proportionality requirements regarding the relation between crime-seriousness and sanction severity.[5]

These further constraints are familiar, and have attracted a considerable literature. To them, however, we want to add two more. One is a constraint of *representative authority*. Criminal prohibitions should be deliberated upon and adopted by a representative body. Where significant sanctions potentially are involved, this should be a high-level representative body, such as the national legislature. Where the particular content of a prohibition is delegated to some lower-level body, any determination of that content should be directed and closely guided by the terms of the delegation. The other is a constraint of *generality*. Prohibitions should be general in character: they may not single out the behaviour of particular persons for proscription.

Taken together, the foregoing requirements play a crucial role in safeguarding the liberty of citizens, both in preserving their freedom of lawful action and in ensuring that they are not undeservingly convicted and punished. But because they can make it difficult to impose sanctions on supposed wrongdoers, there has been a recent temptation to resort to short cuts, most notably *two-step prohibitions* (TSPs). These involve the issuance of (nominally) civil prohibitory orders against persons who have been found engaged in, or who are expected to engage in, undesired conduct. A breach of the order then becomes a criminal offence. The content of the order can vary considerably: it may require the actor to cease and desist from further conduct of the same kind, or it may contain other substantive content, including access prohibitions designed to preventing him from entering certain places where he might engage in that kind of conduct or other conduct that is deemed undesirable. In the United Kingdom, for example, Parliament has introduced the device of an Anti-Social Behaviour Order ('ASBO').[6] In gist, where D has been committing 'anti-social' acts, the local council or chief of police may apply to court for an ASBO restricting D's future behaviour. If D then contravenes the order, he commits an offence imprisonable for up to five years.

[3] See, e.g., *Simester and Sullivan* ch. 5.
[4] See, e.g., P. Roberts and A. Zuckerman, *Criminal Evidence* (2nd ed., Oxford: Oxford UP, 2010).
[5] Above, § 1.1; *Proportionate Sentencing* ch. 9.
[6] Crime and Disorder Act 1998, s. 1; Anti-Social Behaviour Act 2003.

12.2 THE NATURE OF TSPS

We shall consider the appropriate preconditions and content of TSPs in § 12.3. But perhaps their most important feature is their structure. A standard instance of criminal wrongdoing has only one temporal location:

t_{Std}: proscribed behaviour by D occurs, leading to criminal prosecution (predicated on proof of conduct at t_{Std}).

By contrast, the TSP mechanism operates on a three-incident timeline:

t_0: qualifying behaviour by D occurs;

t_1: TSP Order issued (predicated on proof of D's behaviour at t_0, but forward-looking);

t_2: conduct by D occurs in contravention of the TSP, leading to criminal prosecution for violation of the order (predicated on proof of conduct at t_2).

The order made at t_1 is, formally, a civil mechanism, but it is backed up by criminal sanctions. As such, the TSP supplies a means of bringing the criminal law into play (at t_2) in circumstances where obtaining a criminal conviction is difficult at t_1—either because a successful prosecution is impractical, or because the anti-social behaviour at t_0 was not by itself a crime. Effectively, the TSP order (TSPO) supplies a criminal-law bridge between t_0 and t_2. It connects the underlying behaviour at t_0, which supplies the original impetus for the state's intervention, to the possibility of prosecution and punishment at t_2.

a. Why the Desire for TSPs?

The temptation to deploy TSPs arises from two main practical problems about the use of traditional criminal-law prohibitions to regulate some varieties of offensive conduct. The first concerns difficulties of proof, especially in cases of harassment and intimidation. The rules of evidence pertaining to civil processes are less stringent than those governing criminal procedure—for example, they permit the use of hearsay evidence. By adopting a system of civil regulatory orders, the legislature evades the procedural and evidential challenges of using existing criminal law mechanisms to regulate conduct, especially where offenders allegedly intimidate victims and other potential witnesses.[7] Even where the conduct complained

---

[7] See, e.g., *Clingham* [2002] UKHL 39, paras. 16–17 (Lord Steyn): 'Often people in the neighbourhood are in fear of such young culprits. In many cases, and probably in most, people will only report matters to the police anonymously or on the strict understanding that they will not directly or indirectly be identified. ... Unfortunately, by intimidating people the

of at t_0 itself constitutes a criminal offence, the evidential constraints upon criminal trials may mean that, in practice, it cannot easily be prosecuted. In such circumstances, the TSP mechanism means that the court can nonetheless make a civil order against D. In turn, D may be convicted if, at t_2, he breaches the terms of that order (where proof of that breach is subject to rules of criminal procedure and evidence in the normal way). The advantage to prosecutors is that the conduct prohibited by the personal order granted at t_1 may be different, and easier to observe and prove, than was the conduct originally complained of at t_0.

(We note, in passing, a partial response to this argument: that, if the difficulty is procedural, a better and less dramatic approach would be to look for a procedural solution, for example by rectifying difficulties in the laws of evidence concerning hearsay.[8] It may also be worth while to develop and improve community-based witness protection programmes, and to direct greater resources toward fostering a more vocal community, one better-placed collectively to resist intimidation.[9] To the extent that these solutions are effective, they seem preferable to the much more radical and problematic device of the TSP.)

The second perceived difficulty is that the criminal law will obviously be unavailable where the initial conduct at t_0 is not itself a criminal offence. In this case, the impediment is not procedural but substantive. Moreover, it may not always be appropriate to criminalise the initial type of conduct directly. Sometimes, it is only *repeated* instances of an act (which is by itself lawful) that warrant prohibition where, in isolation, the act itself does not deserve to be criminalised. *In aggregate*, a series of minor evils may generate a significant harm to the quality of others' lives.

This possibility finds acknowledgement already in English criminal law. The Protection from Harassment Act 1997, for example, prohibits 'a course of conduct' that is calculated to harass or annoy others. An isolated wrong will not do. In a different context, the common law offence of conspiracy to defraud proscribes conduct by two persons that, when done alone, is not illegal.[10] Both of these offences are controversial, and it is no surprise to find that the concept of criminal harassment lacks satisfactory

---

culprits, usually small in number, sometimes effectively silenced communities. Fear of the consequences of complaining to the police dominated the thoughts of people: reporting incidents to the police entailed a serious risk of reprisals.'

[8] Described by Lord Steyn as 'inflexible and absurdly technical' in *Clingham, ibid.*, para. 18.

[9] It is also worth mentioning that there are specific offences of witness intimidation, in s. 51 of the Criminal Justice and Public Order Act 1994 and ss. 39–41 of the Criminal Justice and Police Act 2001 (the latter pertaining to civil cases).

[10] *Simester and Sullivan* § 15.3.

definition.[11] It verges on the impossible to specify, in general terms, the factors in such cases that turn merely exasperating conduct into a serious wrong. The TSP offers an alternative means to regulate such conduct. It can be used to bring within the criminal ambit a course of conduct where single instances thereof are not suitable for criminalisation; either because they are insufficiently serious wrongs in isolation, or because they are not by themselves wrongs at all, and become wrongs only when done repeatedly and for certain motives. Here, the TSPO offers a flexible—one might say, tailored—means to regulate ongoing courses of conduct without the need to prohibit every instance of that conduct, performed by anyone, *tout court*. As such, its use could even help to avoid over-criminalisation— provided it is used legitimately, and not in abrogation of the objections and limitations to be set out in § 12.3.

b.   The Dual Character of TSPs

The TSPO is designed to be, and is formally, a civil order—it is this very feature that allows TSPs to bypass constitutional limitations such as those governing standards of proof in criminal trials. But what sort of order is the TSPO *in substance*? Is it civil or criminal? This question affects not only the moral debates raised by the TSP mechanism, but also the extent to which the protections of the European Convention on Human Rights (ECHR) are available against TSPOs. From the point of view of the protections contained in the ECHR, domestic law's designation of the proceedings as 'civil' is not dispositive of the matter.

It seems clear that the issuance of a TSPO at t_1 is not *formally* a finding of criminality or a criminal disposal. There is no conviction or formal condemnation of the sort that the criminal law involves.[12] Neither is there anything of the criminal-record consequences that a conviction imports. As the House of Lords observed of one such order in *Clingham*, 'the purpose of the procedure is to impose a prohibition, not a penalty.'[13] The possibility of criminal sanctions such as conviction and imprisonment arises only in respect of *future* conduct, not in respect of the conduct that gave rise to the TSPO. By way of elucidating this point, their Lordships drew a distinction between the making of a TSPO and the disposition,

---

[11] See, e.g., C. Wells, 'Stalking: The Criminal Law Response' (1997) Crim LR 463; *Simester and Sullivan* § 11.8.

[12] Compare, in *Clingham* [2002] UKHL 39, para. 28ff, the discussion of the three categorising criteria laid down in *Engels v. The Netherlands (No. 1)* (1976) 1 EHRR 647, 678–9, para. 82: (a) domestic classification; (b) nature of the offence; (c) the severity of the potential penalty.

[13] *Clingham* [2002] UKHL 39, para. 68.

considered in *Steel* v. *UK*,[14] of imprisonment for refusing to be bound over. Of the latter mechanism, Lord Steyn noted that 'there was an immediate and obvious criminal consequence'—imprisonment—to be imposed in respect of a past wrong, not (unlike the TSPO) for a future wrong. Thus the disposition complained of in *Steel* is, in substance, punitive and criminal rather than civil. At t_1, the TSPO is not.

To this extent, then, making a TSPO is not intrinsically a criminal process or disposal. It lacks most, if not all, of the core features of the criminal verdict. Rather, it is a form of *criminalisation*: an *ex ante* criminal prohibition, not an *ex post* criminal verdict. The TSPO makes it a crime to do Y in the future (at t_2), not a crime to have done X in the past (at t_0). Hence, as we shall see, many of the fundamental concerns about the TSPO arise over its operation as a technique of criminalisation.

That having been said, the issuance of a TSPO may itself have a quasi-punitive effect.[15] The personal order at t_1 is capable as operating as a sanction that is *effectively* like penal hard treatment, even if it lacks the formal element of censure associated with a criminal sentence. The form of a TSPO may not merely be a cease-and-desist order (indeed, it is often not of that form) but rather may be an exclusion order or the like. Hence, in *Clingham* itself, one set of appellants had been barred from the suburb that, until recently, had been their home. Being expelled is a very serious matter: the purpose is preventative, but the state's act is both backward-looking, in that it responds to conduct at t_0, and a significant restriction of D's liberty. It is an unwelcome imposition that sets back D's interests. Lord Hope may have been right to state that 'the *purpose* of the procedure is to impose a prohibition, not a penalty.'[16] But one *effect* of the TSPO can be, and frequently is, to inflict something as onerous as a penalty.

There are, then, two core functions of the two-step mechanism. First, it criminalises *ex ante* at t_1 the conduct specified in the personal order. Secondly, it may have the effect of imposing a deprivation upon D at t_1, predicated *ex post* on D's conduct at t_0. As we shall see, those deprivations may be severe and may not be constrained by requirements of proportionality. The restrictions imposed at t_1 can be, and frequently are, effectively sanctions for the underlying conduct at t_0 to which it responds.

---

[14] *Steel* v. *UK* (1998) 28 EHRR 603, 636, paras 48–49. See *Clingham* [2002] UKHL 39, paras 32 (Lord Steyn), 107f (Lord Hutton).

[15] This point is raised by A. Ashworth et al., 'Neighbouring on the Oppressive: The Government's "Anti-Social Behaviour Order" Proposals' (1998) 16 Criminal Justice 7. On reflection, however, it is not entirely accurate to assert (*ibid.*, n. 4.), that 'an ASBO effectively criminalises those against whom it is issued.'

[16] *Clingham* [2002] UKHL 39, para. 68. Contrast the phrasing by Lord Steyn (*ibid.*, para. 30): 'Here the position is that the order itself *involves* no penalty.' (Emphasis added in both quotations.)

12.3 BYPASSING CONSTRAINTS AND THE POTENTIAL FOR MISUSE

We turn now to consider the safeguards that may be lost through the use of TSPOs. As a penalising sanction for conduct at t_0, the personal order potentially sacrifices such in-principle constraints as fair warning and proportionality. As an act of criminalisation at t_1 (via the content of the TSPO), it ought to be subject to constitutional and other constraints that govern the legitimate criminal prohibition of behaviour by citizens. These constraints should set tight limits on the legitimacy of any two-step mechanism—limits that are, in practice, bypassed.

a. Fair Trial

Because TSPOs are designed to be civil orders, they are said to be exempt from many of the constraints applicable to criminal processes. For example, there may be no requirement of a personal appearance, by either the defendant or a complainant. Moreover, the evidential rules governing proceedings at t_1 are those of the civil law—hence, as we noted earlier, hearsay evidence becomes acceptable.[17] Indeed, this is part of the point of such schemes.

Why is this potentially problematic? Most of us agree that deprivations and sanctions in the civil law may justifiably be imposed without always demanding the special procedural safeguards found in the criminal law. In what way, then, does the TSPO go beyond the ordinary realm of civil law judgments?

The difficulty lies in the range of rights and liberties of which the defendant can be deprived. Even though TSPOs lack the safeguards to which criminal prohibitions are subject, the restrictions imposed by such orders may be no less severe than the sanctions applicable to ordinary criminal prohibitions. In a civil case, following proof under civil rules, a defendant may face deprivation of property rights and, on occasion, an injunction not to commit a specific legal wrong or to perform a specific obligation. But the range of the TSPO may be much greater, including exclusionary orders that deprive D of access to geographical areas and public space. In such cases, as we suggested in § 2(b), the substance of the order, which is driven by retrospective considerations, can be comparable in onerousness to a criminal punishment. At least where the order involves a substantial curtailment of liberty, it seems to us that the civil methods of proof required for issuance of the order at t_1 are inadequate.

---

[17] *Clingham, ibid.* (ASBO proceedings at t_1 subject to civil rules of evidence and procedure, notwithstanding that the *standard* of proof required was, in effect, the higher standard required in the criminal law); above, § 2(a).

b. Representative Authority

Being the product of a civil hearing, the prohibition contained in the TSPO is generally issued by a first-instance judge rather than by a legislative body such as Parliament. Since the TSPO operates as an act of criminalisation,[18] this raises a separation of powers issue: it is no longer appropriate in modern law for the judiciary to create offences.

Admittedly, the TSP process must be initiated by an *applicant*, typically a lower-level administrative official.[19] But even then, the procedure effectively delegates powers of criminalisation too far, unless the legislation includes detailed guidance and constraints concerning the appropriate content of TSPO orders. To some extent, this is a straightforward rule-of-law objection: the lives of individual citizens are not governed by promulgated general law, but rather are exposed to the discretionary initiatives of local officials. While it is an inevitable feature of law that its rules must on occasion be given a more particular content, for example through detailed court orders, the rule of law requires that those orders be shaped and guided, as closely as possible, by more general legislation.[20] Only then can citizens plan their lives in reliance upon stable, promulgated, and predictable law.

Beyond these considerations, however, a requirement of representative authority more directly implicates norms of democracy. A delegated criminalisation technique such as the TSP leaves citizens with reduced opportunities to voice objections, through their representatives, concerning the losses of liberty involved. Because they involve decisions that very significantly affect the personal freedoms of citizens, criminal prohibitions ought to be imposed by a representative body—a body that is directly answerable to the citizens it regulates—rather than (say) by administrative or judicial officials. Not only does this ensure that important decisions are appropriately vested in the democratic polity, it also helps to keep them visible, thereby maximising the opportunities for public debate about the merit or demerit of each prohibition.

It is true that regulatory powers are often delegated in other contexts, e.g. to health and safety regulatory agencies, and the like. But the operation of those agencies is itself under the rule of law: typically, those agencies are fettered by regulatory frameworks and administrative law rules. No such constraints apply to the TSPO. This difficulty is compounded because, unlike the enforcement activities of regulatory bodies—which are confined to particular, directed and specialised, activities—the TSPO framework

---

[18] Above, § 12.2(b).
[19] Under the English ASBO legislation, the initiator is normally a local authority official or the local chief of police.
[20] J. Raz, 'The Rule of Law and its Virtue' (1977) 93 LQR 195, 199–200.

need not be confined to any specific context or type of activity. Hence, individuals do not have the option of taking themselves outside the scope of the criminalisation process by refraining from the relevant specialist activity, an option that they normally have in other regulatory contexts.

One incidental upshot of all this is that it can become possible to use the TSPO to derogate from the decisions of Parliament by prohibiting specific, personal, instances of activities that are otherwise generally permitted: e.g. sexual promiscuity not amounting to criminally proscribed prostitution. Potentially, the TSPOS could even prohibit Xing by D where a criminal prohibition of Xing had actually been considered but not adopted by Parliament.[21]

c. Generality

Another objection to criminalisation through TSPs is that the prohibition is *in personam*, rather than being couched in general terms. This might loosely be termed a bill-of-attainder objection: criminalisation should not be personal. Convictions are personal: prohibitions are not. As we saw in § 1.2(b), criminal proscriptions involve authoritative, condemnatory evaluations of conduct on behalf of the community as a whole. They are, and should be, measures of general application, that govern everyone—or, as a minimum, everyone falling within the relevant class affected by the rationale behind the rule. It is a constitutional, rule-of-law value that everyone is equal before the law. But the TSPO is a form of *ad hominem* criminalisation: it declares, in effect, that everyone else may do X, but that D in particular may not.

Bills of attainder are rightly declared illegitimate by the US Constitution.[22] This is for a complex variety of reasons—very often, bills of attainder impose penalties that bypass the need for a trial and conviction, something the TSP process does not do. None the less, the TSPO shares with bills of attainder the repugnant feature that it singles out individuals and restrict their liberties, thereby differentiating them from the rest of society *ex ante*. In effect, it creates one rule for D, another for everyone else.

The point is one of equality. Apart from certain categorical exceptions, such as children,[23] the members of a modern democracy are—and have a right to be—treated as having equal standing in the community. We no longer segregate citizens into distinct legal and political classes (nobles,

---

[21] This has in fact occurred: below, § 12.5.
[22] Art. 1, § 9, para. 3; together with retrospective laws.
[23] Even then, the distinction is drawn contextually and not for all purposes; and members of such categories are to be treated even-handedly within the category.

clergy, burghers, peasants, women, etc.), but recognise that everyone is equal before the law. This means both that each person has an equal right to participate in the democratic process and, conversely, that the law does not discriminate between individuals.[24] Citizens thereby have a shared responsibility for the law: they are both its authors, through representatives answerable to them, and the joint subjects of its governance. The TSP, by contrast, abandons reciprocity in favour of burdening individual targets.

At a practical level, this technique also means that otherwise unwelcome prohibitions can be more easily targeted upon the unpopular (the so-called 'anti-social') within a society. Thus conduct which many persons are free to do may become prohibited for such 'undesirable' persons, with all the discriminatory potential that this involves. Doing so tends, moreover, to make such prohibitions easier to adopt, since limiting prohibitions to unpopular individuals or groups can render it more difficult to generate effective opposition to their adoption.[25]

d. Criminalisation

Once the making of an TSPO at t_1 is understood as (*inter alia*) an act of delegated criminalisation, certain related constraints become apparent, constraints that are misleadingly obscured by its status as a civil order. Criminalisation restricts liberties—it is meant to. I am not free to discharge my shotgun in your direction, because doing so might interfere with your health. No doubt that is an acceptable restriction. But because it restricts liberty, there are good reasons why legislators should be parsimonious about criminalising conduct. These reasons are in play whenever a freedom is withdrawn. They are especially powerful considerations with TSPs because, in effect, TSPOs can—and frequently do—operate as a form of pre-emptive regulation, for example by excluding D from a public space.

One difficulty with a pre-emptive prohibition is its remoteness from the prospective behaviour by which it is motivated. Depending on its content, a TSPO might prohibit behaviour that is legitimate in itself, such as entering a certain area, merely in virtue of an ostensible risk that the actor might subsequently choose while there to perpetrate undesired conduct. As

---

[24] cf. V. Tadros, 'Justice and Terrorism' (2007) 10 New Criminal LR 658, 683–86, concluding that 'individualized laws violate the basic right of citizens to equal treatment.'

[25] Compare the well-known commentary upon the Holocaust by Martin Niemöller: 'First they came for the Communists, and I didn't speak up because I wasn't a Communist. Then they came for the Jews, and I didn't speak up because I wasn't a Jew. Then they came for the trade unionists, and I didn't speak up because I wasn't a trade unionist. Then they came for the Catholics, and I didn't speak up because I was a Protestant. Then they came for me—and by that time no one was left to speak up.'

we argued in Part II, pre-emptive prohibitions raise concerns of fair imputation, about the extent to which that prospective further wrongdoing provides a reason why D's current conduct, which is itself innocent, should be the subject of a proscription backed up by criminal sanctions.

The concerns about pre-emptive regulation are particularly strong when the technique used is one of exclusion. Prohibitions of this sort deny the moral agency of the defendant, by refusing to recognise her as a morally responsible human being and participant in society—D is not given the opportunity to behave responsibly in public. Once D is found to have engaged in the conduct at t_0, triggering issuance of the order, she no longer has free access to public spaces. Thenceforth, her decision to refrain from committing criminal offences—and even to refrain from committing conduct of the type that gave rise to the order (if that was non-criminal)—becomes immaterial. She is simply excluded from those spaces, irrespective of what her choices would have been had she been permitted access.[26]

This denial of access to public space also raises problems of identity and self-definition. For most of us, our lives involve, and are in part defined by, the interaction and relationships we have with other members of our society. It is through such interaction that a person's membership of her society is affirmed, in the eyes of both the person herself and her fellow citizens.[27] The ability to interact depends, in turn, on access to public space; thus exclusion tends not only to preclude the particular undesired conduct that lies behind the TSPO, and the way of life to which that act gives expression, but also to undermine D's participation in the society itself; and, ultimately, to undermine D's identity as a human being.

e.   Quasi-criminalisation at t_0

It may seem plausible to respond to the foregoing concern (in § 12.3(d)) by highlighting the fact that D becomes subject to a TSPO only if she has perpetrated the qualifying conduct at t_0. In England, for example, the TSP mechanism is engaged only if it is shown that D has done something 'anti-social'.[28] But to the extent that D's conduct at t_0 is relied upon to justify the imposition of onerous and quasi-punitive sanctions such as an exclusion order, the specification of qualifying conduct itself counts as a form of quasi-criminalisation. (And, as we suggested in § 12.3(a), proving that conduct at trial should be governed by criminal rules.) Suppose that

---

[26] A fuller discussion of this argument is found in von Hirsch and Shearing, 'Exclusion from Public Space' in A. von Hirsch, D. Garland, and A. Wakefield (eds.), *Ethical and Social Perspectives on Situational Crime Prevention* (Oxford: Hart Publishing, 2000) 77.

[27] See generally J. Raz, 'Free Expression and Personal Identification' in Raz, *Ethics in the Public Domain* (rev. ed., Oxford: Oxford UP, 1995).

[28] Crime and Disorder Act 1998, s. 1.

φing is prescribed as qualifying conduct, proof of which makes it legitimate to issue a TSPO. In effect, while persons who φ will not immediately receive a criminal conviction, the state announces *ex ante* that such persons will be directly subject to sanctions (at t_1), and will thereafter become liable to criminal dispositions.

As such, the specification of φing itself should be constrained by principles such as the Offence Principle. But the criteria under which a TSPO is available tend to include behaviour at t_0 that is not by itself either wrong or offensive or harmful, and which need not be a criminal offence.[29] The use of a TSPO in such contexts is reminiscent of Robert Ellickson's proposal that 'chronic street nuisances' may be largely excluded from areas of a city's public space through techniques of property-law zoning, whereby persons are regarded as chronic street nuisances if they:[30]

> Persistently act in a public space in a manner that violates prevailing community standards of behavior, to the significant cumulative annoyance of persons of ordinary sensibility who use the same spaces.

Indeed, in England the ASBO criteria go further than Ellickson's, in that the behaviour complained of need not in fact cause any distress; it is sufficient that it be 'likely' so to do.[31] They go further, too, than Feinberg's criteria for the criminalisation of offence.[32] Feinberg required that the affront caused to others by D's behaviour be both grave and predictably widespread across the community; whereas the criteria laid down in the ASBO legislation are satisfied if affront is caused merely to one individual.

This concern must be dissected. It is not inherently objectionable that the qualifying behaviour at t_0 need not actually cause harm or offence. The criminal law frequently prohibits behaviour (e.g. drink-driving, speeding, and the like) without requiring that the behaviour must be *per se* harmful. Indeed, this is generally true of what might be termed 'inchoate' offences: speeding, for example, is rightly proscribed on the ground of its characteristic riskiness. *Per se* harmless or offensive actions may come within the scope of the Harm or Offence Principles where they *standardly* create a risk of harm or offence, even if not in every instance. The justification for criminalising these cases is, in part, practical—it is simply uneconomic to frame and administer laws other than with regard to the standard cases. Even exceptionally able drivers must drive at a speed set with reference to their less competent counterparts.

---

[29] This, especially, because TSPs may be designed to regulate conduct that is problematic only when repeated or sustained: above, § 12.2(a).

[30] R. Ellickson, 'Controlling chronic misconduct in city spaces: of panhandlers, skid rows, and public space zoning' (1996) 105 Yale LJ 1165, 1185.

[31] Below, § 12.5.

[32] *Offence to Others*; above, Chapter 6.

Further, there may also be nothing intrinsically wrong in using TSPOs to prohibit behaviour that, when viewed in isolation, is not a criminal offence. Ongoing anti-social behaviour, at its worst, can significantly affect the lives of other persons—even where any one instance is, by itself, a relatively trivial matter—because it can degrade the quality of life in common public space. It may be that such harm is not a 'direct' and immediate consequence of the anti-social behaviour, but that is not a requirement of the Harm Principle—which is quite capable, in appropriate cases, of extending to remote harms.[33]

Rather, the deeper concern about the preconditions for issuing a TSPO is the requirement that D's behaviour at t_0 be a wrong—again, something obscured by the fact that the TSPO is formally civil. In practice, this requirement is characteristically abrogated by TSP legislation. In England, for instance, the definition of qualifying 'anti-social' behaviour is expressed purely in terms of the reactions of the audience: conduct done 'in a manner that caused or was likely to cause harassment, alarm or distress to one or more persons not of the same household.'[34] As such, it exposes D to the risk that his unconventional behaviour, which wrongs no one, may lead to a personal order purely because it causes, or is likely to cause, distress or alarm in others—whether or not that distress is appropriate or justified. Suppose, for example, that there were a convention in some locality that persons of different races should not have any physical contact in public.[35] If an interracial couple hold hands in the park, they may cause widespread distress amongst others in the park; but it does not follow that behaviour such as this should be prohibited.

In our view, to the extent that the order made at t_1 has the effect of a sanction, by imposing deprivations on D, that order ought as a minimum to be predicated on a wrong. Indeed, this requirement very often applies to civil as well as criminal law. Sanctions in tort ordinarily are imposed only upon proof of a wrong by D—there must be an infliction of personal or property damage, in violation of P's rights, or a failure by D to perform as promised. Like remedies in tort, the personal order mechanism singles D out for *in personam* deprivations. While it need not, as a conceptual requirement, do so on the basis of a criminal offence, the civil order that it constitutes should nonetheless be predicated on a wrong.[36]

---

[33] Provided imputation requirements are met: above, Chapters 4–5.
[34] Crime and Disorder Act 1998, s. 1(1)(a).
[35] cf. above, §§ 6.3(b), 3.2(c).
[36] In the particular case of the English ASBO legislation, the possibility of an order being issued following behaviour that is not wrongful is somewhat ameliorated by s. 1(5) of the Crime And Disorder Act 1998: 'For the purpose of determining whether the condition mentioned in subsection (1)(a) above is fulfilled, the court shall disregard any act of the defendant which he shows was reasonable in the circumstances.' The objection is therefore weakened in respect of the ASBO itself, in so far as s. 1(5) introduces a normative element

f. Fair Warning

Like any sanction, the potential for hard treatment at t_1 should be notified clearly in advance. This constraint demands that the qualifying conduct at t_0 be defined in terms that are sufficiently specific to give citizens an adequate opportunity of shaping their behaviour to avoid running foul of the law and incurring a TSPO. However, the use of TSP mechanisms to regulate conduct that is not in isolation suitable for criminalisation[37] tends to generate vague legislative descriptions of the qualifying conduct. In England, for example, the criteria for issuing an ASBO are defined in loose and sweeping terms. As we noted in the last section, anti-social behaviour is conduct performed 'in a manner that caused or was likely to cause harassment, alarm or distress to one or more persons not of the same household.' This open-endedness was intended as a positive feature, allowing for flexibility in the availability of an order; but it is a serious drawback, in so far as very little is offered by way of guidance to defendants about what behaviour may incur an order. As such, the statute gives inadequate advance warning to D about the potential legal consequences of her behaviour.

Strictly speaking, the objection here is not that the preconditions of the TSPO violate the principle of *legality*, since that principle applies paradigmatically to criminal rather than civil law; and the issuance of a TSPO does not itself constitute a criminal conviction. Moreover, once criminal processes are invoked at t_2, *ex post* the order, there typically *is* good guidance: the terms of the order itself are usually clear and unequivocal.

Rather, the objection is that citizens are also entitled to adequate advance notice before their behaviour incurs substantial civil sanctions. People need to know the legal consequences of their actions, civil as well as criminal, if they are to be able to plan their lives with confidence. It may be that this is a less pressing requirement than it is in the criminal law, where sanctions involve official censure. None the less, to the extent that the terms of a TSPO go beyond a mere cease-and-desist order enjoining

---

into the criteria for anti-social behaviour established in s. 1(1)(a). Nonetheless, it retains considerable force, in that behaviour may be unreasonable (for example, in virtue of being immoral) without it following that the behaviour wrongs anyone. Suppose that D decides to harm himself. His behaviour, in principle, may be unreasonable and distressing to others; but it is not therefore a wrong to anyone else. Still less does it follow that behaviour is a wrong from D's failure to show it is reasonable: it is not clear why the onus of proof should rest on D to establish the reasonableness of his behaviour. Yet a woman who repeatedly attempted suicide by throwing herself into the River Avon was served with an ASBO prohibiting her from jumping into rivers or canals: 'A Triumph of Hearsay and Hysteria' *The Guardian*, 5 April 2005, 20.

[37] Above, § 12.2(a).

behaviour that is already criminal, the personal order imposes a deprivation on the defendant that he ought to have the prior opportunity to avoid. The more serious the deprivation, of course, the more important it becomes that this opportunity be made available. The power to impose them therefore raises issues of the rule of law. If the rule of law is to be observed, persons subject to state deprivations should be dealt with in accordance with determinate and knowable law:[38]

> Stripped of all its technicalities, [the rule of law] means that government in all its actions is bound by rules fixed and announced beforehand—rules which make it possible to foresee with fair certainty how the authority will use its coercive powers in given circumstances and to plan one's individual affairs on the basis of this knowledge.

This means not only that the content of a personal order should be determined in accordance with law, but that the basis of one's exposure to that order should be knowable in advance and not *ex post*. Knowing where we stand augments the ability of citizens to live autonomous lives—indeed, the possibility of being guided by the state's rules is foundational to our capacity as individuals to make decisions. As Joseph Raz puts it, 'This is the basic intuition from which the doctrine of the rule of law derives: the law must be capable of guiding the behaviour of its subjects.'[39] It may be that more precise specification of the criteria at t_0 will allow certain forms of misconduct. But incomplete regulation is sometimes a fair price to pay for the rule of law.

g.   Culpability

There is no reason why mens rea safeguards should be diluted in TSPOs. However, in virtue of the formally civil character of the prohibition, there is a tendency to neglect this essential aspect of criminal liability. By contrast with the criminal law, civil prohibitions lack an expectation of mens rea, and there need be nothing problematic about no-fault liability in tort for hazardous products or high-risk activities.[40] As such, the TSP framework seemingly eliminates the need for mens rea—thus the criminal sanctions for violating an ASBO, for example, do not presuppose knowing

---

[38] F. Hayek, *The Road to Serfdom* (London: Routledge, 1944) 72; compare R. Fallon, 'The "Rule of Law" as a Concept in Constitutional Discourse' (1997) 97 Columbia LR 1, 8.

[39] J. Raz, *The Authority of Law* (Oxford: Oxford UP, 1979) 214; cf. F. Schauer, *Playing by the Rules: A Philosophical Examination of Rule-Based Decision-Making in Law and in Life* (New York: Oxford UP, 1991) 137–38.

[40] As in *Rylands* v. *Fletcher* (1868) LR 3 HL 330.

infringement of the order.[41] Mens rea should, however, remain a require-ment of any TSPO; moreover, criminal-law defences such as self-defence and necessity should be available, in the normal way, for their breach.

h. Proportionality at t_1

Requirements of proportionality tend to be attenuated by the TSP process in two ways. First, understood as a response to conduct at t_0, the hardships imposed at t_1 by the TSPO are not limited by significant proportionality constraints, because of its nominal status as a civil rather than criminal order.[42] Secondly, the criminal disposal following conduct at t_2 can become disproportionate, since the criminal conviction at that point is driven by the fact of D's violating the TSPO, rather than by the wrongfulness of D's conduct *per se*.

Beginning with the first concern, it seems to us that the scope and intrusiveness of the order at t_1 should bear a reasonable relationship to the seriousness of the wrongdoing that D is proved to have done at t_0. It should, in other words, be deserved as well as useful.[43] Otherwise, the intermediate use of TSPOs to enforce existing criminal laws opens up the possibility, for example, that the constraints imposed in the order may run for a very lengthy period (say, 10 years) in circumstances where the maximum permissible penalty under the criminal law for D's underlying behaviour at t_0 is much less (say, a few months' imprisonment or perhaps just a fine).

Additionally, the harshness of the burden imposed by the order ought to be subject to a ceiling, especially if the order is to be made pursuant to civil procedures. Suppose that D is alleged to have committed a serious criminal wrong, justifying a sentence that imposes substantial restrictions on D's freedom of movement.[44] A sentence of this kind ought to be imposed only upon proof, to a criminal standard, of D's wrongdoing. Moreover, we take it that this standard should not be evaded by the device of removing the formal element of the criminal conviction from the process; by establishing a non-criminal exclusions regime within the civil law. Such a substantial deprivation ought to be subjected to adequate fairness constraints, includ-ing those of proportionality. In our view, lengthy exclusion orders from suburbs and town centres in which D resides are sufficiently onerous penalties to warrant similar demands.

[41] Crime and Disorder Act 1998, s. 1(10).

[42] The importance of proportionality in civil law is further discussed in A. von Hirsch and M. Wasik, 'Civil Disqualifications Attending Conviction' (1997) 56 CLJ 599, 612–15.

[43] Or, in the language of the ASBO, 'necessary': below, § 12.5.

[44] Such restrictions need not involve imprisonment: they include, for example, lengthy probation terms with strict conditions that restrict access to public space.

Also problematic is the possibility, seen in the English legislation, that the content of the order at t_1 need only be necessary to prevent 'further' anti-social acts;[45] it need not be confined to preventing the same variety of acts that are alleged already to have occurred. This strikes us as problematic: it exposes D to deprivations that in no way respond to past wrongdoing.

i.   Proportionality at t_2

The second proportionality concern arises in respect of the criminal sanction that is imposed ultimately for violating the TSPO. Like the sanctions for contempt of court, criminal dispositions in such cases are prima facie concerned with the fact of breach of the order at t_2, rather than with the actual nature of the contravening behaviour. Punishment is therefore, at least potentially, underpinned by an authoritarian defiance-rationale, and not by a desert rationale. (Hence punishment for violating an ASBO in English law may involve a prison sentence of up to five years' duration, even where the underlying criminal wrong is not imprisonable, or is imprisonable for a lesser maximum.[46]) This also seems to us wrong, in that it contravenes the fundamental structure of legitimate criminalisation outlined in Chapter 1. Punishment ought, in principle, to be determined primarily by reference to the degree of seriousness of D's actual conduct at t_2, not by reference to the fact *per se* that it is has been prohibited by the order. Otherwise, the TSPO will be operating *in terrorem*: D is directed to desist from certain behaviour, wrongful or not; and is threatened with unpleasant consequences whose severity depends merely on the fact of disobedience. The scheme becomes, in Hegel's well-known phrase, a stick raised to a dog.[47]

12.4   USING TSPS IN SPECIALIST CONTEXTS: THE ACP

The constraints described in § 12.3 militate strongly against a wide use of two-step TSPs to help prevent harmful or offensive conduct. More generally, the use of civil mechanisms to enforce criminal law also risks undermining the moral authority of the criminal law as an institution, through weakening the paradigm distinction between criminal and civil laws, and the association of the former with condemnation of culpable wrongdoing. Blurring the difference between criminal and civil laws risks loss of clarity of the criminal law's distinctively moral voice.

---

[45]   Crime and Disorder Act 1998, s. 1(6).

[46]   In practice, sentences of two or more years are fairly common.

[47]   For further discussion of why defiance of authority *per se* should not be a basis for measuring criminal punishments, see *Proportionate Sentencing* ch. 9.

Despite this, certain more limited two-step schemes do seem to be permissible as ancillary civil prohibitions (ACPs). These schemes operate in aid of particular regulatory or licensing schemes, or as a means for enforcing certain civil causes of action. Examples are disqualifications from certain professions following conviction or determination of professional misconduct, anti-molestation orders, and tree preservation orders.

ACPs also tend to lack the safeguards of the criminal law listed in § 12.1. For example, the prohibitory order normally may be imposed by a lower-level administrative or judicial official, rather than a representative body, and it may be aimed at a particular individual without being general in application. Why, then, are ACPs generally regarded as acceptable? The answer seems to lie in the limited and ancillary character of the regulatory scheme. There is no generalised discretion to issue prohibitory orders. Legitimate ACPs are curtailed in two important respects.

The first limitation concerns the narrowing of the range of behaviour that may trigger an ACP. ACP schemes operate only within specifically delimited areas of behaviour.[48] A professional disqualification, for example, may issue only for persons engaged in certain regulated and licensed professions, who have engaged in particular kinds of malpractice.[49] If one does not wish to be exposed to this kind of disqualification risk, one can engage in other, less regulated kinds of work. An anti-molestation order may issue only if the actor repeatedly harasses a particular person. A tree preservation order may affect only those who own land on which certain kinds of trees grow. If I choose to live in a flat—or live in a house but have no such trees in my garden—I need not worry about being affected.

The second limitation concerns the restricted variety of conduct that may be barred by an ACP order. In ACPs, the prohibitory order should relate only to specified limited types of activity, such as continuing to practice as a solicitor after disbarment; approaching a particular individual whom the actor has harassed before; or sawing off the limb of a tree that is protected by a preservation order. No general good-conduct requirement may justify issuance of an ACP; and the order may involve no general diminution of civil rights.

Provided these limitations are observed, the ancillary character of ACP regimes is crucial to their acceptability: they operate specifically in aid of particular regulatory or licensing schemes (in which case their content and form tends to be tightly confined); or as means of enforcing certain civil causes of action; or they enjoin instances of conduct that is already (and more generally) a legal wrong. It is essential, we think, that administrative and judicial officials do not have a generalised discretion to issue orders

---

[48] On specialised prohibitions generally, see also § 11.2(d) above.
[49] cf. von Hirsch and Wasik, above n. 42.

prohibiting citizens from engaging in conduct at large, and which is not already a legal wrong. No country respecting personal liberty ought to enact a scheme that gives officials a generalised discretion to prohibit conduct.

12.5   ASSESSING THE ENGLISH ASBO LEGISLATION

The foregoing analysis permits us to deal with the ASBO legislation straightforwardly.[50] The ASBO is not sustainable as a legitimate ACP, because of the wide varieties of conduct that may trigger issuance of an order, and because of the vast range of behavior that may be prohibited by the order itself. Indeed, the ASBO confers a very broad discretion to prohibit undesired behaviour, since the triggering conduct includes anything causing, or likely to cause, 'distress' to another,[51] and the order itself may contain prohibitions of almost unlimited scope, constrained only by the requirement that they be 'necessary for the purpose of protecting other persons from further anti-social acts by the defendant.'[52] There is no legislative requirement of proportionality.[53] The order at t_1 can include, for example, a curfew or an exclusion from an area (estate, suburb, shopping mall; even one's home). Moreover, the order can be for an indefinite period and in any event must last for a minimum of two years.

The legislation thus creates the power to issue prohibitions at t_1 of behaviour that is not otherwise criminally proscribed, and which may be harmless (or which, in the case of access prohibitions, merely provides an occasion for subsequent criminal or offensive conduct). Neither the triggering conduct, nor the prohibitory response, need satisfy the Harm Principle or Offence Principle. Moreover, the prohibition shares other problematic features of TSPOs generally, in that it operates *in personam* rather than as a generally applicable prohibition and is issued by low-level officials rather than a representative legislative body. As such, the ASBO bypasses public deliberative processes.

---

[50] For concerns expressed by the European Commissioner for Human Rights, see A. Gil-Robles, *Report on the Visit to the United Kingdom 4–12/11/2004* (Strasbourg: Council of Europe, 2005) paras 108ff.

[51] *Per* Crime and Disorder Act 1998, s. 1(1)(a), the triggering conduct ('anti-social behaviour') is anything done 'in a manner that caused or was likely to cause harassment, alarm or distress to one or more persons not of the same household.' This extremely broad test is ameliorated somewhat, but only somewhat, by the enactment of a defence in s. 1(5): 'For the purpose of determining whether the condition mentioned in subsection (1)(a) above is fulfilled, the court shall disregard any act of the defendant which he shows was reasonable in the circumstances.' See also n. 36 above.

[52] Crime and Disorder Act 1998, s. 1(6).

[53] Home Office guidance on the form of the order nonetheless suggests that proposed prohibitions should be 'reasonable and proportionate'. Home Office, *Anti-Social Behaviour Orders—Guidance on drawing up local ASBO protocols* (London, 2000) § 13.5.

The practical import of this last point is illustrated in three areas of criminal law reform: decriminalisation of self-destructive behaviour such as attempted suicide; exemption from criminal liability of mentally disabled individuals; and the partial decriminalisation of prostitution, including elimination of imprisonment for offences of solicitation. Each of these reforms was achieved after extended public discussion and parliamentary debate. The ASBO device, however, has permitted *de facto* disregard of these reforms, with virtually no discussion. ASBOs have been issued against individuals attempting suicide;[54] against autistic youths;[55] and against prostitutes.[56] Infringement of ASBO directives in these cases will expose the defendant to criminal conviction and imprisonment. No doubt, had comparable proscriptions been proposed as general amendments to the criminal law, strong objections of principle would have been raised—and the chances of their approval would be low.

Might the ASBO scheme fare better if the triggering conduct were limited to behaviour proscribed by the criminal law? This would still not make it a legitimate ACP scheme. Granted, the triggering behaviour would then have to be behaviour that has been adjudged wrongful by a representative body. But the scope of the order's prohibitions still would remain virtually unlimited. This would mean that a very wide swathe of conduct—including access to much public space—could be proscribed *in personam* by unelected decision-makers, without any of the other essential safeguards described in § 12.1 being in place. Moreover, the sanctions for violation need not observe proportionality constraints with respect to the underlying wrong. While this might be tolerable for legitimate ACPs of limited scope, it is not appropriate in broader TSP schemes. For example, the scheme might still result in the issuing of an order prohibiting someone from soliciting (or entering any area where he or she might be inclined to solicit), a minor form of offence, and yet result in a long period of confinement for violations.

By contrast with legitimate ACP regimes, the ASBO exposes citizens to a general discretion of officials. The potential area of coverage of the ASBO is too wide, both because the initial conduct requirement at t_0 is sweepingly defined and because the constraints on the content of the prohibition at t_1 are so minimal.

---

[54] Above, n. 36.
[55] 'Children with Autism the Target of ASBOs' *Observer*, 22 May 2005, 7.
[56] 'ASBOs "are bringing back jail for prostitutes"' *The Guardian*, 25 May 2005, 7.

12.6   CONCLUSION

In this final chapter we have identified a variety of problems with the two-step personal order mechanism. Our concerns include, *inter alia*, the breadth and imprecision of the triggering criteria at t_0; the untrammelled range of the order that may be made at t_1, with its potential effectively to impose substantial restrictions of liberty; the requirement only for civil procedures at t_1, bypassing criminal standards of protection for the defendant's rights; and the potential for substantial punishment at t_2 based on rationales of defiance rather than the wrongfulness of the underlying conduct.

At a generic level, the problem with TSPs is their intermediate character. The TSPO falls between criminal and civil status; and, as such, carries inadequate safeguards. The main problems are twofold. The first difficulty is that a TSPO has the potential to visit significant deprivations without adequate notice and procedural protections. The issuing of a TSPO at t_1 can, without more, impose severe forms of restriction without observing the protections that are and should be demanded by criminal law. The second difficulty is one of criminalisation; especially, infringing the rule of law. TSPOs are an inappropriate means of delegating and personalising the legislative powers to prohibit behaviour by citizens. In our view, the TSPO poses foundational challenges to the preservation of rights and freedoms within a free society.

Some of these objections apply even if the TSPO is deployed only to regulate conduct that is already an offence under existing criminal law. But the personal order becomes a distinctive, and still greater, threat to the rights of citizens when used to regulate more nondescript, unwelcome behaviour that is not itself prohibited as an offence. In our view, two-step schemes cannot be sustainable as proper forms of criminal prohibition— because the order issued is not made by a representative body and is targeted to particular persons. To be legitimate at all, TSPOs would have to be akin to ancillary civil prohibitions. But in that case, their ambit must be substantially restricted, with respect both to the kind of conduct that may trigger an order and to the scope of that order. Moreover, the schemes need also to observe the various constraints, such as proportionality and fair warning, that were noted in § 12.3. As a device, the TSPO is capable of exploiting the poorly understood distinction, between *ex ante* and *ex post* dimensions of the criminal law, to evade some of the standard constitutional limitations on criminalisation. But it cannot evade critical evaluation.

Index